SPECIAL EDUCATIONAL NEEDS IN THE PRIMARY SCHOOL
Second Edition

SPECIAL EDUCATIONAL NEEDS IN THE PRIMARY SCHOOL
A Practical Guide

SECOND EDITION

JEAN GROSS

OPEN UNIVERSITY PRESS
Buckingham · Philadelphia

Open University Press
Celtic Court
22 Ballmoor
Buckingham
MK18 1XW

email:enquiries@openup.co.uk
world wide web: http://www.openup.co.uk

and

325 Chestnut Street
Philadelphia, PA 19106, USA

First published 1993
Reprinted 1995

First published in this second edition 1996
Reprinted in this edition 1998, 2000

A catalogue record of this book is available from the British Library

ISBN 0 335 19656 X (pb)

Library of Congress Cataloging-in-Publication Data
Gross, Jean.
Special educational needs in the primary school: a practical
guide/Jean Gross. – 2nd ed.
p.   cm.
Includes bibliographical references and index.
ISBN 0-335-19656-X (pbk.)
1. Special education – Great Britain. 2. Special education – Great
Britain – Curricula. 3. Education, Elementary – Great Britain.
4. Classroom management – Great Britain. I. Title.
LC3986.G7G76   1993
371.9'0941 – dc20   96-10724 CIP

Typeset by Vision Typesetting, Manchester
Printed in Great Britain by Redwood Books, Trowbridge

CONTENTS

ACKNOWLEDGEMENTS

I am grateful to colleagues in support services in the former County of Avon (Psychology Service, Learning Development Support Service, Service for Special Educational Needs), and to the teachers, parents and children of Wansdyke, for the many ideas and examples of good practice they have contributed to this volume. In particular, thanks go to Christine Humphrey for permission to include examples of her support work using concept keyboard overlays, and to the speech and language therapists in the Bath and District Health Authority Speech and Language Service for permission to use an extract from their guide for teachers.

The author and publishers are grateful to Thomas Nelson and Sons for permission to quote from Westmacott and Cameron's *Behaviour Can Change*, 1981.

· 1 ·

CURRENT PERSPECTIVES ON SPECIAL EDUCATIONAL NEEDS

INTRODUCTION

Teachers have always taught children with a wide range of abilities and achievements. From time to time, a statistic will surface which highlights the extent of this range – from the Cockcroft Report's (1982) estimate, for example, of a seven-year range in maths attainment in an average class of 11-year-olds, to the more recent outcomes of the first standard attainment task (SAT) run for seven-year olds, showing a four-year span, even at this age, in normal reading ability. Before the report of the Warnock Committee in 1978, those at the bottom of this wide range were in turn educationally subnormal, retarded, backward, or slow learners and placed at the margins of the class teacher's responsibility by their perceived in-built blocks and barriers to learning. Post-Warnock, they were children with fluctuating, contextually determined special educational needs; they were promised a brave new future of support in integrated classrooms, only to slip back to threatened marginalization again in the late 1980s, in a climate where children are considered cheap or costly according to the amount of support they require and the gloss they add (or fail to add) to the school's image.

There are, however, still steps that can be taken to hold back the tide of increasing marginalization of vulnerable children. The first is to foster confidence, in all teachers, that they themselves can take effective steps to manage the *whole* range of abilities and needs within their classes. We must never forget how easily work with children who do not learn or behave well can sap adult confidence: their difficulty in learning makes teachers feel like failures too. It is this that can make teachers try to allay these uncomfortable feelings by perceiving the child's problems as intractable, intrinsic, and best dealt with by someone else with appropriate expertise. Teachers who feel confident that they have enough expertise of their own to make plans that will move the child on in learning, even in very small steps, do not need to pass the buck or suggest s/he should be elsewhere. Fostering that personal and professional confidence is vital to ensuring a welcome for all children in all classrooms.

The second element in holding back the tide of marginalization is a collective will amongst school staff, born out of collaborative school development work in special needs, that their school will be a school for all, and that the factors that make for good practice – and popularity with the school's prospective parent clientele – are the same right across the ability range.

In this book, we will look at how such a collective will can be achieved, and seek to give straightforward, practical information that will enable all primary teachers to feel confident in planning within-school supportive action for pupils who, for whatever reason, are not learning as well as they might. To begin with, we will focus on terminology, and the ways in which the words used to describe the hard to teach encapsulate our concepts about learning. We will also look at the current legislative and administrative framework which defines the respective roles of teachers, parents, schools and local authorities in meeting special needs, and which provide the backdrop against which the individual struggle of each teacher to get the best for each child in the class must be set.

WHO HAS SPECIAL NEEDS?

Most primary teachers find it easy to jot down the names of children they teach whom they consider to have special educational needs. The term 'special needs' has an implicit meaning for most of us – but that meaning is hard to put into words, and even harder to agree on. The legislation that followed the Warnock Report, the 1981 and 1993 Education Acts (DES 1981, DFE 1993), is of little help, providing only that a child has special needs if 'he has a learning difficulty which calls for special educational provision to be made for him', and adding that a child has a learning difficulty if he has 'a significantly greater difficulty in learning than the majority of children the same age', or 'a disability which either prevents or hinders him from making use of educational facilities of a kind provided for children of the same age in schools within the area of the local education authority'.

Since the way that attainments are distributed means that roughly half of any group of children will have significantly greater difficulty than the other half in learning any new concept or skill, and since the facilities provided in schools vary enormously from one area to another, it can be seen that the legal definition could embrace anything from a tiny handful to huge numbers of children. Baroness Warnock herself, whose 1978 committee and report first legitimized the special needs terminology, recognized this:

> The concept of 'special need' carries a fake objectivity. For one of the main, indeed almost overwhelming, difficulties is to decide whose needs are special, and what 'special' means.
>
> (Warnock, 1982: 372)

In many primary classrooms today, the meaning is all too clear. Teachers have come to talk of 'my special needs children', or 'my special needs group', in the same way, and in the same tones, with which they once spoke of 'my remedials', or 'my slow learners'. Warnock envisaged special needs as something a child might *have* in certain circumstances, with certain learning tasks. The concept was fluid, implying that any child might experience difficulties at some point, rather than that such difficulties were owned by a fixed group who were in some way different from the majority. Current usage, however, has subtly shifted from the notion of special needs as something we may *have* from time to time, towards the notion that they are something some children *are* – forever.

The difference is subtle, but important to grasp. It can best be understood in relation to our own 'special needs' as teachers. All of us find it fairly easy to acknowledge that these exist – that we have teaching skills that are underdeveloped, areas of the curriculum where we lack confidence. Most would welcome some support in these areas: opportunities to work alongside someone with good practice to share, the chance to spend some extra time catching up on new developments and practices. How many, however, would welcome the headteacher calling us 'one of my special needs teachers'? We may find it helpful to have our learning needs identified, but we do not find permanent labels, attached to ourselves as people rather than to our performance in certain contexts, either helpful or acceptable. Children cannot be expected to feel differently.

Nevertheless, the tendency to label *children* rather than *needs* persists, and because of this many writers in the special needs field would prefer to abandon special needs terminology altogether. Jonathan Solity (1991), for example, argues that the term actively encourages discriminatory practices, such as seating children separately, withdrawing them for their lessons from the mainstream classroom, and giving them work that is obviously different from that of others in the class. A focus on special provision for one in five children with special needs, he feels, distracts our attention from the fact that teachers are not always very good at individualizing instruction for a much larger group. He quotes research by Neville Bennett and his colleagues (1984) – research we will return to in Chapter 3 – which showed that 60 per cent of Year 2 children and 70 per cent of Year 3 children in a range of classrooms were observed to be working on tasks that were either much too easy or much too difficult for them. Given these figures, Solity sees the task for teachers as meeting *all* children's individual needs, not the special needs of a few.

A similar argument derives from the research on school effectiveness, which has in many cases shown that schools tend to be effective or ineffective for all their pupils, irrespective of factors such as social disadvantage which are associated with the incidence of special educational needs (Rutter et al., 1979; Mortimore et al., 1988). If this is so, and what is good for some pupils is good for all, it again becomes less important to identify a special group requiring a different kind of teaching, and more important to identify the features of high-quality education that will mean better achievement for all. From this perspective, pupils who are failing to learn can be seen 'as indicators of the need for reform. They point to the need to improve schooling in a way that will enable them to achieve success' (Ainscow, 1991: 3). Instead of offering extra help and support to identified individuals, the focus will be on work with teachers to increase the range of strategies they are able to use effectively in the classroom. Such school-improvement programmes can produce dramatic results: for example, in one American school (Joyce et al., 1991) reducing the proportion of students who failed their end of grade assessment from 70 per cent to 6 per cent in two years. Such circumstances fundamentally challenge the whole concept of special educational needs – at least as applied to pupils. It is clearly impossible to describe the 70 per cent who previously failed as having special needs: the special needs lay with the school and its staff rather than with the children. If this is so in an extreme case like this one, it is likely to apply in other situations less extreme. Hence the view that we should dispense altogether with the special needs terminology.

The main drawback of the term 'special needs' remains that it still, however well intentioned we are in using it, implies that there is necessarily something intrinsic about a child's learning difficulty. It implies that the special needs characterize the learner rather than the learning situation. This too is an idea so easily challenged that the special needs concept can seem ludicrous: would a child who uses a wheelchair *have* special needs if the local school had a few ramps rather than steps, or would children with a specific learning difficulty/ dyslexia have special needs if a machine were available that could translate speech to print and vice versa? Whether something presents a difficulty or not depends entirely on whether the situation or the environment are enabling or disabling. Yet by describing children as 'special needs' we can absolve ourselves from the responsibility to enable, and reinforce the notions of purely within-child or within-family explanations of learning difficulty. It may have been shown (Mortimore et al., 1988) that school factors can be much more influential than home background factors on the amount of progress made by pupils (four times more important for reading, and ten times more important for maths and writing), but teachers still find it very hard to get away from the idea that learning problems reside primarily in children's individual characteristics and those of their families.

The reasons are not hard to find. Again, it comes back to teacher confidence. If teachers do not feel confident, and supported by colleagues and resources, in planning for children who are not learning, it is entirely natural for them to seek relief from inner discomfort by attributing the failure to learn to factors that are outside their control. What is happening is this:

> Teachers see themselves as significant, or not, in the school and classroom according to whether they are faced with acceptable/satisfactory pupil-reactions to school and academic work, or problematic/troublesome ones. That is, when pupils behave and achieve well, teachers tend to see themselves as important influences. When the opposite occurs, teachers

see themselves as not influential. In the latter situation, pupil-reactions are construed in terms of pupil-'pathologies' or of social determinants beyond the control of the teacher.

(Phillips, 1989)

Given all these arguments against the term 'special needs', with all its risks of labelling and its implied focus on 'pupil pathology', some would maintain that a book like this one, with a title of meeting special needs in the primary classroom, should not be written at all. Instead, we should be writing only about meeting individual needs and making schools more effective.

This too has risks, however. Raising every child's achievement will still leave the gaps between high and low achievers that are vastly hurtful to individual children and their parents. Sharing expertise in meeting special needs may be a better way of promoting the truly inclusive classroom than denying that such expertise exists at all. Asking teachers to focus on individualizing programme planning and instruction for all 20 to 30 (or more) children in their class may be asking more than is humanly possible. Since the majority will be able to learn incidentally – that is, from brief, loosely focused exposure to appropriate experiences, rather than needing multiple exposures and direct, tightly-focused teaching – it may be better to use limited time in making detailed plans for this kind of teaching for three or four children in a class rather than for them all.

Further arguments in favour of using special needs terminology could be found if it were possible to show that there are some special sorts of teaching that some children require from time to time, while others do not. This is a sensitive and contentious issue, but on balance, the evidence from research is that there are such special requirements – though not nearly so many of them as were once thought. All children require some things once thought to be the particular province of special education – for example, systematic procedures for monitoring progress, parental involvement in their learning, differentiated tasks, and the 'climate of warmth and support in which they feel valued and able to risk making mistakes as they learn, without fear of criticism' (NCC, 1989). Nevertheless, it is possible to identify some special approaches which some children require more than others. These include:

- The provision of special means of access to the curriculum, as outlined by Warnock – for example, the use of a specialist communication system such as Braille or a sign language.
- The use of bypass strategies to ensure that difficulties in one area of the curriculum do not hold a child back in other areas – for example, oral presentation of material for a pupil with reading difficulties.
- A bias towards somewhat more structured teaching methods (Cronbach and Snow, 1977), especially in specifying the small steps within the broad ladder of learning targets outlined for all children in the national curriculum, and in providing for overlearning (that is, continuing to practise new skills long after the point at which they appear to have been mastered).

- A focus on increasing the time that the child spends on task, which research has shown to be particularly low in children with learning or behaviour difficulties, and which correlates highly with academic success (Bennett et al., 1984).
- A focus on increasing the child's self-confidence and self-esteem, which again feature prominently in research on the characteristics of children who are not learning or behaving well, and which teachers are uniquely able to influence as a route to enhancing achievement (Gurney, 1988).

These, then, are the arguments for continuing to think in terms of some children's special needs rather than simply all children's individual needs. How can the debate be resolved? The answer is probably to continue to identify situations where some children will have special requirements, but to locate the special needs in ourselves as teachers, and in schools as organizations, more readily than we locate them in children. Seen this way, children with special needs are, as Solity describes them, children that teachers experience difficulty in teaching. This is the best meaning for the term 'special educational need', and the one that is implied throughout this book.

The best practice in relation to special needs will also be based on the notion of minimizing teachers' difficulties in successfully working with the whole range of children in their classes. A real-life example from one junior school (Ainscow and Muncey, 1989) illustrates how this can come about, without unnecessary labelling of children, or imposing fixed conceptions of their intrinsic difficulties. In this particular school, planned programmes of work in various curricular areas were drawn up by teams of staff on a termly basis. Once the programme had been agreed, the team would go through it point by point to identify parts that might prove difficult or inadequate for some pupils, and plan alternative ways in which these parts of the curriculum could be delivered or in which pupils could respond. The need for different ways of organizing pupil groups and staffing arrangements, and for special teaching resources, would be considered. For the moment, some pupils and their teachers would be identified as having special needs – but only for the moment. Through this system, the best aspects of the concept of special educational needs – extra planning and resourcing – could be maintained, but the worst aspects of labelling avoided.

ROLES AND RESPONSIBILITIES: THE LEGISLATIVE FRAMEWORK

Chris is 10. His speech is not always clear, because of articulation difficulties; he uses short, sometimes ungrammatical sentences and finds it hard to process and remember classroom instructions. His reading and written work are poor (he is working towards Level 2 in these areas of the national curriculum), but with support in writing things down he can do as well as most others his age in science and technology. He has infrequent speech therapy at a local clinic: his speech therapist is keen to devise a programme of language work for Chris to do in school. A special support teacher visits once a week to help Chris with his reading. The class teacher is relieved that he is having extra help from a specialist outside the school, so that she can concentrate on the needs of others in the class. She wonders, though, how Chris will manage in the forthcoming SATs, which are expected to be largely written. The headteacher feels concern about whether a child with such a low level of literacy skill should be expected to undertake SATs at all, and would like Chris to be exempted from the assessment tasks if possible.

Up to the end of the last financial year, Chris also had help from the school's own special needs support teacher, who worked with Chris for a short period each day, in class, on reading and with written work. Now this has become more difficult to arrange, as the school has had to reduce the hours attached to her post. Some parents have complained to the school governors about this, but the governors feel it is not their responsibility, and that they have done all they can within the locally managed budget.

Chris is making only very slow progress. The educational psychologist is consulted, and at a meeting involving Chris' parents and teachers, it is agreed that his needs should be assessed to determine whether the local education authority (LEA) should provide for him through a Statement of Special Educational Need. The subsequent multiprofessional assessment makes clear Chris' needs for increased access to specialist language programmes, intensive literacy support, and classroom bypass technology such as a hand-held tape recorder and electronic spellchecker. The local authority, however, is overwhelmed with requests for extra support and technology for children in mainstream schools, which they must meet from the limited funds left over from an educational budget mostly devolved to locally managed schools. They do not employ their own speech therapists, nor is there a language unit available in the area. In their view, Chris' needs should be met locally from the school's own resources.

Where should the responsibility for providing extra resources for Chris lie? And equally, who should be responsible for *managing* the provision made for him, and monitoring its effectiveness? The type of scenario described here for Chris is increasingly common. The advent of local management of schools (LMS) has turned an already complex situation into a veritable minefield, with children and their families as the potential casualties. To find their way in situations like this, all concerned need a very clear picture of their respective responsibilities. Schools need to know what can legitimately be expected from them, and where the boundaries of their role should lie.

The role of the class teacher

The class teacher's role in relation to special needs is spelled out in the DFE's Code of Practice on the Identification and Assessment of Special Educational Needs (DFE 1994). He or she is responsible initially for identifying a child's special needs, and gathering a range of information about the child's attainments and behaviour. This information should include the views and perspective of the child's parents, and the child's perceptions of his or her difficulties and how they might be addressed. The class teacher is also responsible for registering the child's special needs with the school's special needs coordinator (SENCO), carrying out planned strategies for meeting the child's special needs, and monitoring their effects. Initially the planned strategies may be simply increased differentiation of regular classroom work; if difficulties persist they may include specific programmes, activities or resources, sometimes involving extra adult support or advice from an outside agency. The class teacher's role, however, does not cease when outside agencies become involved as it seems to have done with Christopher; he or she, as the person in most regular contact with the child in school, retains a pivotal role in implementing and evaluating support strategies.

The role of the school governors

School governors are required under the 1993 Act to:

- Do their best to ensure that the necessary provision is made for any pupil who has special needs.
- Make sure that the needs of such children are made known to those who teach them.
- Make sure that teachers in the school are aware of the importance of identifying and providing for children with special needs.
- Make sure that children with special needs can join in with other children in school activities, within the limits of efficient use of resources.
- Draw up a policy for special educational needs and report annually to parents on the implementation and effectiveness of their policy.

The Code of Practice also indicates that governors should, in conjunction with the headteacher, establish appropriate staffing and funding arrangements for special needs. They are not required to nominate one governor with responsibility for special needs, but are encouraged to consider appointing a committee to take a particular interest in this area.

The role of the school as a whole

Through their special needs policy, schools are required to publish information for parents on the allocation of resources to and amongst pupils with special needs. They must identify and name a teacher or teachers responsible for the day to day coordination of arrangements for supporting these children (the SENCO or SENCO team), and for advising and supporting colleagues. They should set up a staged procedure which will make sure that first simple interventions, and later (if these have not proved effective) more detailed strategies are put into place for any child whose progress is a cause for concern. After the first simple interventions, later strategies should be recorded formally through an Individual Education Plan (IEP) for the child, setting out roles and responsibilities and arrangements for monitoring progress. Schools will generally need to provide evidence of this planning for staged support in school, of regular reviews involving parents, and of seeking advice from outside agencies, before asking for additional support from the LEA through a Statement of special educational needs.

Schools are responsible (DES 1989a) for coordinating and recording the work that has to be done before the requirements of the national curriculum can be modified or disapplied for a pupil, either temporarily by a headteacher's direction or through a Statement of special educational needs. Generally however, the need for any such formal procedures can be minimized by making use of the flexibility provided in the revised curriculum for pupils to work on material outside their key stage where this is necessary for them to progress and demonstrate achievement. Additional flexibility is provided by the special arrangements available for assessment in standard attainment tasks.

Schools are obliged to contribute their professional written Advice to the LEA when a pupil is being assessed for a possible Statement. If a Statement is issued, they must prepare reports for the annual review of the Statement and coordinate the annual review meeting to which parents and relevant agencies must be invited.

The roles and rights of parents

Parents' views must be taken into account when planning appropriate provision for children with special needs. Anyone with parental responsibility for a child (not just the people the child lives with) should be consulted and involved where practical in the school-based stages of assessment and provision; they must be formally informed of any proposal to assess the child's needs for a possible Statement, or of any proposal to modify or disapply any aspect of the national curriculum. Parents can request the LEA to assess their child's needs, and the LEA must comply with that request unless they have already made a statutory assessment in the last six months or unless, after examining all the available evidence, it is their opinion that such an assessment is unnecessary. Parents are entitled to be present at any examination related to the assessment procedures, and to receive copies of all the professional Advice received in the course of the assessment. They can specify which school they would like to see named on the Statement; the LEA are obliged to comply with that preference unless the school is unsuitable or the placement would be incompatible with the efficient education of other children in the school or the efficient use of resources.

Parents can appeal against an LEA's refusal to make a formal assessment or reassessment of the child's special needs, or to issue or maintain a Statement. They can appeal against the content of the Statement, or the school named by the LEA. Appeals are to the Special Educational Needs Tribunal, a national agency set up by the 1993 Education Act to hear parents' appeals.

For children with special needs who do not have a Statement, parents are entitled to information – in a range of community languages and on tape – on:

- the school's special needs policy;
- the support available in school and from the LEA;
- procedures for acting on parental concerns;
- the involvement they can expect in assessment and decision making, emphasizing the importance of their contributions;
- how to complain if they are not satisfied with the arrangements made by the school for their child;
- services provided by the local authority for children 'in need';
- local and national voluntary organizations which may be able to give advice, information or counselling.

The role of the local education authority

The local education authority has a responsibility to assess children's needs under the 1981 and 1993 Acts. If it is shown that a child has a learning difficulty (as defined in the Acts) that cannot be met from normally available resources (which are taken to include outreach and peripatetic support and advisory services) the authority has a responsibility to determine the additional special educational provision for the child. It is placed under a duty to educate the child in an ordinary rather than a special school, providing that this is compatible with:

- his receiving the special educational provision he requires,
- the provision of efficient education for the children with whom he will be educated, and
- the efficient use of resources.

When the 1981 Act came into force it was anticipated that the numbers of children with Statements would be similar to the numbers who had hitherto been placed mainly in special schools and units – about 2 per cent of the school population. Statements would be required, said guidance accompanying the Act, for pupils still placed in special schools and units, and also for some pupils with 'severe and complex' difficulties requiring extra provision in mainstream. In practice, 'severe and complex' has proved difficult to interpret. Many LEAs have greatly exceeded the anticipated 2 per cent numbers, and find themselves under increasing pressure to guarantee, via Statements, ever more central resources to children in locally managed mainstream schools. In response, many have sought to develop tighter guidelines on the types of need that schools should expect to meet locally, and those which might require central resources. The 1994 Code of Practice provides a framework (albeit a loose one) for such criteria.

In the past, a child's Statement would specify only those additional, central resources provided by the LEA to meet the child's needs. Since a 1990 appeal ruling, this position has become more complicated. The Statement now has to specify *all* the provision required to meet a child's needs, even if some of that is provided by the school. This means that the school as well as the LEA might be in breach of the law if they ceased to be able to provide what the Statement specified.

In making an assessment of a child's special needs under the 1993 Act, the LEA must as a minimum seek advice from the child's parents and school; from the health service and social services; and from an educational psychologist. The advice from professionals should include details of the child's strengths and weaknesses, relationships with the environment at home and at school, relevant aspects of his or her past history, the aims of any special provision for the child, and the facilities and resources required to achieve these aims. The time span between notifying parents of the intention to assess and the issue of a draft Statement should not exceed six months. The LEA has a duty to keep the Statement under annual review, and to coordinate a full multi-agency review in the year after the young person's fourteenth birthday.

With regard to the provision of services – such as speech therapy – which have in the past been regarded as falling outside the LEA's responsibility, recent appeal judgements have made it clear that they can be considered as educational, and should be provided by the LEA if the assessment shows a need.

Once an LEA has assessed a child's needs, decided to issue a Statement, and asked the parents to indicate the school they would like their child to attend, it must consult the governing body of the school it proposes to name in the Statement. It must give consideration to the views of those consulted, but has the right to direct admission if there is a place available. A governing body cannot refuse to admit a child because of his or her special educational needs.

For pupils without Statements, but with special needs, the LEA is required by Circular 22/89 to 'help governors to fulfil their duties by providing guidance to all county and voluntary schools in their area on the arrangements and procedures for identifying, assessing and meeting special educational needs'. They can devise a set of weightings for pupils with special needs, with or without Statements, in order to allocate moneys to schools to meet special needs from their own resources via the LMS budget. They must, however, monitor the effectiveness of such provision.

The weightings have most commonly been based on the numbers of pupils in each school taking up free school meals – a crude measure of social disadvantage, but one that nevertheless seems to work as well as many more complex measures. In some areas, however, an internal audit by each school of the number of pupils with learning difficulties, and the level of support they require, is moderated by the LEA and used as the basis for allocating funds.

Finally, local authorities as a whole (not just their education departments) have a range of duties under the 1989 Children Act (Dott 1989). They must provide services such as advice, guidance, counselling, day and after school care, home helps, family centres, and assistance with holidays to the families of children defined as 'in need'. The definition of 'need' is as unclear as the 'special need' in the 1981 and 1993 Acts, but will encompass children who are living in situations where their health (physical or mental) or development (physical, intellectual, social or emotional) is likely to be significantly impaired for reasons of disability, neglect, or acute family difficulties. Many children with Statements of 'special need' may also be entitled to services as children 'in need' under the Children Act – but not all. The two concepts differ in intent: while 'special needs' are linked to education provision, the term 'in need' is intended to lead to a wider range of support services to enable families facing troubles of different kinds to look after their children themselves. The main overlap of the two concepts is in their provision for children with disabilities. Here, the Children Act introduces the important new principle that local authorities should provide services to disabled children in their area that will minimize the effects of disability and allow them to lead lives which are as normal as possible.

School inspection and special needs

Responsibility for monitoring the extent to which a school is fulfilling legislative requirements in respect of special needs lies partly with the LEA (for example, through monitoring annual reviews of Statements) and partly with Ofsted. School inspectors will be:

- Verifying the SEN provision made by the school, and the use made of any SEN funding.
- Making judgements on the quality of that provision – asking, for example, whether it allows pupils to access a broad and balanced curriculum, and whether pupils make progress commensurate with their abilities.
- Commenting on the extent to which the identification and assessment processes set out by the Code of Practice are in place, inform the SEN policy and are understood by all teachers.

They will be looking for evidence of positive attitudes towards children with special needs, close partnership with parents, and judicious use of outside support services and voluntary help. Crucially, they will want to know whether the special needs coordinator is provided with authority, time and resources to discharge the role and support colleagues. They will look to see whether children with Statements are receiving the provision set out for them, and may ask to see examples of Individual Education Plans. They may interview or observe support agencies working in the school, and will look at the accommodation provided – for example, for withdrawal teaching. In the course of classroom observation they will examine curricular provision – for example, how the school makes texts accessible or offers alternatives to written recording for children with literacy difficulties.

CONCLUSION

Definitions are difficult. It is hard to pin down just who has needs, and even harder to determine whose responsibility it is to meet them or how well those responsibilities are being fulfilled. The legislative framework attempts this; its intention – to safeguard the rights of children – is admirable, even if by its focus on identifying and providing for certain children with 'needs' that others do not have, it runs the risk of distracting attention from an equally pressing question addressed in this introductory chapter – how schools and society can adapt themselves better to individuals so that ultimately no one needs the stigma of being special. In the next two chapters we will return squarely to this alternative question, as we focus on the school and the curriculum rather than the individual child in need.

FURTHER READING

Ainscow, M. (ed.) (1991) *Effective Schools For All*. London, David Fulton.

· 2 ·

DEVELOPING A WHOLE
SCHOOL POLICY

WHOLE SCHOOL POLICIES AND SCHOOL MANAGEMENT

Writing whole school curricular and policy statements is a familiar exercise for most teachers these days. A mainstay of the new approach to school improvement and school self-management (Hargreaves et al., 1989), school policies cover everything from parental partnership to the storage of PE equipment: the 1993 Education Act followed this trend in making the publication of a whole school special needs policy a legal requirement for all schools.

There is a danger, however, in requiring a policy if those who contribute to its development do so because of perceived external demands rather than because of the kinds of internal processes which make the need for a coherent, shared policy clear to all. In these circumstances, there are great temptations to adopt an off-the-peg policy, from another school or published source, adapted slightly to meet local needs. Such policies, however good they look on paper, may never make the leap from paper to classroom practice. If they are to affect practice, and meet the real needs of children, parents and staff, it will be necessary to focus on the *process* of policy development, rather than the outcome, and to start the process with a real awareness of the reasons why whole school policies are needed and the benefits they can bring.

WHOLE SCHOOL POLICIES: THE RATIONALE

In one school, a recently-appointed teacher of Year 5 has several children in her class whose reading skills have not yet developed beyond level one in national curriculum terms, and whose written recording is usually restricted to a few short sentences. The children go out once a week for extra help with their work, but their teacher feels this is not enough, and wants to do more. When she asks in school about appropriate reading material for the children, she finds there is a shortage of anything other than simple stories with an infant interest level. There is no one who can advise her on how to overcome the children's dislike of writing. They all say they would like to improve their handwriting and spelling; there are resources for the combined practice of handwriting and spelling patterns in school, but each teacher keeps his or her own favourites in their own classroom.

In another school nearby, the same problem meets a different response. Here the designated teacher with responsibility for special needs meets with the class teacher to plan a project where the children with literacy difficulties will be included in mixed-ability groups to write (on the word processor) and publish personalized story books for each member of the reception class. There is a central resource bank of spelling and handwriting materials, coded against the small steps which staff have worked out to bridge national curriculum attainment levels. The problem of shortage of books at appropriate reading and interest levels has been identified by all staff, but not yet solved: ordering books will have to wait till funds permit. Meanwhile, when the class teacher raises at a staff meeting the problem of developing these children's reading, colleagues suggest that each child is linked with a reading partner from a Year 6 class for regular paired reading of books that would be too difficult for the younger children to manage alone, but possible given the older child's support. Finally, the new teacher meets with the support teacher who has been withdrawing the children for extra help. The support teacher explains that her role in the school is to work with identified children to help them reach learning targets they have set with their class teacher; there will be regular review meetings to monitor progress.

The difference between these two schools is one of individual versus collective responsibility. In one, we can imagine each teacher withdrawing to his or her own room and closing the door: what happens inside to any children who have special needs will be determined by the knowledge, skills and resources available to that classroom teacher – perhaps supplemented by the separately-held knowledge, skills and resources of a support teacher. In the other, responsibility is shared: advice is available; resources are commonly held; lines of responsibility are clearly outlined, and systematic procedures in place for monitoring and recording pupils' progress.

The benefits of such a whole school response to special needs are obvious. Outcomes for children will be better; staff satisfaction greater; opportunities for lack of communication and piecemeal, inconsistent responses to children's needs fewer. What is also clear, however, is that the benefits for the school in the second example did not come about without a good deal of hard work: these were staff who had together committed time and energy to the process of policy development.

DEVELOPING A WHOLE SCHOOL POLICY: MANAGING THE CHANGE

Reflecting on major changes they have had to make to their own professional practice, most teachers agree that they were most willing to commit themselves to proposed changes, and most willing to see them through, when the following conditions were present:

- The impetus for change was at least partly internal rather than external, offering the people involved the chance of solving problems that were genuinely problems or 'points of pain' for them.
- Solutions were not imposed from above: ideas were generated, discussed and evaluated by everyone involved.
- The proposed changes were supported by people in positions of power.
- Resources – including time for those involved to learn new skills, observe each other in classrooms, and meet regularly to share ideas – were available to support the change.
- Changes were not expected to take place overnight, but were spread out over time.
- Elements of accountability (targets to be achieved and deadlines met) were built into the plans for change.

This teacher-generated list of necessary preconditions to successful change, which is supported by the outcomes of several large-scale research studies (Fullan, 1991), has many implications for the development of a whole school special needs policy. Such a policy, if it is to be effective, will almost always involve major changes in attitudes or practice for at least some members of a school staff.

Very often, such staff will have worked for much of their school career in a climate where special needs are attributed exclusively to factors within the home background, where understanding children's special needs and proffering appropriate teaching has been seen as the province of 'experts', where the ideal is one-to-one or small group teaching outside the classroom or in a special school, and where classroom teachers feel minimal confidence in their ability to help the child, and minimal personal responsibility for so doing.

We cannot expect those accustomed to this model to adopt overnight the post-Warnock concepts of the interactive nature of special needs, and the crucial responsibility of the classroom teacher for curriculum-based assessment and curriculum planning – not unless we build in the preconditions for successful change, and plan policy development as a process owned by and actively involving all staff, which will take place over an extended period of time. Such a process will start by establishing a shared perception of the pressing problems that need to be tackled, through the mechanism of reviewing the school's present strengths and weaknesses in meeting children's special educational needs.

Step one: reviewing practice – where we are now

The overt purposes of reviewing current practice in school are twofold: to define any problems that the school is experiencing in providing for special needs (so that key areas can be highlighted for development and actions planned), and to identify the things that are already going well (so that these can be incorporated into the school policy document). There can also be a third, less obvious purpose, which is to promote changes in attitudes through the feedback on current practices that is gathered – particularly from pupils and parents – in the course of the review.

Extensive school development programmes are available (Gross, 1991) which provide a range of suggestions for reviewing and reflecting on existing practice in the area of special needs. At a minimum, however, the review and reflection phase should include:

- Gathering information and perceptions from as wide a group as possible – staff, parents, pupils, governors, external agencies who visit the school.
- Asking staff for their perceptions of the school's strengths and weaknesses in meeting special needs: if a questionnaire is to be used, it should include questions on the availability of information on pupils' special needs and appropriate teaching approaches, availability of materials and resources, the role of the special needs coordinator, the use of additional adults in or out of the classroom to help individuals or groups, the role of outside agencies, and the links made with parents.
- Gathering information on current staff levels of confidence and professional development needs in key areas. One way of doing this is to ask each member of staff to sort cards (Table 2.1) into three piles: 'things I feel very confident about', 'things I feel moderately confident about' and 'things I do not feel confident about'. An exercise like this will make it possible to identify patterns in staff development needs, and also to identify strengths in collective expertise – areas where colleagues can act as a support and reassurance for one another.
- Considering the perspective of children in the school who have been identified as having special needs, for example by discussing with them things that they enjoy and look forward to in school, and things they do not, who they sit and work with in the classroom and how they feel about that, how they feel about any extra support provided to them, how they feel about themselves as learners, and anything they would really like to achieve or change about themselves in school.
- Meeting with parents of children with special needs to ask about their perception of positives and negatives in the ways in which their children's

Table 2.1   A card sort to assess staff levels of confidence and professional development needs

Legal requirements and LEA special needs procedures	Diagnostic assessment
Planning schemes of work for all abilities	National curriculum assessment for pupils with special needs
Breaking the curriculum down into small steps for children with learning difficulties	Groupwork and special needs
Identifying special needs	Managing in-class support
Making action plans for individual children	Ways of working with the special needs coordinator
Involving other children in helping pupils with special needs	Involving parents
IT and special needs	Other resources and materials
Support services I can call on	Integrating children with disabilities
Helping children with behaviour difficulties	Self-esteem and special needs
Listening, counselling, circle time	Helping children with language difficulties
Helping children with literacy difficulties	Helping children with physical difficulties or sensory impairment

difficulties have been discussed with them, the ways in which information has been shared, and the ways in which they have been involved in forward planning.

- Examining existing curricular policy documents and programmes of study to see how they address the issues of special educational needs.
- Gathering and looking together at examples of current records of assessment and action for children with special needs.
- Looking at the way children with special needs currently spend their time in school, by recording their activities in the form of running diaries, pupil logs or blocked in timetables.

The outcomes of this information-gathering phase need then to be shared (again, as widely as possible) with all staff and governors, through displays, presentations, and written reports.

Step two: developing a vision – where we would like to be

Having gathered and shared information on the school's existing response to special educational needs, the next step is to establish the broad vision which the school holds for meeting children's individual or special needs: the values and principles it would wish to adhere to, and its view on the entitlements of children and parents.

It will be useful to consult policy guidelines developed by others – for example, the LEA – but the vision *must* be personal to each particular school, and owned by those who work there. For this reason, the discussion and activities which will develop the vision should be shared by all staff and governors.

Activities should focus attention on the needs of children who have difficulty in learning, but can usefully draw on adults' own experience as learners. For example, staff and governors might discuss in pairs an experience of a time when they were trying to learn something new which they found difficult: points to talk about include how this made them feel and behave, and what kind of help they wanted and did not want. Alternatively, they might try out some difficult tasks (like writing at speed to dictation using the non-preferred hand, or reading aloud from a text which is partly obscured, or working in small groups on a task where some groups are given only part of the information they will need to complete the task), then discuss any negative feelings or behaviours that result, and ways in which these might have been avoided. Put together with information from the review phase on the perceptions and experiences of children and their parents, activities of this kind will help the group to formulate their ideas on the general principles for the school in delivering the curriculum and offering support to children with special needs.

Step three: comparing vision and practice

It should now be possible for staff to consider together the information from the review of current practice, in the light of the agreed general principles for meeting children's individual needs in school: to compare the 'where we are' with the 'where we would like to be'. One way of doing this is to list individually and as a group the strengths in current practice, which should be incorporated into the whole school policy document under relevant headings (see below), then the major gaps or problem areas. The group can work to agree several key problem areas which should be prioritized in the policy document for action and development, and then work on these one by one using the four-stage problem-solving process (Cameron and Stratford, 1987):

- What exactly is the problem? (getting it clear)
- How would we like things to be instead?
- How can we get here? (brainstorming solutions)
- Which is the best solution? (evaluating possible solutions)

Step four: drafting the policy

The minimum content of a special needs policy should include, under government regulations:

Basic information
- the objectives of the SEN policy:
- the name of the SENCO or teacher responsible for day to day implementation;
- the arrangements for coordinating provision;
- information on any SEN specialism or special unit the school might have, on special facilities increasing access to the school for pupils with SEN, and on relevant admission arrangements.

Identification, assessment and provision
- how resources are allocated to and amongst pupils with SEN;
- arrangements for identification, assessment and review;
- how pupils with SEN will be enabled to access a broad, balanced curriculum including the national curriculum;
- integration arrangements;
- how any complaints about provision can be made;
- criteria for evaluating the success of the policy.

School staffing and outside links
- SEN INSET arrangements;
- use made of support services and other teachers and facilities from outside the school;
- links with special schools and other mainstream schools; transition arrangements;
- partnership with parents;
- links with other agencies – health, social services, voluntary organizations.

Additionally, many schools will want to include their own working definition of special needs, the vision and values they hold for their provisions, and details of the roles and responsibilities held by school staff and governors.

Step five: evaluating the policy

Since schools have been asked to report on the effectiveness of their special needs policy each year they have begun to give thought to the difficult question of evaluation. Many are setting themselves targets – for example, to raise measured achievement in less able groups; to achieve a certain percentage of objectives set in children's Individual Education Plans; or to reduce the number of children progressing upwards through the Code of Practice stages from school based interventions to interventions requiring outside agency support.

Other possible performance indicators could include:

- pupil self esteem
- parental participation
- parental views
- pupil views
- resources acquired
- resources actually used
- number of pupil exclusions
- evidence of integration
- evidence of curriculum breadth for pupils with special needs
- lesson plans showing evidence of differentiation
- staff confidence in meeting particular kinds of special needs.

AN EXAMPLE: DEVELOPING A WHOLE SCHOOL POLICY AT GLENDOWN PRIMARY SCHOOL

Glendown is a seven-class, 210-pupil primary school in a small town. It serves a mixed area with both owner-occupied houses and a small council estate where many of the children take free school meals. The school has a (part-time) special needs coordinator whose role includes collating special needs records, and discussing with other staff whether children require withdrawal teaching support (which she does with groups of four or five children, mainly on literacy skills), and whether/when to refer to outside agencies.

Information from the review of special needs provision came from a survey of staff opinion, an interview with individual pupils undertaken by the special needs coordinator, discussion with outside agencies, a survey by the special needs coordinator of resources in school suitable for children with special needs, a check on existing curricular policy documents and on programmes of study, and finally a log completed by all teachers of the tasks set to a pupil with special needs, and a pupil of average ability with no special needs, at fixed points in the day over a two-week period.

The log of tasks revealed that in many classrooms, children with special needs were spending more time completing written tasks than were other children, and correspondingly less time on such activities as individual reading, using the computer to input and print out work, and group discussion. They were often engaged in relatively routine individual tasks rather than investigative or group projects.

The staff questionnaire indicated that most teachers felt the school was good at helping children with literacy problems. They also felt that parental involvement for parents of children with special needs was high, with parents being drawn in early to discuss their child's difficulties through the school's system of regularly recording and reviewing plans for individual children, and through the paired reading home programme set up by the special needs coordinator. Staff felt that children with special needs were generally identified at an early stage. Several staff mentioned as a strength the initiative by the school's information technology (IT) coordinator, who had invited the advisory teacher for IT to come to a staff meeting and demonstrate useful software for children with special needs; they felt that the software was now well used in several classrooms and that the children enjoyed it.

As for weaknesses, staff felt that they lacked knowledge of other resources that might be useful for children with special needs, and of general strategies for teaching slow learners. Helping children with behaviour problems was another area where staff felt they needed more advice and training. Several teachers said that they felt there should be more sharing of expertise and resources in school, rather than just expecting the special needs coordinator to do everything. Others (possibly as a result of logging children's activities) felt that the school should look at the curriculum offered to children with special needs, and try to make it more interesting and relevant.

Current school policy documents and programmes of study included few references to meeting special learning needs – with the exception of the science documents, where staff had made use of the suggestions in the NCC booklet *A Curriculum For All* (National Curriculum Council, 1989) to produce guidelines on ways in which materials and tasks could be adapted to meet the needs of children with a wide range of difficulties.

When the special needs coordinator interviewed groups of children, they mentioned not enjoying or looking forward to tasks involving a lot of writing, spelling and times tables tests, being kept in to finish work, and (for junior-aged children) having to fetch their new reading books from the infant area of the school. All the children said they sat and worked in class with the children with whom they also went to their withdrawal teaching sessions. They were not unhappy about this, regarding these children as their friends, but they did not like being referred to as 'Mrs Thorne's group' (the name of the special needs coordinator): one child said 'the others . . . 'cos we have to have help – they say we're Mrs Thorne's thickies'. Most of them said they felt they were not as clever as others, and that they did not often feel proud of their work. When the special needs coordinator asked them if there was something they would really like to achieve or change about themselves in school, the most common wish was to be on the same maths book/reading colour level as others in the class. This was particularly true when there were very few children in any one class on that book or reading level.

External support agencies said that they felt the school was very strong in parental involvement and in its use of written action plans for individual children. Also mentioned were its structured approaches to literacy for children who had difficulties, and the fact that the school had chosen to spend money on a special needs coordinator and given her an important role. Areas where the school was perhaps not doing so well were highlighted as the low self-esteem and lack of opportunities for success for many children with special needs in what was basically quite an 'academic' school. Support staff also reported feeling isolated from the class teachers, whom they rarely seemed able to talk to on visits.

The survey of resources by the special needs coordinator brought to light a cupboard full of materials for language and listening skills ordered by a teacher who had left, and a very unequal provision between classes of games and worksheets to support basic skills. A local special school kept a permanent display of materials for children with special needs, but no one from Glendown except the special needs coordinator had yet visited or borrowed equipment.

In working on the general principles for their special needs policy, the Glendown staff found some aspects easy to agree. These included full access to the whole range of curricular experiences for all children in the school; a curriculum that offered opportunities for success to all; an acceptance by the class teacher of ultimate responsibility for coordinating systems to meet the special needs of individuals in the class.

There was considerable debate on whether support should be offered to children on a withdrawal basis or in class, and on whether priority should be given to supporting children still experiencing difficulties at the upper end of the school, or to younger classes. Eventually it was agreed that priority for support in English and maths should be given to younger children, but that there should still be provision for particular children's ongoing and individual needs in older groups wherever possible. Initially, learning support would be offered within the classroom, but regular discussions between class teacher, child and support teacher would be used to monitor its perceived effectiveness.

There was also debate over the principle of integration. Some staff felt strongly that for some children special schools and units were the only answer; others felt that all children should have a right to be educated in their own local schools. There was a general concern that the requirements for schools to publish the results of national curriculum assessments could mean that they would be less willing to integrate children with special needs. Glendown staff and governors decided that their policy should be to base decisions on integration on the needs of individual children and of others in their class, and not on considerations about overall achievement levels within the school.

In their policy document, staff went on to record and expand on existing good practice under headings of parental involvement, record keeping and differentiation of the curriculum (using the work that had been done in Science as a model).

They made a long list of areas that were seen as problems: over-reliance on the special needs coordinator at the expense of sharing expertise, inadequate and unevenly distributed resources, support limited to children with literacy problems, an often unstimulating curriculum for children with special needs, low self-esteem and lack of opportunities for success for some children, policies for pupil groupings and assessment and provision of materials that singled out children with special needs in unhelpful ways.

It was felt that by re-defining the role of the special needs coordinator to include working alongside the class teacher and helping to adapt materials and schemes of work, many of these problems would be tackled. Three other key areas were identified as priorities for further development work in school in the next six months.

1 For the first, the problem of *pupil groupings*, staff decided that the best strategy would be a plan to develop mixed-ability group work throughout the school, using the expertise of two members of staff who regularly worked with their classes to help the children learn the skills of effective group work.
2 For the second, that of the *low self-esteem* of children with special needs in the school, staff brainstormed all the ways they could think of to celebrate children's successes in and out of school, and their progress in work or in behaviour. This led to several developments, including a board on which photographs of children

were pinned next to positive things which other children and teachers had written about them, and records of special talents or successes.

3 For the third problem area, that of *resources in school*, it was decided first to ask teachers from the resource base at the local special school to bring a selection of materials to a staff meeting and talk about their use. Eventually staff planned to develop their own resource bank of materials, centrally held and indexed according to national curriculum programmes of study.

In the light of their work in these three areas, they later revised and added to their whole school policy. The final version was then used as a basis for a leaflet for parents explaining what the school could offer to children with special needs, and as a tool for evaluation when the policy was reviewed.

CONCLUSION

The example of Glendown highlights many of the important issues in developing a whole school policy for special educational needs. The school might have chosen to base their policy on an off-the-peg model, and probably agreed an elegant, comprehensive and clear document in half the time. That they did not take this route reflects the relative importance they placed on process rather than product, in ensuring maximum commitment to the policy from all those involved. Finding the 'points of pain' for children and staff through the review of practice, negotiating priorities together, and allowing time for further development all meant that this particular policy was more than just another piece of paper; instead it represented the staff's real efforts to work collectively rather than individually to meet the whole range of needs in the children they taught.

FURTHER READING

Stobbs, P., Mackey, T., Norwich, B., Peacey, N. and Stephenson, P. (1995) *Schools' Special Educational Needs Policies Pack*. London: National Children's Bureau.

· 3 ·

SPECIAL NEEDS AND THE NATIONAL CURRICULUM

INTRODUCTION

The introduction of the national curriculum has brought many benefits to children with special educational needs. It has enriched the range of curricular experiences available to children in special schools, units and classes. It has made it easier for children to move between such special provisions and mainstream classes, because of the increased continuity of learning experiences across different settings. It has sharpened assessment and definition of need, by providing a shared vocabulary: there is at least some agreement on the interpretation of national curriculum attainment levels, whereas previous descriptions of children 'on red book four' or 'infant level maths' often had meaning only for a particular teacher or particular school. National curriculum assessment has also helped teachers to see more clearly how a child may have special needs in one area or subject, but not in others. Teachers' enhanced expertise in assessment of all children's progress through detailed observation within the classroom has been particularly helpful for children with difficulties in learning – for whom detailed observation of this kind is an essential pre-condition to offering timely and appropriate forms of support.

The most important contribution the national curriculum has made to the development of good special needs practice, however, is not in continuity or assessment or the shared vocabulary: it is, rather, in the emphasis it has brought on how to adapt tasks, and teaching and learning styles, to make the *same* overall programmes of study, specified for each key stage, accessible and meaningful to all children in a class. The word for this is differentiation, and differentiation within the national curriculum is the main focus of this chapter.

DIFFERENTIATION

Research has shown that on the whole primary teachers find differentiation very difficult. The studies of British classrooms in the 1980s by Neville Bennett and his colleagues (1984) provide the evidence. In observations of maths and language work among 6- to 8-year-old children, Bennett found that, on average, only around four out of ten tasks given to children were matched to their level of ability. Nearly half the tasks given to low attainers were too hard for them; 40 per cent of tasks given to high attainers were too easy for them. In classes of 8- to 11-year-olds, nearly two-thirds of all tasks given to the lowest attainers were too difficult. This applied particularly to written work: the children found practical tasks very much easier. When they were asked to write, they 'typically had limited memory for the stimulus to writing . . . performance on the task was slow: less than one word per minute of allocated time was produced' (Bennett, 1991: 125).

The introduction of the national curriculum initially appears to have decreased rather than increased teachers' confidence in their ability to adapt tasks and teaching and learning styles to meet the very wide range of ability in their classes. Over three-quarters of a large group of primary teachers surveyed when the national curriculum was introduced (Wragg et al., 1989) felt that including children with special needs in the national curriculum would be difficult.

Yet in principle, the ladder of learning steps prescribed by the national curriculum offers a great deal of practical support to teachers, in helping them to be aware of the things some children lower down the ladder may still need to be learning, and of the steps further up the ladder that some very able children may be ready to take. Here is an example:

> In planning topic work in her Year 4 class on the theme of clothes
> and coverings, one teacher first mapped her scheme of work to check
> for coverage of foundation subjects and cross-curricular themes. Her
> next step was to record the range of levels of attainment which the
> work in each subject area could involve. In science, the investigations
> she had planned of the properties of different fabrics would provide
> scope for children to make the kinds of simple observations and
> deductions required at Levels 1 and 2 in the attainment targets on
> scientific investigation, and on materials and their properties.
> Experiments on fabric strength and porosity would allow for Levels 3
> and 4 work on deduction, fair testing, and linking the properties
> of materials to the uses made of them. Some children, however,
> would need opportunities to take the work further, formulating
> simple explanations of findings about insulation (AT1 Level 5).
> In maths, the children's tests of the porosity of different fabrics
> would provide work on the need to use standard measures, from
> Level 2 of the shape, space and measures attainment target, right up
> to Level 6 for a child in the class with particular mathematical gifts,
> who would need to be challenged to devise a compound measure of
> porosity using volume and time.
> Work in history would be aimed for the majority of children at
> Level 3, helping them make deductions (for example, about social

groupings in Victorian Britain) based on the clothes people wore, while a child in the class with severe learning difficulties and a statement of special need would be able to work at Level 1, talking about clothes in pictures and photographs and comparing them with her own.

In geography, work would include a range of levels, with all the children able to find out (as part of their wider study of a developing country) about the clothes worn in different parts of the Indian subcontinent (Level 2), and some linking these with the climate and religious beliefs (Level 4). The study of the materials and processes used in making clothing would extend some pupils at Level 5 (offering explanations for the ways in which human activities affect the environment).

This teacher used the national curriculum documentation as a framework to help her identify opportunities for broadening what might have been a fairly mundane piece of topic work to stretch some children in particular directions, and to include work properly matched to the needs of children with learning difficulties. We will return to her topic planning later in the chapter to see how she went on to use other forms of differentiation, but first we need to consider in more detail the issue of matching task to learner.

Differentiation by task: the small steps approach

The most basic strategy for differentiation of the curriculum is differentiation by *task* – that is, offering children tasks of varying difficulty within the same broad scheme of work, as in the example of the topic on clothes and coverings. The national curriculum attainment targets and associated programmes of study can, as we have seen, support this approach, in that they break down curricular areas into roughly hierarchical steps, with ideas for appropriate tasks at each level. The difficulty, however, is that the gaps between the steps of the ladder are very wide, and there is little information on intermediate steps and associated tasks.

As an example, we can look at the measurement work that would be involved in the science experiments for the topic on clothes and coverings. It is a large leap for any child between ordering objects using direct comparison (AT3 Level 1), and using everyday standard units to measure length and mass (Level 2). Bridging steps are needed – and for the child with learning difficulties, the bridging steps may need to be very small and tightly documented.

In order to be able to differentiate by task, then, the teacher needs to know how to work out the bridging steps that will lead up to a particular skill, concept or level description. Let us see how this might be done for one aspect of the measurement work, telling the time (AT3 Level 3).

The teacher's first step is to consider the range of sub-skills necessary to be able to tell the time. She will recognize that the child must be able to understand

Table 3.1 Small steps to target. Maths AT3 Level 3: telling the time

Associates regularly occurring events with particular times – at one o'clock we eat lunch, etc.	☐
Understands vocabulary long and short	☐
Understands vocabulary near and nearest	☐
Recognizes and names numbers 1–12	☐
Tells time by the hour	☐
Understands concept of half	☐
Tells time by half hour	☐
Understands concept of quarter	☐
Understands language of past and to the hour	☐
Tells time by quarter past and to	☐
Counts aloud in fives	☐
Writes number sequence in fives	☐
Tells time to nearest five minutes past the hour by counting round in fives	☐
Matches appropriate digital times to analogue clock face	☐
Tells time to nearest five minutes to the hour by counting back in fives	☐
Automatically associates clock positions with times past and to the hour without needing to count round or back in fives	☐

and use certain language concepts, such as 'long' and 'short' (for the hands of the clock), and 'near' and 'nearest' (for when the short hand is nearest to . . .). S/he must be able to name written numerals to 12, to count in fives, and to have some understanding of simple fractions (one-half and one-quarter). The teacher's next step is to put these sub-skills into roughly hierarchical order of difficulty. She will end up with something like the steps in Table 3.1 – though not necessarily exactly like this, since there are always several equally valid ways of breaking down a task. Now, it will be possible to locate the point at which tasks should be pitched for each child in the class: sorting strips of fabric for a weaving project into long and short piles for one child, perhaps, while another group works on the counting in fives sequence, and in another corner children take turns to set times on an analogue clock for the rest of the group to reproduce on a digital one.

Most teachers are very familiar with the idea of sub-skills and small steps for concepts as clearly defined as many in the maths curriculum. The same approach, however, can be applied in other less clearly-defined areas. Take, for example, a year 4 class, where all the children have been given a worksheet involving putting keywords for the topic they are studying into alphabetical order, and looking up their meaning in the dictionary. For a third of the class

the task is just about manageable. Another third find it easy and finish quickly. Quite a few children, however, do not really know where to start. Amongst them are children who do not know the sequence of letters of the alphabet, and children at an even earlier stage who are not sure of all their letter sounds. For them, the task they have been given is widely adrift from the prior knowledge and skills they bring to it. This teacher urgently needs a mental map of the small steps that lead up to the ability to 'check spellings or meanings of words, using dictionaries where appropriate' (English AT3, Key Stage 2 Programmes of Study), in order to plan differentiated tasks for the class. Using such a mental map (Table 3.2), s/he will be able to offer a range of activities from sorting the words on the worksheet by initial sound, to entering them into personal alphabetical word books, to looking them up in simple children's dictionaries or in adult versions.

Learning how to break down skills and concepts into small steps takes practice. It is, however, an essential competency for special needs work. It is also an immediate confidence-builder for both teachers and pupils, shifting as it does the emphasis from what the child cannot do to what in the earlier small steps he or she *can* do, and what the next learning step might be.

It is not, however, necessary for every teacher or group of teachers to re-invent the wheel by working out for themselves the small steps for every core skill and concept in the national curriculum. Published materials are readily available: some sources are listed at the end of this chapter. The school special needs resource area should include some of these materials, alongside the home-grown versions which individual teachers in the school may have produced in relation to particular schemes of work.

Differentiation within a task: input, approach to learning, and pupil response

Differentiation is not just a matter of providing children with tasks matched to their status on a hypothetical learning ladder. Were it so, we might as well return to the practice of streaming, with children pursuing largely separate curricula and with status accorded mainly to high-fliers. Fortunately, however, the national curriculum is open to forms of differentiation other than by task: to situations where the task stays the *same* for all children, including those with special needs, and where the differentiation strategies are applied within the shared task, by varying the way in which the task is presented to the children, or the way they are asked to approach it, or the ways in which they record their learning (Table 3.3).

These approaches to differentiation are used when a child *can* actually cope with a task, given a little extra planning and support from the teacher. A child with a visual impairment, for example, is provided with texts that have been enlarged on the photocopier; a child with language difficulties is given the instructions for a task one by one, instead of all at once; a group of children who cannot yet tell the time but need to be able to read a clock face for a science

Table 3.2 Small steps to target. English AT3: using a dictionary

Understands concepts of print – front/back, page, word, letter	☐
Identifies the first sound of a word on an auditory basis: 'bag' begins with the sound 'buh'	☐
Matches auditory to written sounds (buh-b) using picture cues (e.g. picture of Bouncing Ben next to 'b')	☐
Uses alphabetically ordered word bank (on a card, or using Breakthrough materials), with picture cues for each letter	☐
Can point to the right written letter for each letter sound, without picture cues	☐
Uses alphabetically ordered word bank without picture cues	☐
Uses simple alphabetical picture dictionary	☐
Matches sound-written letter-letter names (buh-b-bee)	☐
Recites alphabet in order	☐
Writes alphabet in order from memory	☐
Orders plastic or wooden letters in an arc in front of him	☐
Quickly finds a named plastic or wooden letter from the arc in front of him	☐
Says whether a letter falls into the first, second or third quartile of a dictionary and can open dictionary to this quartile	☐
Orders words alphabetically on the basis of second letter when first is the same	☐
Orders words on the basis of third letter when first and second are the same	☐
Quickly locates such words in children's dictionary	☐

experiment uses a clock on which the teacher has stuck peel-off labels saying 'five past', 'ten past' next to the relevant numbers; a child who finds writing difficult works with a more fluent writer who acts as scribe.

This kind of differentiation needs to be built into the teacher's planning at an early stage, in relation to the particular needs of children in the class. This was the approach taken by the teacher earlier in the chapter for her topic on clothes and coverings, and these were some of the ideas she came up with:

> For one week's work in English, she used some ideas she had read about in a special needs magazine (Evans, 1990). In order to practise writing descriptively, the children all brought in a photograph of themselves for a wall display, and wrote a description of their appearance and clothing: each description was read out and the rest of the children had to match it to one of the photographs. To support children with spelling difficulties, the teacher supplied a word bank of descriptive adjectives. Other children were given a prompt sheet

Table 3.3   The differentiation menu

Presentation
- Simplifying verbal instructions (short sentences, simpler vocabulary)
- Demonstration
- Writing down and leaving up instructions after saying them
- Reading aloud key text or instructions before the children read them
- Putting up a glossary of word meanings for difficult vocabulary
- Simplifying written workcards and texts (short sentences, active not passive verbs, making instructions stand out boldly)
- Supplementing information in books with tapes, video, pictures, charts and diagrams

Approach to learning
- Choosing more motivating activities by linking tasks to children's individual interests
- Dividing longer pieces of classroom work into shorter tasks, each with its own endpoint
- Increasing the use of active learning approaches (brainstorming, drama, role play, card sorts, making posters or a display, group discussion, group problem-solving activities)
- Providing opportunities for repetition and reinforcement – the same type of activity presented in different ways, reviewing earlier learning regularly, giving child the opportunity to teach something newly learned to others

Response
- Using alternatives to written recording: oral presentation, tape recordings, video recordings, dictation to a helper, dramatic presentation, pictures/diagrams/flow charts, computer-aided recording
- Providing prompt sheets for writing: questions to answer, key words to build each section or paragraph around, sentences or paragraphs to put in the correct order
- Providing clue cards
- Using cloze procedure, where the pupil fills in missing words from text rather than writing up from scratch
- Using cooperative writing in groups or pairs

with a framework to help them with their description, or worked from a concept keyboard overlay prepared by the teacher.

Another week, the children collected examples of uniforms of various kinds and discussed in groups why they thought people wore uniforms. The groups then had to debate the issue of school uniform, with each child putting forward their point of view. The teacher knew that several children would find this aspect of speaking and listening difficult; she planned to give each of them a set of cards on which were written statements about school uniform which they could sort into two piles, those they agreed with and those they disagreed with. They would then discuss with a friend their reasons for agreeing or disagreeing with each statement, and use all this as a basis for their contribution when it came to discussion in larger groups.

Maths work on the uniform theme included a survey of the views of parents and pupils on school uniform. To help everyone participate, the teacher decided that the initial work of planning the survey and deciding how to record the data would be done in mixed-ability groups. Later, however, a group of more able mathematicians would be given an open-ended opportunity to extract comparisons from their data using percentages, means and ranges while others worked with the teacher to prepare block graphs.

For geographical and historical work on clothes and costumes, she made sure that books available included several with large clear print and plenty of illustrations. A display of the processes involved in making silk with real cocoons and different types of silk to handle was interesting, but involved a lot of reading: the teacher asked a group of moderately good readers to prepare, then make, a tape of the text and captions on the display, so that other children could listen to it while handling the materials. Before they watched a television programme about wool production, she planned to give some children with difficulties in picking out key features of inputs a card specifying key things to look out for.

The teacher thought the work on clothing from different historical periods would need quite a lot of differentiation. She wanted to increase the use of active learning opportunities for some children whom she felt would not be very motivated by drawing or writing about how clothing has changed over time. In the end, she decided to follow up a local museum visit with a challenge to groups of children to research and present material on the clothing of a particular period using their own choice of media – drama, role play, tape or video recordings, posters and drawings, descriptive writing. One group chose to present a fashion show with a prepared commentary; another group collected photographs and made a tape recording of interviews with grandparents and neighbours who talked about the clothes they wore as children and special memories such as washday and shopping.

The main need in science, the teacher felt, was to provide a step-by-step description of how to go about the experiments on the properties of different fabrics, and make sure that the children could understand the science scheme workcards. She rewrote sentences like 'in this experiment you will be comparing the insulating properties of various materials' to say 'you are going to find out which materials (fabrics) are best at insulating (stopping heat getting out)'. During the practical sessions, less able children worked with a partner of higher ability, with the simplified instructions (accompanied by diagrams) to refer to. Afterwards, they could choose to record their work on a pre-prepared sheet. Sometimes this supplied a framework of headings (of the 'what we used', 'what we did' type); sometimes it took the form of a cloze passage – a piece of text in which the teacher had blanked out keywords and written them at the bottom so that the child could choose which one should go in each space.

Finally, in her planning, the teacher wanted to take account of the needs of a child in her class who had quite severe coordination difficulties. He found handwriting a struggle, and was routinely allowed to use the computer for word processing wherever possible. For the clothes topic, the teacher felt his main need for differentiation would be in some of the art and design work she had planned. Though he would cope well with fabric collage with help from a friend on cutting out the materials, he would probably prefer to use strips of fairly sturdy fabric rather than fine materials for the weaving project, and should be encouraged to produce his design for a fabric pattern using computer software rather than hand drawing.

ORGANIZING THE CLASSROOM FOR DIFFERENTIATION

Classrooms offering an undifferentiated curriculum require relatively little prior organization and planning: the teacher has to plan one scheme of work, make one master of each worksheet, and order one set of materials. The demands on the teacher are likely to be of a reactive rather than proactive kind, as s/he grapples with the insistent demands for help and the behavioural difficulties that are likely to arise when tasks are not matched to individuals. For the teacher offering a differentiated curriculum, the situation is reversed – far fewer on-the-spot demands for explanation and help, but a great deal to do before the children arrive. The necessary organization and planning *is* time consuming; the bonus is that once it is done, the stress on the teacher is likely to be a lot less.

What forms of organization will make for easier differentiation? In *A Curriculum For All* (1989), the National Curriculum Council (NCC) have provided some guidelines. These include:

- Written schemes of work which specify the way in which some activities will be broken down into a series of small steps, and the ways in which different ways of presenting tasks, different ways of approaching learning, and different types of pupil response will be used to ensure that a wide range of children can achieve success.
- Effective management of support from classroom assistants, parents and volunteers, and special needs support teachers.
- Easy access to classroom resources, including information technology.
- Cooperative learning among pupils.
- Flexible pupil groupings.

Let us look at these organizational issues one by one. First, to achieve differentiated schemes of work, groups of teachers (including the relevant curriculum coordinator and the special needs coordinator) can work together to plan schemes that will, as we saw earlier in the chapter, allow access to a broad range of national curriculum attainment levels. This is the first step. The next is for the working group to pose a series of questions in relation to the main types of special need encountered in school. How will the scheme work for pupils with short concentration spans, or a difficulty in working as part of a group? How will it be differentiated for children with poor listening skills, or minor hearing problems? For children who need help in expressing themselves orally, or in structuring their ideas for writing? For children who find it hard to see the purpose in much everyday classroom learning? For children with reading difficulties, or those who have plenty of ideas for writing but lack the mechanical skills of spelling and handwriting needed to get things on to paper? For children with poor memory and a need for repetition and reinforcement? For children with difficulties in picking out key features from the environment, in learning from abstract experiences, or generalizing from one experience to another?

Once the working group has planned the way in which strategies from the differentiation menu will be used to meet the variety of needs, they should make sure that the scheme of work includes identified opportunities for tackling the cross-curricular theme of personal and social education which is particularly important for many pupils with special needs. Finally, the group should consider and record particular books, materials, computer software and any other equipment which will be needed to meet the whole range of special needs within the scheme of work.

Once planned, these centrally held records of differentiated scheme of work will form a long-term resource for staff, and a central part of whole school response to special needs. They will also allow each teacher who uses them to see how s/he can best deploy any available extra *human* resources – either to support individuals or groups in class, or to prepare differentiated materials for the pupils to use independently.

Then there is the question of easy access to resources within the classroom. Considered in more detail in Chapter 5, this means making sure that pupils can be truly independent in accessing hardware they may need, such as tape recorders and calculators, that they know where to go for word banks and picture dictionaries and prepared glossaries of topic words, that they can easily find a tape to go with a particular book, or the concept keyboard overlay they need, or the back-up simplified work cards or clue cards they may want to refer to. It also means spending as much time initially in teaching the children where to look for the support they need as is spent in teaching the actual curriculum.

Finally, in organizing the classroom for differentiation there is the over-whelming need identified by the NCC for cooperative learning among pupils, and flexible pupil groupings. Such cooperative learning is not the traditional answer to differentiation in British classrooms. Croll and Moses (1985), for example, found that children with special needs were given *less* time on work involving cooperating with other pupils than were their classmates without special needs. Seven years later, giving children with special needs a series of individual and individualized tasks (often in worksheet form) was still the preferred teacher response to special needs in most primary classrooms.

Such approaches can, however, deny the children who most need it the opportunity to learn from the kind of social dialogue with 'more knowledgeable others' which is fundamental to human learning and development (Bruner and Haste, 1987). As Diane Montgomery (1990) argues:

> Children with learning difficulties need classrooms in which there is collaborative learning, negotiation, oral problem solving and discussion between pupils. The individualised programme and remedial tutorial are generally unsuitable as the *main* teaching vehicle for them, for they limit the communication channels which are open for learning, and throw them back on their own limited cognitive resources.

Cooperative groupwork, then, fosters learning in children with special needs because it increases the resources they can draw on. It is also particularly beneficial for children with special needs because it works on the particular attitudes and behaviours that have been shown to be problematic for them: it enhances self-esteem (Johnson and Johnson, 1987) and increases engagement with learning tasks by as much as 20 per cent (Bennett, 1991).

What does collaborative group work for pupils with special needs actually mean? First, it does not mean just seating groups of pupils together to do their work. As observational research has repeatedly shown, the kinds of cooperation this leads to are most often chat among the children about what was on television last night, what page they are on and who has hidden the rubber. The ORACLE study (Galton et al., 1980) showed that children spent up to five hours a week interacting with each other in class, but three-quarters of these interactions had nothing to do with the task in hand. In many situations that pass as groupwork, children sit together but do individual work; the grouping is purely an organizational device allowing for occasional economies of direct teaching input.

To achieve genuinely collaborative groupwork, children need to be given the kinds of challenging tasks with a common goal that are encouraged by the national curriculum. These can be language based: buzz and brainstorming groups, collaboration around an adventure game on a computer, group story composition, critical support for each other's writing, providing a forum to share responses to a story or poem, standpoint taking, group prioritizing and ranking of issues and concerns. Or they can be of the practical, problem-solving variety: design a home for yourself given information about climate, terrain and tools available, find out how many children in the class are left and right handed, make a cart that will roll down a slope, fill three boxes $\square + \square = \square$ with cards numbered 1, 2 and 3 to make the largest and smallest possible answer.

The next essential for successful collaborative work in a differentiated curriculum is to plan the composition of the groups. Here the message from research is becoming clear: for cooperative learning where the teacher acts as facilitator but not instructor, mixed-ability groups work better than single-ability groups for children of average and below-average ability, and at least as well as single ability groups for children of above-average ability. Swing and

Peterson (1982), for example, found that both high- and low-attaining children learned more in mixed-ability groups, and hypothesized that the more able children gained a deeper understanding of, and a greater hold on, new learning through explaining and justifying their ideas to the less able. Bennett (1991) analysed the kinds of talk in groups of all high-, all average- and all low-ability children. He found that if grouped together, the low attainers tended to use low-quality discourse, with very little sharing of explanations or knowledge. Low attainers in mixed-ability groups, however, benefited from the more sophisticated talk and achieved more. High attainers performed well whichever group they happened to be a member of – an important finding that should help to allay the widespread fear that mixed-ability groupwork may hold back the more able children.

Bennett's research also looked at different types of mixed-ability group, some with two more able children to one less able, and some with the reverse. He concluded:

> On every criterion it was the two low and one high group which was superior. What appeared to happen in the other combination is that the two high attainers talked together whilst the low attainer was ignored, or opted out, and as a consequence misunderstood the basis on which decisions were being made. In the two low and one high combination, on the other hand, the high attainer took on the role of peer tutor and support.
>
> (Bennett, 1991: 586)

Other strategies which will help children with special needs to get the most out of cooperative learning include preparing them ahead of time for their contribution to the group, and allocating tasks and roles within the group. Less confident children can be asked to talk, plan, or research first in a friendship pair, before joining up into fours or sixes to complete the task as a group. Or the teacher can use the jigsaw technique, where small groups of four or five are given a topic, and each student is made responsible for becoming an expert in a particular aspect. The children go off to do their research, coming together at the end to teach each other the information or use it for a task. For example, if the class is going to find out about materials that dissolve in water (Norman, 1990), the children start in what are called 'home' groups to discuss the kinds of things they may do and be allocated a number. Then children from across the home groups with the same number join up as an 'expert' group with a particular investigation to do. When the investigations are finished, the children return to their home groups, where they are able to take an expert role in contributing their own findings to the discussion that puts all the pieces of the jigsaw together.

Participation within the group can also be encouraged by allocating children to particular roles: materials gatherer, reader, scribe, checker, timekeeper, chairperson. Sometimes these roles will rotate; sometimes they will make use of children's individual strengths on a more permanent basis. Even children with

Table 3.4   Coverdale structure

What helped ...	What hindered ...
When we decided that Alison would be the leader	We kept on chatting
When we split up to do different jobs	We didn't listen to Andrew's idea
	We took too long to do the measuring

major special needs and abilities very disparate from those of other group members can be successfully integrated if they are provided with a useful group-process role. Johnson and Johnson (1987) describe strategies such as asking the pupil to be responsible for explaining the group's decision, checking that everyone in the group has understood the decision, or praising members for their contributions.

Using cooperative groupwork, then, as a means of increasing access to the curriculum for children with special needs will involve setting up mixed-ability groups, in which more-able children are in the minority, and in which everyone is encouraged to participate by developing prior expertise and taking on clear roles. Such groups will function best if they have the opportunity to work together on a variety of tasks for a term or more, so that they can profit from the experience of developing effective teamwork over a period of time. One way of encouraging this is to use the Coverdale structure (Coverdale Organisation, 1986), where group members review, after each task, the way they worked together and organized themselves (Table 3.4). Also helpful is having one member of the group in turn act as observer during the group's work, perhaps focusing on individuals' contributions using a rating sheet based on the ground rules the group has adopted (Table 3.5).

Just as adults do, children need to learn to work together: for some children with special needs, the opportunity to learn over time, through actual experience and constructive feedback from peers, may be particularly important – and worth any amount of adult lecturing on how to behave in groups.

Work with one mixed-ability group over an extended period, however,

Table 3.5 Rating sheet

WORKING WELL TOGETHER

Name _____

Group _____

Activity _____

Date _____

Did this person

1 Listen to others?   😊 YES   😐 A LITTLE   🙁 NO

2 Praise others' ideas?   😊 YES   😐 A LITTLE   🙁 NO

3 Give some ideas?   😊 YES   😐 A LITTLE   🙁 NO

4 Help sort out arguments?   😊 YES   😐 A LITTLE   🙁 NO

5 Help the group get the job done on time?   😊 YES   🙁 NO

needs to be balanced with opportunities to work in other types of grouping. Flexibility is the key to success: there is no reason to believe that working all day, every day, in one mixed group will meet all the needs of pupils with learning difficulties, any more than will asking them to work all day, every day, in one 'slow learners' group. Given the evidence that many children with special needs require a greater structure to their learning, and more opportunities for repetition and reinforcement than their peers, time needs to be found for direct instruction of groups of children who are all at a similar stage in their learning, and a similar rung on the national curriculum ladder. Bringing together a group of children around a 'big book' which the teacher is using to introduce concepts of print, or teaching a group of children about place value, are examples of this very necessary kind of work. For children with special needs, increasing the amount of time spent on such groupwork (with the teacher present throughout in an instructional role) is not just economical of teacher time; it can also make a big difference to their concentration and achievement. Croll and Moses (1985), for example, showed that for slow learning children and children with behaviour problems, whose overall levels of time spent concentrating on the task in hand were below average, a shift to group work with the teacher rather than individual seat work or class work meant a very big rise in their engagement with learning.

CONCLUSION

This chapter has focused on the benefits – some potential, some actual – of the national curriculum for children with special educational needs, particularly the encouragement of groupwork and the emphasis on planning for differentiation within programmes of study that are meant for all. The negatives have not been emphasized, partly because they are already widely understood, and partly because a theoretical discussion of the problems inherent in a curriculum largely geared towards narrow academic success would be out of place in a practical guide of this kind. Nevertheless, the negatives cannot be ignored: most particularly, any expectations we may have of the amount of time teachers are able to spend with individual pupils with special needs must be set in the context of the absurd demands on their professional energies made by the requirement to assess the progress of 20 or 30 (or more) children against numerous but nebulous attainment target level descriptions for the purpose of reporting annually to parents. Assessment has become the tail that threatens to wag the dog; in the next chapter, we look at some of the implications of national curriculum assessment for children with special needs, alongside other forms of assessment that have a better pedigree and greater potential for ensuring their progress.

FURTHER READING

Lewis, A. (1995) *Primary Special Needs and the National Curriculum*, 2nd edn. London, Routledge.

RESOURCES

Source materials for small steps within the national curriculum:

Avec Designs Ltd, P.O. Box 709, Bristol BS99 1GE.
Dudley Learning Support Service, Saltwells Educational Development Centre, Bowling Green Road, Dudley, West Midlands DY2 9LY.
Education Department Psychology Service, Tyne House, Hepscott Park, Stannington, Morpeth, Northumberland NE61 6NF.
Humberside LEA (1991) *Recording Progress Using Small Steps*. CASS, Humberside LEA.

· 4 ·

ASSESSMENT AND SPECIAL
EDUCATIONAL NEEDS

INTRODUCTION

Assessment has recently become a key area for school development work. Concerns remain, however, about how far the systems put in place to monitor the progress of all children within the national curriculum will meet the needs of children with difficulties in learning. The assessment arrangements may help to identify pupils who are failing to make progress, so that appropriate support can be given at an early stage, and may help pupils and teachers to target more clearly the next steps in teaching and learning. Nevertheless, there are risks that for children with special needs the targets may seem unreachable, and the experience of assessment an experience of failure. The learning steps within the national curriculum are, as we have seen, very large, and some children will need to have their achievements monitored in greater detail if progress is to be adequately demonstrated. It will be important to find ways of celebrating progress that is made in small steps, and of recording a wide range of achievement. We will need to watch carefully to see whether the less specific language of the revised national curriculum level descriptions leads to global teacher judgements of 'level-ness' across subject areas, rather than precise analysis of the child's strengths and weaknesses. Most importantly, the focus on assessment of achievement within the national curriculum should not lead us to lose sight of other kinds of assessment, notably the Warnock and 1993 Education Act concept of assessing needs, not children – of asking the question not of 'what can this child do and not do?' but of 'what does this child need from us in terms of resources, tasks and differentiated teaching approaches in order to make progress?'

IDENTIFYING SPECIAL NEEDS

All schools are required by law to identify special educational needs, and place children so identified on their SEN register. The risks of labelling and creating negative expectations implicit in all such systems need to be balanced by a clear picture on the part of the school of the purposes to be served in identifying special needs. Staff should discuss for themselves what they see as the intended positive outcomes, and regularly monitor the system used to identify needs to make sure that it is fulfilling agreed purposes. These might include:

- Ensuring the effective deployment of resources, both from within the school and from external support agencies.
- Ensuring continuity of response when the child moves from one class or school to another.
- Ensuring that parents or carers are involved very early on in discussions about the best ways to support the child.
- Initiating further, more detailed, assessment of the child's needs.
- Providing the school with information about areas where the curriculum or teaching approaches may be creating difficulties for pupils.

A major issue in identifying special needs is whether the teacher's own judgements are sufficient, or whether more objective screening instruments should be used. The evidence we have suggests that subjective teacher assessments are quite discriminating: teachers do not just pick out a fixed proportion of children in their classes (the 'bottom end') as having special needs, but instead nominate numbers that vary widely from class to class (Croll and Moses, 1985). Diana Moses (1982), however, has shown that when making judgements about whether a particular child has special needs, teachers are heavily influenced by whether the child shows a particular behaviour pattern – low work rate, fidgeting and restlessness – which they associate with the slow learning child. Children who do not show this behaviour pattern, but who are nevertheless picked out as having difficulties on the basis of standardized attainment tests, tend to be missed in the teacher judgements of special needs.

The introduction of national curriculum assessment may help to highlight the needs of such children. It may also highlight another group sometimes missed by teachers – those with *specific* learning difficulties, whose performance perhaps in reading or written language may not be very much out of step with that of other children in the class, but where there are significant discrepancies between these literacy attainments and the child's own performance in other areas of the curriculum, such as science or speaking and listening.

National curriculum assessment, however, is unlikely to be sufficient on its own to make sure that all special needs come to the notice of the teacher and the school. Many schools will want to plan for support and differentiation from the moment of school entry, long before national curriculum assessment begins. For this purpose, some local authorities are developing their own school-entry assessment systems; there is also a range of commercially available screening instruments available, for example:

- *The Bury Infant Check*, published by NFER-Nelson, which is intended for 5-year-olds in their second and third terms at school. It includes a quick check of items rated by the teacher, which will highlight children who need more detailed assessment. The quick check includes language items and learning behaviours, such as whether the child is able to concentrate, ask for help when needed, or begin an activity when requested. The full check requires an adult to work individually with the child for about 20 minutes, using a picture booklet and a series of structured tasks to assess language, learning style, memory, number concepts and perceptual motor skills.

- *Early Years Easy Screen*, from the same publisher, which is for 4–5-five-year-olds. It covers pencil coordination, active body skills, number skills, oral language skills, and visual and auditory reading skills, and can be used with small groups of children for ongoing informal assessment over their first six months at school. The materials include picture cards and lotto board, photocopiable worksheets and an audio-cassette tape.
- *COP*, the classroom observation procedure developed by the Inner London Education Authority, which provides a structure for informal assessment of language, visual discrimination, motor, auditory and reading skills in children across the infant age range.

Screening instruments that focus on specific areas that are not likely to be covered by national curriculum teacher assessment include:

- Behaviour checklists (Rutter et al., 1970), indicating which children have behaviour difficulties outside the ordinary range expected in their age group. Importantly, Rutter's checklist includes the difficulties of quiet, withdrawn children as well as more overt behaviour problems.
- Learning behaviour checklists, such as *The Guide to the Child's Learning Skills* (Stott et al., 1988), which will pick up faulty or inappropriate behaviours in such areas as concentration, coping with new demands, cooperation within a group and independent learning.
- Language screening instruments, such as the AFASIC checklists published by Learning Development Aids, or the whole class screening system in NFER-Nelson's Teaching Talking scheme.
- Checklists for indicators of minor visual or hearing impairment (see Tables 4.1 and 4.2).
- Checklists for indicators of specific learning difficulty/dyslexia (see Chapter 11).
- Checklists for indicators of minor motor difficulties of a 'clumsy' type (see Chapter 12).

FURTHER ASSESSMENT

Having identified children who may have special needs, using informal teacher judgement supplemented or moderated by some of the more formal screening instruments, the next step is further, more detailed assessment:

Mr James had noticed that out of all the children in his Year 2 class, Adam seemed to be making the slowest progress with his maths,

Table 4.1   Checklist of indicators of possible visual difficulties

- Slower than expected educational progress
- Finds it hard to copy from books or the board
- Handwriting difficulties – unusually large, small or poorly formed letters
- Rubs eyes frequently
- Holds reading material at an unusual distance or angle
- Peers or squints at near or far objects
- Appears clumsy and uncoordinated; often trips or stumbles
- Often loses place or skips lines, letters or words when reading
- Confuses visually similar letters and words
- Tires easily when looking at print or fine detail
- Takes longer than other children to complete reading assignments

Table 4.2   Checklist of indicators of possible hearing loss

- Slower than expected educational progress
- May not respond when spoken to, often says 'What?' or 'Pardon?', asks for things to be repeated, or gives answers that seem unrelated to the question
- Tends to ignore, mistake or forget instructions
- Watches the speaker's face for clues
- Seems in a world of his/her own; daydreams; switches off
- Shows signs of irritability, frustration, temper
- Behaviour erratic; worse when s/he has a cold, or in listening situations
- Speaks unusually loudly, or indistinctly, with parts of words missing
- Has difficulty acquiring phonic skills for reading and spelling
- Has a history of repeated ear infections; appears catarrhal

particularly number work. Mr James decided to make Adam the focus of classroom observation for a few days. Using a notebook and sticky post-its, he jotted down things he noticed as they happened; he also made time to sit with Adam while he was working on his maths. The observations showed that Adam worked hard and concentrated well when writing or doing practical work, but appeared to daydream when he had to do any work involving written numbers. Listening to him talking about some addition on a page of his maths book which had a number line, Mr James noticed that he used the number line to count right through the number sequence and arrive at the numeral he needed for the sum – thus, for 7 + 2 he would count 1-2-3-4-5-6-7 before saying, 'It's seven add two'. Following a hunch, Mr James wrote down the numbers 1 to 10 in random order and asked Adam to name them. Adam could only name a few. He clearly had a real difficulty in remembering the names for numerals, but had managed to get by without this being noticed because he *could* recall their names if they were in order or if he referred to a number line and went through the whole number sequence. Mr James wondered if Adam might have some visual difficulties which made it hard for him to tell one number from another, and decided to try him on a test where he had to find the right match for written numerals – for example,

$$5 \qquad 2 \quad 7 \quad 5 \quad 3 \quad 8$$

Adam had no trouble at all with this. Mr James was puzzled, but when he shared his observations with Adam's parents, they told him that Adam often seemed to forget the names for things: he sometimes took a long time to get his words out, and would express himself in a roundabout way – 'It's in the place you wash dishes' instead of 'the sink', for example. He had been late in talking and had a period of speech therapy before starting school. Mr James contacted the speech therapist who had worked with Adam. She felt that his difficulties with numbers were a legacy of his earlier language difficulties, and probably part of what she called 'word-finding' problems. She and Mr James discussed some strategies that would help, such as providing Adam with a ruler clearly marked to at least 30 as an always available reference point, and teaching key points (5, 10, 15, 20, 25) from which he could count on to arrive at the number name he needed. She also suggested that Adam practise number naming in relaxed contexts far removed from ordinary number work – playing dice games with numbers rather than dots on the dice, playing dominoes with dots to be matched to numerals, using coins in shopping games with purchases marked in amounts like 12 p, playing darts with his Dad, or collecting information about car number plates. Mr James recorded a plan of action based on these strategies, and discussed it with Adam's parents; they agreed to review the plan together in six weeks. If it seemed to be helping, they would know that they and the speech therapist were on the right track in their initial assessment of the reasons for Adam's slow progress in maths.

Sadiq was 7, and his teacher was concerned about his immature behaviour; he found it hard to sit still for any length of time in the classroom and didn't always do as he was told. He had, she felt, poor motor control which caused him to struggle with handwriting and drawing. She discussed her concerns with the headteacher and special needs coordinator. The coordinator asked if she could spend some time in the classroom observing Sadiq, and then free the class teacher to do some work with him on his own. The coordinator was able to feed back to the teacher the contrast she observed between Sadiq's unsettled behaviour in the rather formal atmosphere of the classroom and his behaviour in a PE lesson, where he produced very creative ideas and worked well with a group. She suggested that he might need shorter tasks with a more active learning style, and offered to look at the teacher's topic plan with her to identify opportunities for this. The class teacher, alone with Sadiq, asked him to finish a piece of work. She noticed that he really seemed to be struggling to get his drawings and writing into the small paper in his exercise book. His letters were erratic in size, with no clear distinction between ascenders and descenders. She asked Sadiq to tell her how he felt about writing. 'It makes my hand hurt', he said. When she suggested that he tell her the rest of his story so that she could write it down for him, he produced some ideas and vocabulary which really astonished her. They agreed that in future Sadiq would use bigger paper and a larger pencil for some of his work, and would tell her when his hand hurt so they could finish the work together. In addition, the teacher would provide him with special handwriting sheets where he could practise getting his 'monkey', 'turtle' and 'giraffe' letters the right size.

In their assessments, these teachers made use of most of the main strategies which can help us to gain a clearer picture of the situation when a child seems to have special needs:

- Classroom observation of strengths as well as weaknesses, and of factors in the learning *context* that may be helping or hindering the child's progress, as well as of factors within the child.
- Child–adult conferencing, to obtain a 'window into the child's mind'.
- Miscue analysis: looking at the child's apparent mistakes to see what light they shed on the strategies and thought processes s/he is using.
- Using an analysis of the small steps leading up to mastery of a particular skill, in order to see if there are significant gaps in the child's prior knowledge and understanding that make him or her unable to cope consistently with the task.
- Assessing underlying skills (in perception, memory, motor coordination) to see if there are weaknesses which might be affecting school learning.
- Gathering information on the child's strengths, weaknesses and interests in other situations, notably the home.
- Assessment through action planning: finding out what works and what does not, through deciding on a strategy to support the child, trying it out, and evaluating it.

Diagnostic assessment methods

Let us look now at each of these diagnostic assessment methods in turn.

Classroom observation
Classroom observation can include making notes or keeping a diary, making a tape recording of the child reading or talking in a group, making a video

recording, or using a structured format for observing specific behaviours. A record of a child's contribution to group processes (Chapter 3) would be one example of a structured format; another might be a sheet on which the teacher notes whether a child is on or off task at set intervals during the day; another a sheet on which the teacher records the ABCs (antecedents, behaviour, consequences) for a particular classroom behaviour problem over the course of a week. In all such classroom observation, it is important to gather information on the types of task or setting where the child *succeeds*, as well as the areas of weakness: such observations provide vital clues to contextual factors which might be contributing to the child's difficulties – such as the over-long tasks Sadiq's teacher was using.

Child–adult conferencing

Through conferencing, the teacher aims to gain a clearer picture of the child's misunderstandings or misconceptions – for example, that s/he believes that the amount of water changes when it is poured from a tall narrow container into a shallow wide one, or that hitting people at school is morally acceptable if someone else started it. Through conferencing, the teacher should also be able to discover how the child *feels* about certain tasks or situations, and about him or herself as a learner. Direct, closed questions are avoided; instead, the teacher uses openers such as 'tell me about how you feel when . . .' ('you're listening to me reading a story', 'you're writing in your journal'), or invitations to complete sentences ('the trouble with having to sit and listen to stories is . . .'; 'it would be better if . . .'; 'I feel happy at school when . . .'; 'I feel sad/angry/worried/ embarrassed in school when'). The child's self-esteem can be explored, using questions like those in Table 4.3, or a card sort like the one in Table 4.4 can be used to elicit perceptions of the self as a learner.

Conferencing is easier to fit into the busy classroom if teachers use the popular idea of 'magic bubble time': the rest of the class are told that for the moment the teacher and the selected child are talking together inside a magic bubble, which will burst if other children break in to ask for the teacher's attention.

Miscue analysis

Miscue analysis is by now familiar to most primary teachers as a window into the child's reading strategies. It can also be applied, however, to other areas. Sadiq's teacher, for example, used it when looking at his handwriting, asking herself whether it looked messy because of

- erratic letter sizing?
- erratic letter spacing?
- no spaces between words?
- letters not aligned to a baseline, with correct ascenders and descenders?
- ascenders and descenders not straight and parallel?

Table 4.3   Exploring the child's self-concept (adapted from Rogers Personal
Adjustment Inventory, revised by P. Jeffery, NFER-Nelson)

1 _____	is very good at sports.
Are you like him/her?	
2 _____	is always helpful.
Are you like him/her?	
3 _____	is very good at school work.
Are you like him/her?	
4 _____	usually behaves well.
Are you like him/her?	
5 _____	is very clever.
Are you like him/her?	
6 _____	is very good-looking.
Are you like him/her?	
7 _____	is a very happy person.
Are you like him/her?	
8 _____	is very strong.
Are you like him/her?	
9 _____	has lots of friends.
Are you like him/her?	
10 _____	is a kind person.
Are you like him/her?	
11 _____	is good at _____
Are you like him/her?	

Ask the child to choose someone in school who fits each description (the same name can
appear more than once) and write the name in the blank spaces. For Question 11, fill in
the second space with an activity that you know is currently very important to the child
and peer group, e.g. karate, maths, skipping. Then ask the child to mark 'Yes', 'No'
or 'Somewhere in between' for each of the questions.

Miscue analysis also works well for spelling; studying the child's invented
spellings (or, from another perspective, spelling mistakes) will yield all the
information needed in order to plan a teaching programme for the child:
keywords and letter strings not yet mastered, a need for practice in listening to
the sounds in words, or for help in developing visual recall where a child's
approach is totally phonetic. Different spelling miscues indicate different
teaching strategies – 'sotr' for 'story', for example, indicating a need for help in
developing auditory strategies, while 'store' might lead to teaching the final -y
pattern in a word family like 'story', 'baby', 'lady'.

In maths, miscue analysis (particularly if children are asked to explain how
they reached a particular conclusion or answer) can indicate anything from
simple misunderstandings about place value or four-rule procedures, to a
difficulty in retaining number bonds, or a need to learn to estimate before
calculating.

Table 4.4 Card sort

The child is asked to sort statements into yes, no, maybe
- I usually do as I'm told at school
- I am interested in learning and finding out about things
- I often day-dream or mess about instead of doing my work
- I work well with a group
- I work best on my own
- I usually have a try at things before asking for help
- I am often unkind to other children
- People like me to play with them
- My teacher thinks I do good work
- My teacher likes me

Using the small steps approach to identify gaps in prior knowledge or understanding

Adam's teacher used this strategy when he found that Adam could match written numbers and name them when in order, but not manage the next step of naming them when presented out of sequence. Once he had established this, he could easily see why Adam took so long to cope with simple addition and subtraction – tasks for which number naming is an essential prerequisite skill. Sadiq's teacher might have used the strategy to see if Sadiq could correctly form the pre-writing shapes which are the precursor to correct letter formation in handwriting (Table 4.5).

The ability to analyse task demands to find out where the obstacles may lie for a child is a fundamental tool of diagnostic assessment that needs no special tests or techniques. It is not difficult – but it is not always done. A teacher may wonder why a child cannot seem to start sentences with capital letters even after being told many times, but not think to check whether the child understands what a sentence is, or whether s/he actually knows how to write all the capital letters without a reference model. Or a teacher may feel that a child lacks ideas for story writing when a finer task analysis would show that it is *ordering* ideas that is the real problem, and that he cannot yet cope with the very fundamental step of sequencing a set of pictures into chronological order.

It is particularly important to look for gaps in a child's prior knowledge and understanding when his or her performance seems erratic: good one day, but all to pieces the next. As Ireson et al. (1989) aptly observe:

> The child's performance of a complex task is impaired when a component of that task has not been mastered. This is a very common problem in human learning. It is like asking a learner driver to negotiate a roundabout before he has mastered gear changes; he may manage to go safely round a large roundabout if there is little traffic so he does not need to slow down, but the car will go out of control on a small roundabout where he needs to change gears.

Table 4.5 Small steps to correct letter formation

Holds pencil correctly
Traces pre-writing shapes   ◯ ∣ — ⋂ ⋃ ∧ ∨ Ꮥ ᒐᒋ
Copies pre-writing shapes   ◯ ∣ — ⋂ ⋃ ∧ ∨ Ꮥ ᒐᒋ
Has established left to right direction of writing
Forms letter group 'a c d o' correctly
Forms letter group 'g q' correctly
Forms letter group 'b f h l t' correctly
Forms letter group 'j p y' correctly
Forms letter group 'k v w x z' correctly
Forms letter group 'i m n r u' correctly
Forms 'e, s' correctly

Identifying the gaps in a child's understanding will be easier if the school has access in its resource base to some of the commercially-available breakdowns of core attainments into the small steps that lead up to them. Some of these materials, specifically linked to national curriculum attainment targets, were referenced at the end of Chapter 3; others which pre-date the introduction of the national curriculum but are still useful and widely available include Ainscow and Muncey's (1986) Small Steps Workshop Programme from the SNAP materials, the Early Learning Skills Analysis materials (Ainscow and Tweddle, 1984), DATAPAC (Ackerman et al., 1983) and its successor the Special Needs Spelling, Reading and Maths materials produced in Hampshire (Bentote et al., 1990).

Assessing underlying perceptual, memory and motor skills
This was the approach used by Adam's teacher when he wondered whether an underlying difficulty in visual discrimination was making it difficult for him to distinguish similar numerals. It was Sadiq's teacher's approach when she felt that his handwriting difficulties were due to poor motor coordination. It was some years ago an approach much favoured by remedial specialists, at a time when the prevailing model for special needs was a quasi-medical one of diagnosis and cure. Popular assessment tools such as the Aston Index (from Learning Development Aids) are based on the idea of identifying underlying difficulties. Covering such areas as auditory and visual discrimination and memory, they aim to help the teacher devise a programme that will remedy any deficits discovered, whilst directing the main thrust of teaching towards the child's stronger perceptual channels.

Such approaches, whilst superficially attractive, have tended to fall out of favour over the past decade. Partly, this has been in response to the considerable body of research which failed to show any differential effects of teaching programmes matched to underlying strengths and weaknesses (Kavale and Forness, 1985). Partly, it has been a consequence of the shift away from locating special needs wholly within the child, towards assessment which focuses on factors in the task, the classroom context or the curriculum which contribute to difficulties in learning or behaviour.

More recently, the underlying skills model has begun to make a come-back. Some research findings – such as those by Bryant and Bradley (1985) on children's auditory perception of sound patterns in words – have begun to show that there may be some underlying perceptual skill deficits that *can* be successfully remedied, with long-term positive effects on children's learning. It is also true that while some of the internal processes assessed using tools such as the Aston Index are still unproven as prerequisites of progress in attainments like reading and writing, there may nevertheless be more direct and 'surface value' implications of such assessments which are useful for teachers. For example, finding that a child has poor auditory sequential memory may help to explain why s/he has such difficulty in following a series of instructions given to the whole class, or sitting quietly in listening situations like assembly or story time. And while an action plan including auditory memory training may not be very useful as part of the child's *reading* programme, it could be very useful in helping develop listening skills.

For the most part, however, assessing underlying skills does not require expensive tests or special equipment. Auditory sequential memory can be assessed as well through seeing what happens when a child is asked to follow progressively more complex classroom instructions as it can through special tests; visual discrimination through asking the child to match a word on a card with similar ones in his reading book, and so on. This is called curriculum-based assessment, and is the most useful focus for the classroom teacher. The outcomes of such curriculum-based assessment need to be firmly tied in to the child's ordinary, everyday learning. Formerly, if a child was thought to have difficulties in a process like visual discrimination, the remedial teacher might prescribe an elaborate series of activities related only very indirectly to the classroom tasks of learning to read, write, count, measure, and so on. For example, the child would be given worksheets where s/he had to match squiggles in varying orientations. Nowadays, it is recognized that there may be little or no transfer from such activities to regular classroom learning, and that skills are better practised 'on the job' – for example, through activities that make children look very closely at real words rather than geometric shapes or meaningless squiggles, if they have poor visual discrimination. Put another way, this means that even though she felt he had underlying difficulties in motor coordination, Sadiq's teacher did better by helping him directly with his handwriting than she ever would have through a programme of activities in general motor skills.

Gathering information from parents

Parents are the real experts on their own children. Any assessment which fails to take into account their historical understanding of the child's difficulties, their perception of the child's strengths and weaknesses, behaviour and interests *outside* the confines of school, risks missing the essential elements that will lead to successful action planning. Parents know what their children enjoy doing, and what might motivate them to give of their best in school. They know what teaching styles and classroom contexts have in the past suited their child best. They know, like Adam's parents, about potentially significant factors in the child's pre-school development and experiences which may not have got as far as school records. They know about out-of-school stresses which may be making it hard for the child to concentrate on learning. A semi-structured interview with the child's parents or carers, using some of the starting points in Table 4.6, with the issues of confidentiality discussed and agreed information clearly recorded for long-term reference, should be part of the assessment process early on for every child whose progress causes concern.

Finding out what works and what does not: assessment through
action planning

Linked with the parental interview is the approach to assessment which rests on identifying key problem areas causing concern to parents, teachers and the child alike, planning a strategy to deal with these problems, and meeting again at a predetermined interval to evaluate the effectiveness of what was planned. Assessment here is through action, and is a matter of checking on hypotheses about the nature of the difficulties experienced by child or teacher, and the support required to ensure progress. Adam's teacher and speech therapist, for example, felt that his word-finding difficulties became more acute when he was put on the spot to provide answers; if he coped better in the more relaxed and game-like learning situations they planned for him, their hypothesis would be confirmed. Sadiq's teacher felt that she might be contributing to his apparent motor difficulties by asking him to use inappropriate tools; his response to her intervention strategy would tell her if she was right.

Assessment of this kind focuses much more on the context than on the child. The question it seeks to answer is not so much 'what is wrong here?' as 'what will help?' It is about differentiation: assessing, through trial and error, which particular adaptations to tasks, inputs, teaching and learning styles or pupil response will best ensure curriculum access.

Its outcome is a clearer picture of the strategies that have proved successful, *and those which are not so useful*; the action plans that do not work well are as important an element in the assessment process as those which do. This is a message that needs to be put across to parents and to the child: we are going to try out a plan, and even if it does not work we will all have learned something that will help us plan better next time.

Assessment through action planning is rarely a one-off process. It forms part of a cycle that can be repeated as many times as is necessary to establish

Table 4.6 Exploring the parents' point of view

- How does _____ feel about school?
- What does s/he like and dislike at school?
- What sort of teaching do you think works best for him/her?

- What is s/he good at?
- What is s/he interested in outside school?
- Are there any ways you wish s/he would change, were different?

- Is s/he fairly independent and socially competent?
- How do you think his/her friendships are going?
- What are his or her relationships like with other members of the family?

- What can you tell us about his or her history: health, hearing and eyesight, separations, major events or stresses in his/her life, school changes?

---

effective support mechanisms. It also does not stand alone: it forms part of a tripartite assessment strategy, drawing on and feeding into the other types of information gathering which we have looked at in this chapter.

Parents and teachers
sharing information

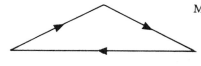

Assessment using
classroom observation,
conferencing, miscue
analysis, small steps
approach

Making and trying
out action plans
at home and at
school

NATIONAL CURRICULUM ASSESSMENT AND SPECIAL NEEDS

How does the tripartite assessment strategy suggested here fit in with national curriculum assessment? And how can national curriculum assessment – both teacher assessment and formal assessment through SATs – be made into a useful experience for children with special needs and their parents? In this section we will try to draw out some common threads from national curriculum assessments and assessments of special needs, and look at possible ways of reconciling their very different purposes.

The first point to make is that national curriculum assessment does share at least one purpose with the special needs assessment strategies we have described here: it is in its formative sense intended to help the teacher, child and family establish what their next steps should be in teaching and learning. This is the common ground. Special needs assessment is simply a more fine-grained and frequent application of the same formative process that all children should now be experiencing.

Most of the assessment methods suggested here, moreover, are those with which teachers are becoming increasingly familiar as they gain experience of national curriculum assessment focused classroom observation, child–adult conferencing and miscue analysis.

The only real differences, then, between assessment of special needs and teacher assessment for the national curriculum is the addition of some assessment methodologies – notably the small steps approach – which will not be necessary for the majority of children, and the intimate involvement of parents in information exchange at every step.

If children's progress is recorded against small steps rather than the broad rungs of national curriculum attainment levels, many of the potentially damaging effects of the summative aspect of national curriculum assessment can be avoided. Schools should not be satisfied with end of year reports to parents that carry dispiriting messages like 'still working towards Level 2 in English', or 'some progress towards Level 3 has been made'. For children with special needs, they should employ recording and reporting systems that are a great deal more fine-grained – if possible managed by the children themselves. Some examples, adapted from work in special schools (Hunt, 1992), are shown in Figures 4.1 to 4.3. This kind of self-assessment leads naturally into children setting their own targets, and enlisting the help of available adults – parents, support teachers, classroom assistants – to work with them towards achieving their goals.

For more general profiling, some children with special needs will benefit from using pre-prepared templates on the word processor, finishing sentences such as 'I can now . . . because . . . ', and 'I have most enjoyed . . .' and 'I need to improve . . .' (Hanson, 1991).

Combined with a record of achievement in which the child notes *all* aspects of personal success in and out of school, not just the purely academic, such records of progress towards attainment targets can help to make the national curriculum assessment process both positive and motivating. Also particularly useful for children with special needs is the now widespread practice of choosing samples of work for individual portfolios, and annotating them with the help of the teacher – noting perhaps what the child felt was good about the piece, what s/he thinks in general about his or her work in the area, and how it might be improved. The aim of such discussions for children with special needs is to establish and record together what exactly the pupil will be aiming to achieve next (working faster, listening better, mastering joined writing . . . perhaps in the form of a target sheet for the record of achievement file), and what sorts of experiences and teaching will be needed to ensure success.

All these forms of assessment are aimed at preserving the child's self-esteem through following certain fundamental principles:

I am a story writer. I can _____

- draw pictures of something I did and put them in order ☐
- talk about it to my teacher ☐
- put comic pictures in order to tell a story ☐
- tell this story to my group ☐
- think of an end for a story ☐
- make up a story with my group ☐
- use a story planner to draw a story beginning, middle, end ☐
- tell my story to a friend ☐
- write my story using a magic line for words I don't know ☐

_____ agrees with me.

Signed _____

Date _____

English AT3 Level 2

Figure 4.1 Example of recording and reporting system.

- Self-assessment wherever possible.
- The experience of success through reaching small achievable targets.
- Reporting in a style which demonstrates achievement.
- A focus on the joint responsibility of child *and* teacher for achieving change.

Use of these principles can be readily observed in properly managed teacher/assessment within the national curriculum.

The one-off forays into children's understandings represented by standard assessment tasks may well turn out to be a different matter. With no opportunity here for breaking the task down into small steps, for self-assessment or for joint forward planning, supporting children with special

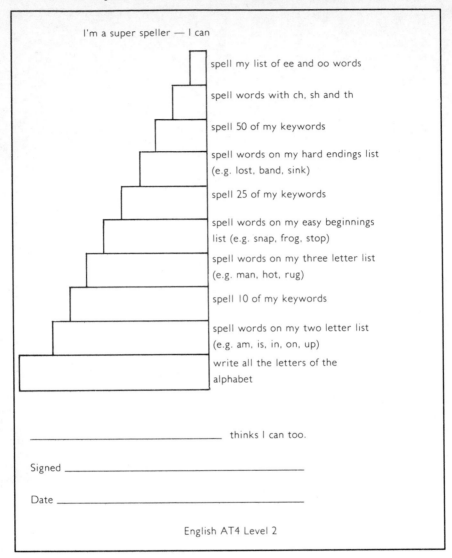

I'm a super speller — I can

spell my list of ee and oo words

spell words with ch, sh and th

spell 50 of my keywords

spell words on my hard endings list
(e.g. lost, band, sink)

spell 25 of my keywords

spell words on my easy beginnings
list (e.g. snap, frog, stop)

spell words on my three letter list
(e.g. man, hot, rug)

spell 10 of my keywords

spell words on my two letter list
(e.g. am, is, in, on, up)

write all the letters of the
alphabet

_____ thinks I can too.

Signed _____

Date _____

English AT4 Level 2

Figure 4.2   Example of recording and reporting system.

needs in the SATs becomes an exercise in damage limitation. The teacher must
seek to preserve self-esteem through making maximum use of the opportunities
provided in SATs guidance to enter and leave the tasks at points appropriate to
the individual pupil, to intervene and help the child complete the task after the
point of failure, and to assess individually or in small groups wherever staffing
will allow.

It will also be important to ensure that children with special needs have fair

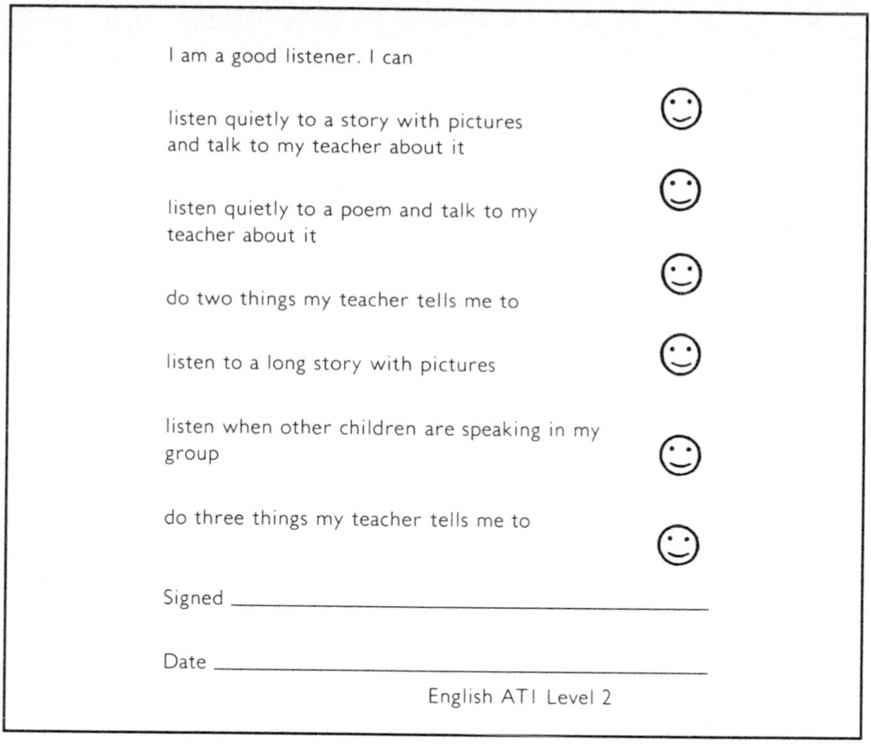

I am a good listener. I can

listen quietly to a story with pictures
and talk to my teacher about it   ☺

listen quietly to a poem and talk to my
teacher about it   ☺

                                                            ☺
do two things my teacher tells me to

listen to a long story with pictures   ☺

listen when other children are speaking in my
group   ☺

do three things my teacher tells me to
                                                            ☺

Signed _____

Date _____

English ATI Level 2

Figure 4.3   Example of recording and reporting system.

access to the assessment tasks. Here we are looking to make sure that the assessment criteria used relate to the subject and statement of attainment being assessed, and not to any other factors which may disadvantage children with special needs. For example, it means making sure that in science, the children's understanding of scientific concepts is being assessed, but not their listening or writing ability; in maths, the children's grasp of probability or data handling, but not their reading ability.

All of the documentation on assessment within the national curriculum to date has made it very clear that strategies which bypass particular special needs – for example, modified verbal instructions for children with language difficulties, or oral reporting for children with difficulties in written recording – are legitimate, so long as listening or writing or whatever are not actually being assessed in the activity at issue. Outside of specific writing, or speaking/ listening ATs, children can 'convey what they know . . . by any means appropriate to them: talk, writing, gesture, pictures, models'. Differentiation of the child's mode of response is encouraged. So is differentiation of the input or mode or presentation: outside of reading ATs, all written instructions can be read to pupils, worksheets can be enlarged or cut up or made concrete by replacing pictures with models, verbal instructions simplified or repeated. Differentiation of the process between input and response is also to some extent allowable: children who find it hard to work in a group can be assessed individually, and breaks in the assessment built in for those with a shorter concentration span.

As for technological and human support, the general principle expressed in the guidance is that if the child normally has the help of a classroom assistant, or uses a typewriter or word processor for recording, or any other aid to mobility or the manipulation of objects, then that support should continue to be available for assessment as well as learning. If there is a helper, he or she must make sure that any interventions, however, 'stop short of direct or indirect help. For example, if your support breaks the activity into such small steps that it leads the child to the response required, it invalidates the observation' (SEAC, 1992).

In keeping with the spirit of the national curriculum as a curriculum for all, the recommendations for differentiation of presentation or response, and extra support from adults or technology, are intended to ensure that almost all children can participate in the assessment tasks with some degree of success. It is not envisaged that children with special needs will be exempted in any large numbers from any aspect of the SATs, either through Statements of special educational need or through temporary headteacher directions. The few references to disapplication of assessments in NCC and SEAC guidance refer only to obvious areas such as handwriting for children with severe physical disabilities, or aspects of speaking and listening for some children with hearing or communication difficulties.

Table 4.7 gives a summary of the guidance on permissible differentiation of assessment tasks, grouped by broad areas of special need, and drawn from SEAC's teacher handbooks for the key stage one SATs in 1991 and 1992. An essential role for special needs coordinators will be to abstract each year further general and specific guidance as it appears for newly-introduced SATs, and to plan jointly with class teachers any adaptations that will be necessary for individuals or groups of pupils in the school when they undertake the assessment tasks. The consultative role of the special needs coordinator should also extend to planning for teacher assessment: bypass strategies are equally legitimate here, and equally essential if teachers are to avoid the global perceptions of children's ability, heavily influenced by their written language skills, which have traditionally determined their judgements of pupils in the past.

CONCLUSION

In this chapter, we have looked at some ways in which the potential of assessment for enhancing learning can be realized for children with special needs and their teachers – assessment not just of what children know and can do, but also of factors in the learning environment which will best help them

Table 4.7 Differentiation of national curriculum assessment

Difficulties in language comprehension
- Use whatever terminology you and the children are used to, and repeat or rephrase your instructions; use gesture or drawing to get across meaning.
- Check for understanding by asking the child to explain what he has to do.
- Use signing if this is the child's normal means of understanding.
- For a complicated task where several operations are to be carried out sequentially, provide prompt cards using signs or simple words.
- When assessing reading ability, choose books from the recommended list that have simple, literal language and don't place undue demands on rote recall.

Difficulties in verbal expression
- Use an 'experienced listener' to translate what the child says.
- Children can communicate in their usual way, including signing.
- Children can demonstrate understanding with a few simple words in conjunction with mime, drawing, or moving objects (for example, moving toys or models when retelling a story, or placing numbers or pictures in labelled sorting rings).
- For tasks requiring an ordered account of events, take the child through one example of sequencing before they begin writing or oral reporting.

Literacy difficulties
Except in specific English ATs:
- Children may convey what they know by any means appropriate to them – talk, gesture, pictures, models.
- Children can dictate written and numerical recording to an adult scribe.
- Pupil sheets can be read to the children, and picture clues added to text.
- Word processing packages that produce whole words can be used.

Visual impairment
- Pupil sheets can be enlarged or cut up, or turned into models, or into tactile form.
- Specially made equipment, such as embossed dice, can be used.
- A sighted helper can review orally groups of objects the child has to describe or classify.

Hearing impairment
- Children can communicate in their usual way, including signing.
- Assessment can be on a one to one basis in a quiet environment.
- The adaptations described for pupils with language difficulties can all be used.

Physical impairment and coordination difficulties
- Children can use any aids to mobility or manipulation of objects they normally employ, including a typewriter or word processor.
- Children can position concrete objects, as an alternative to drawing or mapping.

Emotional and behavioural difficulties
- Conduct the activities on a one to one basis.
- Give extra reassurance and encouragement.
- Use breaks in the assessment; discontinue if you feel it is a bad time for a particular child, and try again later.

---

make progress and demonstrate their learning. We have touched on record keeping in the context of self-assessment, and on action planning in the context of finding out what works and what does not for a particular child. In the next chapter we return to these issues in more detail, in describing a flexible structure for planning and recording intervention for children with special needs, that can be used to ensure efficient transfer of information both within and between schools.

FURTHER READING

Ainscow, M. and Tweddle, D. (1979) *Preventing Classroom Failure*. London, John Wiley.

· 5 ·

ACTION PLANNING AND RECORD KEEPING

ACTION PLANNING

The problem-solving approach

The idea of developing and evaluating action plans for children with special needs at a series of stages or levels, beginning within school and widening progressively if necessary to involve external agencies, was a key concept of the Warnock Report. Well before the 1994 Code of Practice sought to formalize the staged approach, many LEAs had incorporated the concept into systems used throughout their schools. Most systems had in common the use of the problem-solving approach, a cornerstone of special needs practice which has been discussed by most of the leading authors in the field (e.g. Pearson and Lindsay, 1986; Ainscow and Muncey, 1989).

The essential element of the problem-solving approach is developing an action plan – or, in the language of the Code, an IEP (Individual Education Plan) – for a particular child based on the answers given by parents, teachers and child to a series of questions, never better described than by Westmacott and Cameron (1981) as shown in Figure 5.1.

Listing assets
Starting an action planning meeting by listing a child's assets has many advantages. First, it sets a positive note that makes it clear to parents and to the child (if present at the planning meeting, as many older children should be), that he or she is valued and appreciated. Second, it provides information that will be helpful in developing the action plan – about what the child finds motivating, what strengths s/he might share with others in order to build self-esteem, what interests the teacher might work through, what classroom (and home) contexts help produce the best learning and behaviour.

Figure 5.1 The problem-solving approach (Westmacott and Cameron, 1981).

Listing and prioritizing problems

Listing problem areas is the easiest part of the problem-solving process, for teachers, parents and the child alike. We are all practised in identifying deficiencies in ourselves and others, often much more so than in identifying strengths. What is not so easy is making sure that the language we use to describe problems is precise and accurate, and narrowing down long lists of problems into a manageable few.

Yet the process of prioritizing a few key problems, and working on those, is a real confidence builder. Much of the sense of inadequacy and lack of confidence felt by many classroom teachers working with special needs stems from the simple problem of not knowing where to start. When a child experiences difficulties in many areas of the curriculum, and perhaps in behaviour and relationships as well, it is easy to feel overwhelmed by all that needs to be done. The problem-solving approach prevents this: it enables all concerned to acknowledge that there will be many areas that they *cannot* tackle for the moment, but one or more on which they will all concentrate. It increases the chance of success because it ensures that energies are not dissipated over too wide an area, and that there is consistency: parents, teachers and the child are all working towards a common goal.

Which problems should be prioritized? It is best to choose:

- Those which the child feels are important and wants to work on − that is, those which tie in with their main life concerns at the time. This might, for example, be reading at the point where a child realizes a younger brother or sister is overtaking them, and suddenly begins to care passionately about doing better; it might be 'neat writing' if that is the one thing that matters to the child about his or her work at the moment.
- Those where there is some chance of success within a reasonably short time scale: for example, tackling an immediate problem of helping the child learn to control his or her temper, rather than a much more long-term problem in making and maintaining friendships.
- Those problems which underpin others − for example, low self-esteem or inappropriate learning behaviours (concentration, personal organization, willingness to tackle something new), which lead to poor performance in a wide range of social and learning situations.

The language in which the priority problems are expressed should be free from ambiguity. 'Can't concentrate' could mean anything from day-dreaming to wandering the classroom to talking or interfering with other children's work. 'Aggressive' could mean that the child shouts at other children, or hits them, or swears at the teacher. 'Immature' could mean anything from not being able to do up buttons on a shirt to not being able to tolerate losing in a game. In all of these examples, the action taken to resolve the problem would depend on which of the several interpretations most accurately described it. This is why it is important to use words with only one interpretation wherever possible.

Problems often become clearer if they are described in terms of what the child or teacher *does*, using verbs rather than adjectives: 'Julie talks to her friends when she should be working', 'Darren often pushes other children over', 'Paul doesn't make use of meaning or phonic cues when reading'. Such language avoids negative labelling of children's personal qualities; it means that everyone is tackling the same problem; it is non-emotive and comes across as less critical and negative than language like 'lacking in confidence', 'withdrawn', 'disruptive' or 'a poor reader'.

Specifying a desired outcome: setting targets and agreeing strategies
Once one or more priority problems have been agreed, the next step is to establish a goal or target for the action plan that will try to tackle them. The question here is 'What do we want the child to be doing *instead* of what is happening now?' The goal is also a yardstick for measuring progress, answering the question, 'How will we know if we have succeeded?'

If a child has repeated temper outbursts when teased or when other children will not do as she asks, what might be wanted instead is for her to develop and successfully use a range of other behavioural strategies to cope with provocation. If a child waits to be told what every unfamiliar word says when reading, the target might be that he would regularly try a guess based on initial letter and reading on and back. If he has difficulty in working independently, the target might be that he would start each piece of work unaided and only ask for help after trying alone for at least five minutes.

Once again, targets need to be specific and clearly defined: they must describe an end state that everyone can see and agree on. Sometimes this will mean unpacking a vague description into something observable: 'develops a love of books', for example, into 'asks for stories to be read to him at home'; 'chooses to spend some time each day at school in the book corner'; 'handles books without damaging them'.

Sometimes the process of defining a target is enough in itself to ensure success – just because for the first time, perhaps, everyone has agreed and shared with the child what they actually want him or her to do, rather than what they are fed up with him or her not doing. Sometimes, however, plans need to be made and recorded for particular strategies which parents, teachers and the child will use to reach the target – paired reading at home each night, regular praise from the teacher for starting work unaided, practice in deep breathing and relaxation to control temper outbursts, and so on.

Finally, a review date should be set and recorded, when all concerned will meet again to see if the strategies are working, and consider whether to discontinue the plan, make a new one, or seek further advice from outside agencies.

An example

Alan Morris was in a Year 6 class; he was having extra help with his reading but was also about a year behind others in his class in maths. He was a very well-liked child, popular both with other children and with adults. He was good at all forms of sport, and showed considerable interest and aptitude in work with computers. At a meeting attended by his parents, class teacher, the school's special needs coordinator and Alan himself these strengths were listed: everyone began by saying something they valued in Alan or something he was good at. Going on to the problem areas, Alan said he thought that his biggest problem was his writing: though he felt he was quite a good reader now, his written work was no good. His teacher said that from her point of view the main concern was that Alan seemed to be falling further and further behind in all the basic subjects, and that she was not succeeding in getting him to finish things off. His tray was always full of uncompleted bits of work. He was also very disorganized. Often he could not find the things he needed to tackle a piece of work, or would forget to bring things from home that he needed.

Mr and Mrs Morris said that they thought a lot of messages from school never reached them: Alan had always been a one for losing notes he was meant to bring home – and losing everything else, like his reading book. His room was always a mess and he would not make any effort to sort it out. He never seemed to know what day it was or when he had PE or swimming and needed his kit. They did not know how he was going to cope when he went on to secondary school; he had a sister there, so they knew how much the children were expected to do in the way of organizing themselves with what they needed each day, and with homework.

The special needs coordinator suggested that they make a list of everyone's concerns, and then try to decide which were the most important ones to tackle. Alan's teacher and Mr and Mrs Morris agreed that though there were problems in specific areas like maths, it would be better to choose a more general priority like helping Alan to get more work finished, since this would help him to do better in all his school subjects. They also felt that because he was coming up to secondary school transfer, it would be extremely important to help him learn to organize himself for learning. The special needs coordinator suggested they add a third priority, Alan's writing, since this was what mattered most to him at the moment. Some further discussion led them to the conclusion that the real problem here was not so much that he could not produce good written work (which he could, from time to time), but that he did not feel he was any good as a writer. He did not like the look of his work, or the fact that his friends wrote loads while he just did half a page or so.

The coordinator summed up the priority problem areas: Alan often does not finish his work, forgets messages and does not have the right equipment at the right time, and is not proud of himself as a writer. From there it was easy to answer the question, 'What do we want to see him doing instead?' Everyone, including Alan, agreed that they wanted to see him finishing more of his written work, relaying messages accurately between home and school, knowing what he was doing each day and organizing the things he would need, and being able to feel he was a good writer.

Alan's teacher thought it would be useful if she helped him to make a checklist of jobs to be done at the start of each day in class. The special needs coordinator suggested that it should have drawings or a keyword for each task to act as prompts. Alan would tick off each job as he finished it. If at the end of the day he had done everything on the checklist he would be allowed to use Pendown on the computer to type in the day of the week and colour it, a privilege he much enjoyed.

Mrs Morris wondered whether it would help Alan if he had an in-tray for unfinished work, as do people in offices, as well as his ordinary tray, instead of everything being jumbled up with his bags of crisps and pencils and reading books. The teacher thought that this was a very good idea, and would stop his work getting so messy. She asked Alan what he thought he should do if the in-tray began to pile up. He said he thought it would be fair for him to have to stay in at lunchtime to catch up a bit. This was agreed.

It was also planned to use a home–school diary, similar to the one Alan would use at secondary school, to record messages in. Alan would staple letters home into the diary. Mr and Mrs Morris would ask to see the diary every night; they would also make a weekly calendar with him to stick on the inside cover of the diary, showing what activities he had each day at school and what he would need. Alan agreed to check the calendar and organize his equipment before bed every night. To help him get better at remembering things, his teacher would send home a verbal message every Friday and his parents would note in the diary whether he remembered it.

To help Alan feel more positive about his writing, he would do one piece of work a week, from first draft to published version, entirely on Pendown, and have this work displayed. He would also be given opportunities to tape record some longer pieces of work which either a classroom helper or his parents would type on the word processor for him: it was stressed that real, adult writers often have people to type things for them like this.

Alan's parents agreed to come into school again at the end of term, to discuss whether the planned strategies were working, and what should happen next.

Recording action plans

Action-planning meetings should lead to a formal written record (IEP) which sets out:

- the nature of the child's learning difficulties;
- a record of the child's strengths and areas of success;
- the specific targets to be achieved, within a given time;
- the programmes, activities and strategies which will be used to achieve the targets – these might distinguish strategies which will be used to bypass particular priority problem areas and help the child access the full curriculum (such as use of a tape recorder or scribe for a child with writing difficulties), as well as the strategies that will be used actually to overcome problems (such as extra work on spelling or handwriting);
- staff involved (from within the school or external agencies), including frequency of support;
- any special materials or equipment needed;
- any help needed from parents at home;
- any special pastoral care or medical arrangements;
- arrangements for monitoring, including how success/progress will be measured;
- review arrangements and date.

Table 5.1 Individual Education Plan

Name: Lorraine Carter   **Date of birth:** 3.1.90

Current difficulties: Speech very hard to understand, tempers in school almost every day – usually when we can't understand what she wants. Has seen a speech therapist (report on file).

Strengths and areas of success: Play cooperatively with other children. Draws very well. Tempers rare when more adult attention available, e.g. when classroom assistant is there.

Targets for change: By the end of term . . .
1 Increase in the number of occasions when Lorraine is able to communicate effectively with adults in school.
2 At least four out of five days each week without tempers in school, on three successive weeks.

Programmes, activities and strategies:
- Home school diary so class teacher knows what Lorraine is trying to tell her about events at home, and vice versa for parents.
- Classroom assistant to have time each day to talk with Lorraine over a shared experience (cooking, making, pretend play) where the context will help make Lorraine's meaning clear.
- Special time (and sticker) from headteacher if Lorraine hasn't had a temper all day.

Staff involved: Classroom assistant for half an hour every day.
Materials and equipment: Diary, stickers.
Help from parents at home: Will try to take Lorraine to her speech therapy sessions regularly.
Pastoral care or medical arrangements: Monthly speech therapy, six monthly hearing check.
Monitoring arrangements: Class teacher will help Lorraine with a weekly chart for her stickers and will note successful communication in home school diary ('Lorraine told us about . . .').
Review: Meeting in school 2.6.95.

Table 5.1 gives an example of an IEP on these lines. Many other formats, however, are possible: formats for **group** action plans, for example (where several children have similar difficulties and receive support in a group); formats with space for short term objectives representing intermediate steps to the IEP targets (for example, weekly lists of keywords to be learned); and formats which give the child greater ownership of the plan, like the 'My Point of View' format, designed by the staff of Barrs Court Primary School in Bristol (Figure 5.2).

Reviewing the IEP need not necessarily mean masses more paperwork. If the IEP is designed with plenty of space under its main action headings, all that

Figure 5.2   Format for involving child in action planning.

really needs to happen at review is to note next to the targets set, and in a different colour, whether or not each has been achieved. Post-its can then be stuck over relevant sections to add new targets, strategies, resources and roles where necessary. Later on, affixed to blank paper and photocopied, each set of post-its provides a permanent record of each IEP.

The benefits of action planning

IEPs work because they focus attention and effort in a coordinated way on key problem areas, and because the in-built review system ensures that everyone concerned feels accountable for outcomes. As one teacher put it: 'They stop things being so vague, and help me home in on the particular problem. If I write something down it makes sure it happens. And then it passes on to the next teacher so what has been done isn't forgotten.'

IEPs work, too, because they are essentially optimistic, and make people feel they can actually do something about a problem themselves rather than just wait for outside intervention. They reduce feelings of helplessness and inadequacy, and at their best – when the chosen targets are closely linked to the child's own purposes, and are aimed at promoting the child's self-confidence as a learner – have been shown to work small miracles in situations where change had seemed impossible.

RECORD KEEPING

The special needs summary card

The IEP is a central plank in any system of record keeping – the working document kept by the class teacher along with a monitoring sheet for noting evidence of progress towards targets. Over the years however, the child's SEN file can accumulate numerous IEPs and monitoring sheets, and all sorts of papers recording information from health records, school assessments, and discussions with the child and parents. For this reason many schools have found it useful to keep a special needs summary card for each child who has been on the SEN register (Table 5.2). Its purpose is to provide information at a glance, for each incoming teacher and for external agencies, about the child's main areas of difficulty, what has been tried so far and with what result, what external agencies have been involved, and what may need to be done in the next school year.

Record keeping for secondary school transfer

Record keeping for secondary school transfer is an area that requires particular care. Currently, in many schools two philosophies operate: either the 'clean slate' philosophy, where it is felt that little or no information about special needs in learning or adjustment should be passed on in case it creates negative expectations, or a belief that information should be passed on as a kind of warning to secondary teachers about what to expect of the child.

The first philosophy does have some advantages, and works well for a few children; for most, however, it prevents the secondary school from appropriately deploying at an early stage the resources that might enable them to smooth the child's transition to secondary school, and ensure full access to the curriculum.

The second philosophy is also well-meaning, but often unfortunate in its effects. A recent study in Nottinghamshire (Nottingham County Council Advisory and Inspection Service, 1990) of the records passed on to secondary schools about pupils with behavioural difficulties, for example, noted that most

Table 5.2 Format for special needs summary card

Child's name Jessica   Date of birth 21-8-87   Telephone _____

Parental responsibility held by _____

	R	Y1	Y2
Action planning and within school support		In-school action plan started Oct. 92, reviewed once	Action plans made and reviewed termly
External agencies and external support	Speech therapy – ended Dec. 91		Learning Support Service consulted for advice Nov. 93
Health, hearing, eyesight	Speech difficulty. Hearing loss in r. ear. Grommets inserted summer 92	Hearing OK, speech clear. Missed a lot of school autumn term because of asthma	Hearing still OK
Main strengths and interests recorded on action plans		Good relationships peers. Takes in maths ideas quickly	Very good at maths. Gets on well with others
Main concerns on action plans		Poor listening skills and concentration	Very slow progress with reading. Can't remember how to write short words. Concentration erratic
Differentiation: what has worked		Giving instructions in short chunks, prefaced by her name	Concept keyboard writing works well. Still needs instructions in short chunks
Action plan strategies: what has worked		Listening skills games in group; use of tapes at listening centre. Parents have successfully read to her each night for longer periods (now up to 15 mins sustained concentration)	A teaching to targets programme with daily practice of writing her name and keywords from memory. Letterland for learning initial sounds
Reminders		Annual hearing check needed. Suggest further in-school action plan next year	Next review with parents, Learning Support Teacher due October

Address _____

Y3	Y4	Y5	Y6
Action plans reviewed termly	Action plans reviewed half termly		
Extra help with reading from Learning Support Teacher, all year	Discussed with Ed. Psych. Sep. 95. Extra help from Learning Support Teacher, all year		
Nice art work. Works hard. Good progress in maths	Art good. Helpful to adults. Lots of interests outside school – Brownies, First Aid course, swimming club		
Reading – little progress despite a lot of effort	Reading and written work. Also maths – falling behind because can't read scheme? Lots of quarrels with other children		
Needs to dictate some work to a scribe	Cloze procedure when writing. Needs a peer as reading helper, esp. in maths		
Paired reading at home has helped, and the multisensory work the support teacher has done on sight vocabulary and phonics	Strategies to boost self-esteem – she's been helping Y1 children with their reading, did the art-work for school Christmas card etc. Support teacher has used ARROW machine for literacy work – seems to be working, but slowly		
Review with parents, Learning Support Teacher due November	Review with Ed. Psych. autumn term – parents want need for Statement to be discussed		

were written 'in such a way as to assign a label to the child, and sometimes their parents . . .'. There were few indications in these records of the actions that had been taken in the primary school or of their outcomes. There was a preponderance of negative statements like 'disruptive', 'sullen', 'insolent behaviour', 'nuisance', 'argumentative' and 'flimsy grasp of basics'. Even where statements in such transfer records are positive, they are often couched in such vague and general terms as to be virtually useless: one-liners like 'nice boy; has some special needs' are by no means uncommon.

The most helpful transfer records are those that make positive suggestions about how teachers might deal with specific difficulties previously experienced by the pupil. One way to achieve this is to attach a separate front sheet to the special needs summary card, detailing:

- the most helpful ways of differentiating the curriculum for the pupil;
- whether the pupil is likely to need in-class support;
- in which areas the need for support will be greatest;
- in which areas the pupil may need structured programmes in academic, social or behavioural skills, delivered on a withdrawal basis;
- any other special needs, for example particular types of pastoral support, group or individual counselling;
- the pupil's own feelings about in-class support and withdrawal help, and the pupil's main concerns about secondary transfer;
- the parents/carers' main concerns about secondary transfer, and views about the type of support required.

Other forms of record keeping

So far we have looked only at record keeping that focuses on the individual child. There will be a need also for record keeping focused on the curriculum: class or subject teachers will want to keep records of their plans to differentiate schemes of work, and of what they actually did, along with some evaluative comment that will help colleagues implementing similar schemes of work in the future. And at the level of whole school planning and resource management, the head or special needs coordinator will need to record numbers of children in each class or year group identified by their teachers as having special needs, details of the stage of assessment reached – whether this be internal, or at the level of consultation with outside agencies, statutory assessment, or Statement of special needs – and of review dates. This particular type of record keeping is well adapted to the use of information technology, but in smaller primary schools all that is probably needed is for class teachers to take a copy of their class register, highlight the names of children with SEN in different colours according to the stage of assessment reached, and add review dates. The SENCO can then simply summarize this information for checking the SEN register and providing information for the LEA and governing body as required.

CONCLUSION

In this chapter, we have considered some formats that schools might want to use to keep track of the response they make to special needs. Aspects of these might well be incorporated into their whole school special needs policy: each school will need to design a system, however, that meets its own unique requirements, and those of the local authority. Each school will also need to build into its plans a regular review of the chosen system for making action plans and keeping records, perhaps by sampling records from time to time to make sure that they meet criteria of orderliness, objectivity, and above all usefulness.

We should never lose sight of the principle that like good action planning, record keeping is only worth while in so far as it provides a guide on what to do next – for parents, teachers and children. The question of how to adapt the curriculum so that it is maximally responsive to the needs of the whole range of children can only be answered if there are records of what has proved successful and unsuccessful in the past. Equally, at a time of limited financial resources for schools, good record keeping is essential if scant support teaching time or extra equipment is to be targeted where it will do most good. It is to this issue, of managing limited resources, that we turn in the next chapter.

FURTHER READING

Ramjhun, A. (1995) *Implementing the Code of Practice for Children with Special Educational Needs.* London: David Fulton.

6

MANAGING TIME

INTRODUCTION

The first question asked by teachers in relation to any special plans for supporting children with special needs is 'where can I find the time?' Lately, it has been asked on an increasingly urgent note, as budgetary restrictions on individual schools force larger classes and cuts in any extra staffing which has traditionally been used for special needs support.

In this climate, it has become ever more important to look at the best ways of using any limited support teaching time available, and to look creatively at all the alternatives to the kinds of one-to-one or small group support long held to be the panacea for all special needs. It has become important to consider which elements of this kind of help (careful target setting, immediate feedback, close monitoring, positive input to the child's self-esteem) each child actually needs, and what flexible ways there might be of providing these elements within the classroom, using a mixture of physical resources (information technology, specially-designed materials) and accessible human resources (peers, parents, classroom helpers).

FINDING THE TIME

Something most schools will want to do when developing or reviewing a policy on allocating time to special needs support is to brainstorm collectively, at a staff meeting, all possible times in the school day when teachers could find time to spend short periods with an individual child or group of children who need an extra boost, and all possible ways in which staff could collaborate to free each other for such work. There may be times when classes can be shared – for story or television time, music practice, putting on a performance for each other or showing work they have done. There are rarely any magical solutions, but at least everyone will know that they have looked as creatively as possible at what might be achievable. Whatever is agreed, it is important that it is reliable: it is no good the headteacher promising to come in and free the teacher to work with a group if half the time s/he will be called away by other more pressing commitments. Many action plans for children with special needs fail because they are founded on something that proves impossible to deliver regularly: more than many other children, they need consistency of input, and in these cases it may be better to make a small scale plan that can be relied on rather than a more ambitious one that cannot.

Other ways in which it may be possible to create extra time for children with special learning needs include looking critically at the amount of time the teacher spends in class dealing with managerial and resources-related queries from children, rather than work-related questions. This means noting, over a day or two, the types and frequencies of questions the children bring to the teacher: if s/he is spending more than a few minutes at the beginning and end of work periods dealing with issues like pencil sharpening and paper and whose turn it is to press the button on the tape recorder, it may be time to reorganize the classroom so that the children can access the resources they need more independently, and teach the children rules and routines for using equipment.

Another idea is to organize the day so that there are times when children work in groups requiring different levels of supervision. One teacher, for example, sets useful but low supervision board work (such as handwriting practice, or dictionary skills) for the first half hour of each day, while she supervises a small group of children with special needs more intensively on individualized programmes of daily activities. Another identifies a time each day when she works with a particular group of children (not always those with special needs) while the rest of the class are engaged in collaborative problem-solving activities, with the brief of only approaching the teacher for help when they are sure that they have exhausted all possible knowledge and expertise within their working group.

Time for individualized programmes can also be created by looking at how children spend any spare time in the classroom. Many of the difficulties in learning which have traditionally been ascribed to a failure in the child to take in and remember new ideas actually occur because of the way in which learning has been structured: the teacher has moved on when a new skill or concept has been acquired, but not practised to the point where it becomes fluent and automatic. Without such extra practice in 'fluency' (Haring et al., 1978), the learning may not stick. Ann Lewis (1995), in her book on primary special needs and the national curriculum, suggests that to help pupils reach the stage of fluency teachers plan games, quizzes and timed tests to be done in pairs, which children use when they have finished set tasks and have a few minutes to spare in the classroom. One teacher uses this idea regularly with her class: spare time has become known as 'top-up time', and children know where to go for games and ideas cards that will help them top up on acquired skills in maths, handwriting, spelling and reading.

MANAGING SMALL AMOUNTS OF
TEACHING TIME

If, despite teachers collaborating to share classes, and reorganizing the way children work, only a small amount of teacher time can be freed, then the best use of it may be to work out (perhaps with the help of the special needs coordinator) a plan involving short periods of daily tightly-focused activities which the child can manage to do independently in class, or manage with the help of a peer, a volunteer helper, or a classroom assistant.

Such programmes require the very clear targeting of exactly what it is hoped the child will achieve, which was described in Chapter 5:

> Mrs Castle, a Year 3 teacher, was concerned about Ben's slow progress with reading and the technical aspects of written work. Her 'bypass' strategies for differentiating the curriculum were working well: she was careful about the level of difficulty of anything he had to read in his maths, science and topic work, and he was increasingly managing to record his ideas using process writing with invented spellings, magic line and support from a friend when editing a draft. In English, however, he was stuck at a level of very simple reading books: he made very good use of context when reading and his miscues invariably made a kind of sense, but he made little or no use of phonetic strategies. His sight vocabulary did not seem to be growing. In his invented spellings he also seemed to be stuck; he was not showing spontaneous use of any common early letter patterns such as 'sh', 'ee', 'oo', or of longer letter strings like 'and', 'all', or 'ing'.
>
> His teacher decided to target his knowledge and application of these phonetic skills in her action plan. No extra teaching support was available, and the special needs coordinator warned that Ben might need a lot of repetition and reinforcement: he has done some work last year on the Sound Sense workbooks, but with little success. She gave Mrs Castle a list of letter strings to work on, and suggested some suitable materials. Mrs Castle decided to arrange for Ben to practise a new letter string each week, with a break every third week when he would review words from lists he had worked on previously. She discussed with Ben some of the ways in which he might work on learning the letter strings, and agreed with him a daily sequence of activities as follows:
>
> *Monday.* Copy list of words into exercise book, using joined writing and look-cover-write-check. Read through the words with Sam.
> *Tuesday.* Work with Sam to make up a silly sentence or rhyme linking as many of the words as you can: write it on a card, illustrate it, and put it on the wall.
> *Wednesday.* Use the computer to input and practise the list on the Complete Speller software (Northern Micromedia).

Thursday. Use Letterland materials or A Hand for Spelling sheet to
practise the letter string.

Friday. Have Sam ask you to make each word on your list with plastic
letters.

Every day, Sam and Ben also tested each other on the word list, and
quickly went through a pack of cards that had letter strings written on
one side and a key clue picture and word for each on the reverse: Ben had
to say each sound and record how many he got right.

The teacher wrote what Ben had to do on the first page of a special
exercise book, and had him add drawings to help him remember each
day's instructions. On the next page she put a format he could use
independently to record his progress:

	Date		
	---	---	---
Target	*Working on*	*Mastered*	*Checked*
I can spell words with the 'sh' pattern			
I can spell words with the 'ee' pattern			

The remainder of the book was used as a weekly diary, in which Ben
entered the week's word list and his scores on the daily sound check.

All this took the teacher about 20 minutes, with an additional 10
minutes each week to sort out a word list and supporting materials, and to
monitor Ben's work through the diary from time to time. Ben's parents
were asked to help by looking in the diary to see which letter strings he
had mastered, and praising him for any attempt to apply them when
doing shared reading at home.

Another way of managing a small amount of teacher time is to use what are
sometimes called use *precision teaching* or *teaching to targets* approaches. Here,
the teacher chooses a small-scale teaching target, based on an identified gap in
the child's knowledge or skills. The target needs to be something that it is
important for the child to learn, and achievable within a time scale of a few
weeks. A useful suggestion (Ireson et al., 1989) is to set targets at the limit of
what the child can do *with help*.

The target – for example, that the child will 'complete correctly addition
within twenty sums, counting on from the larger number', or 'spell correctly
words with the letter string "all"' – is recorded on a learning chart, as in the
example in Table 6.1. Then the teacher records on the learning chart the
instructions s/he or another helper will use when working with the child: for
example, 'add these two numbers', or 'write these words as I say them', and the

Table 6.1 Learning chart (adapted from Jewell, 1986)

Learning Chart   **Child's Name:**

1 Target for the week: **4 When to stop:**

                                        5 Rewards:

2 Instruction:

                                        6 Back up resources for independent
                                           practice:

Materials:

3 How many times each day:

                                        Next pupil target:

Mon   Tues   Wed   Thurs   Fri   Mon   Tues   Wed   Thurs   Fri

Key: √ if correct ● if help needed

---

materials needed – a number line, perhaps, or a prepared list of five words. S/he decides how often it will be possible to work with the child on the learning target: perhaps once a day in school, and once a day at home. S/he next sets a criterion which will indicate when the child has reached mastery of the learning target: in this case, 'when he has got nine out of ten sums right on four successive days', or 'when he has spelled all five words right on three successive occasions, and can also generalize to a new word with the "all" letter string'. This criterion is recorded on the chart under 'when to stop'. Teacher and child determine a way of celebrating success: for example, taking the chart and his work to show another teacher, or having some extra time on the computer with a friend, or a gold star. The teacher adds any relevant materials that might be useful for the child to work on independently, to back up the work on the learning chart – for example, playing a number game, or using spelling worksheets.

Once the learning chart has been filled in, the child spends a few minutes each day working with a helper (the teacher, a classroom assistant, volunteer helper or peer), on the task on the chart, until he reaches the mastery criterion. The role of the support person is to correct any mistakes straight away, and immediately help the child to the right answer. The helper puts a tick or a star on the learning chart for each correct unaided response, and a dot if help was needed. Table 6.2 gives an example of a learning chart completed in this way.

The advantages of this kind of approach are that it provides a structure which any helper coming into the classroom can easily learn to use, and that it makes sure that teaching goes on until the child has actually mastered the piece of learning, rather than stopping (as is usually the case in classrooms) when some of the class may have got the idea, and some not – or only half learned it, so that it still has to be thought about rather than having become automatic.

The difference between learning something to the point of mastery, and other types of learning, can be illustrated by an analogy – that of teaching children to cross the road safely. This is something we naturally teach to the point of mastery: we give the child plenty of opportunities to practise the skills of looking right, left and so on with our support, and would not dream of stopping the teaching until the child has fulfilled our own implicit success criterion – getting the whole process right independently several times without a slip-up. This can be contrasted with our more hit-and-miss approach to teaching many other skills, when we may show the child how to do something once or twice, hope they have got it, and then move on to something else. For some children, this will work. But for many children with learning difficulties, it does not: they have not a sufficiently secure hold on a new skill to remember it for very long, and become easily confused by the introduction of something new.

For some children, then – particularly those who seem to know something one minute and forget it the next – the consistency of precision teaching using a learning chart can be very helpful: indeed there is much documentary evidence, from the Portage pre-school home teaching scheme, and from work with older children (Miller et al., 1985), to show that it is. There are also many objections to the approach (Ainscow and Muncey, 1989): that it, is narrow, overly prescriptive, and above all boring for children. And so it can be, if used without regularly checking with all those involved (helper, parent and child) how they are feeling about it, and if used across the curriculum rather than for just a few key skills which underpin much of what a child will learn subsequently. But given these preconditions, it can be a sensible way of making

Table 6.2 Completed learning chart

Learning Chart — **Child's Name:** Gemma P.

1 **Target for the week:** Gemma will complete addition within 20 sums correctly, counting from the larger number.

2 **Instruction:** Add these two numbers

Materials: Number line, sums (ten a day)

3 **How many times each day:** Once.

4 **When to stop:** When she gets nine out of ten sums right on 4 successive days.

5 **Rewards:** Take sums and chart to show Mrs K.

6 **Back up resources for independent practice:** Cambridge Primary Maths Games pack; LDA Puzzle Tables.

Next pupil target: Addition to 20 without number line.

Mon	Tues	Wed	Thurs	Fri	Mon	Tues	Wed	Thurs	Fri
•	√	√	√	√	√	√	√	√	√
•	√	√	•	√	√	√	√	√	√
•	√	√	√	√	•	√	√	√	√
•	√	•	√	•	√	√	√	√	√
•	•	•	√	√	•	√	√	√	•
√	•	•	•	√	√	√	√	√	√
√	•	√	•	•	√	√	√	√	√
•	√	•	√	√	√	√	•	√	√
•	•	•	√	√	√	√	√	√	√
•	•	√	•	√	•	•	√	√	√

Key: √ if correct • if help needed

---

maximum use of the few minutes a day of individual teaching help which can realistically be expected for children with special needs in busy classrooms.

MAKING USE OF PEER TUTORING

One readily available source of support for children with special needs is peer tutoring: asking one child (either from the same class, or from another age group) to take on a direct teaching role with another. Many teachers, however, feel that this is somehow unethical – that the child who is the helper is wasting valuable learning time, that s/he would feel put upon or held back, that his or her parents would mind.

Fortunately, the research evidence makes it so abundantly clear that peer tutoring benefits the tutor as much and very often more than it benefits the tutee, that such objections can be easily answered.

Projects in which children tutor others of their own age or younger in reading typically demonstrate that tutors make substantial gains in their own learning – around two-and-a-half times the gains they would normally be expected to make over the project period; tutees make about twice the normal gain (Limbrick et al., 1985). There have been similar results reported from studies of peer tutoring in many other curriculum areas: mathematics, spelling, language development, computer skills, problem solving (Topping, 1988). It is thought that the enhanced self-esteem engendered by acting as teacher to another child may be one reason for the powerful positive effects on tutors; other explanations advanced include the opportunities that tutoring provides for consolidating the tutor's own learning; as any teacher knows, there is no better way of obtaining a sure grasp of a concept than to have to teach it to others.

An example of a project in one primary school illustrates the impact on children of being chosen as peer tutors:

> A teacher of a Year 6 class was very concerned about the very poor reading skills of a group of children in her class. She decided to pair each of her poor readers with a child from an infant class. The aim, the older children were told, was 'to help the infants with their reading'. The younger child would choose a book and the older child talk about the pictures and story with them, or the pair would read what they could together. The older group were given a lot of praise, from their own teacher and the infant teacher. They were told how well the younger ones' reading was coming on, and of changes in their attitude to books and to learning. After a few months, the teacher reassessed the reading skills of her class. The children who had acted as peer tutors had made rapid progress. One boy, for example, had gone from being nearly three years behind in his reading to being only a few months behind.

Low-achieving, poorly-motivated children have most to gain by acting as tutors; schools can make use of this by forming partnerships between Years 5 and 6 children and those in younger groups, as with the teacher in the example, or in setting up a scheme with a neighbouring secondary school involving their older pupils. Maher (1984) reports several highly successful projects on these lines, in which 14–16-year-olds with a history of disruptive behaviour and underachievement tutored 9–11-year-old slow learners. He found that the older pupils made surprisingly good tutors, and showed massive gains in school attendance and performance. The tutees showed improvements of 15–20 per cent in task completion and performance on attainment tests over the ten-week tutoring period, with two 30-minute tutoring sessions per week.

While cross-age tutoring has particular benefits for enhancing self-esteem and motivation, same age tutors can be just as effective in enhancing learning (Sharpley and Sharpley, 1981). Same age-tutoring projects are also easier to organize: there have been many reports of successful schemes that have divided classes or year groups into two, on the basis of reading ability, and established hearer–reader partnerships involving every child (Horner, 1990; Leeves, 1990). These are described in more detail in Chapter 11 along with some of the techniques (like cued spelling, paired reading and pause, prompt and praise) which lend themselves to peer-tutoring projects.

Peer-tutoring components

The essential components of a successful peer-tutoring scheme have been described by Topping (1987). On the basis of research evidence, he suggests that projects should be time-limited, running initially for about 6–10 weeks, after which the teacher seeks the views of tutor and tutee and decides with them whether the tutoring should stop, continue as it is or continue in another form. The tutor and tutee should work together regularly, for 15–30 minutes, at least three times a week in class time, supplemented if they wish by more work in their free time. Careful training of tutors is vital: peer tutoring works best if the tutor has a clear structure to work from, which is demonstrated by the teacher and then practised under guidance. The tutor should also be provided with simple written instructions in the form of a manual or handbook. Tutor and tutee must have some way of recording progress, and the teacher must plan to monitor the tutoring by looking at these records, observing occasional sessions and holding review meetings.

Parental involvement

Peer tutoring is one way of increasing the amount of individual attention available to children with special needs. Others include having classroom assistants and volunteer helpers work with the child on materials and activities planned by the teacher, and involving parents more actively in their children's learning. This can have benefits beyond the merely instructional: the opportunities it provides for parents and children to learn more about each other, spend more time together, and share both the struggle and the pleasure of learning can lead to changes in the child's self-acceptance that unlock whole areas of hidden potential.

It can only do this, however, if the experience of parental involvement is one which makes the child feel valued and successful. It is the fear that this will not be the case that makes many teachers shy away from setting parents and children tasks to do together, as part of an action plan: despite the massive amount of evidence on the effectiveness of parental involvement projects (Young and Tyre, 1983; Topping and Wolfendale, 1985), they are aware that in individual cases parents can find getting their child to do a set task a battle that spoils rather than enhances their relationship, can find it hard to tolerate the child's mistakes or remember to praise them for successes, and can, on occasion, push the child too hard to the point where all learning becomes an anxious chore.

In these circumstances, it is all too easy to back off from asking parents to become involved. To do so, nevertheless, risks depriving the child of a readily available and often highly-motivated source of support. It means leaving parents and carers who on many occasions want very much to do something to help with little guidance about what might be best, so that the field is open for inappropriate teaching methodologies or targets. Instead of forgoing parental involvement, it may be better to negotiate something – however small – which the parent knows s/he can do without becoming anxious or angry, and which the child will be willing to do without argument. By asking three questions – 'How does it go when you try to work with your child at home?', 'What helps it go well?', 'What makes it go badly?' – the teacher can find out which problems might be solved, and which side-stepped. If getting the child to work at home is a battle, the answer might be sending home educational games, making the amount of time spent initially very small, or using a contract with the child linked to a reward system at home or school. If the parents say the problem is their own impatience, it may be possible to find someone else (grandparent, brother or sister) who can work with the child, or use a technique (like paired reading) where the importance of mistakes is minimized, or offer the parents training in noticing and praising success.

What about parents who appear not to want to be involved in their child's learning? It is certainly true that on the surface, at least some parents of children with special needs seem unwilling to engage in active plans to support the child: their feelings about their child's difficulties in learning or adjustment are often those which cause awkwardness in their relationships with the school, and make the establishment of a working partnership a particularly sensitive issue. Appearances, however, are sometimes deceptive. Dorothy Hamilton (1987), reflecting on her work on parental involvement in inner city areas during the PACT (Parents, Children and Teachers) project, has much that is useful to say about this:

> In practice . . . teachers fears in this respect are often unfounded: many schools have contracted and worked with all their parents successfully. It is important to start with the recognition that there is (of course) no difference between the parents of children with special needs and other parents; it is just that some of the former are likely to be further along a continuum of distance from schools, often because of their own unmet needs. But the lessons we have learned about approaching parents and

maintaining contact with them apply here as elsewhere. The chief requirements for success appear to be that the school has the will, and is prepared to suspend the myth of parental apathy.

Schools that have been willing to persist in their efforts to involve all parents in particular projects – using evening as well as daytime group meetings, small informal groups with class teachers, home visits from the education welfare officer or teachers – have in practice succeeded, even in deprived inner city areas, in reaching almost all their parents. There are certain necessary preconditions for engaging and maintaining high levels of involvement: there needs to be a clear structure in what the parents are being asked to do to help the child, that is demonstrated, practised and later on monitored in some way by school staff. There also needs to be an effort to maintain the impetus of any parental involvement scheme by varying and developing the work done at home: one year paired reading, for example (Topping and Wolfendale, 1985), another a paired maths scheme (Arora and Bamford, 1989), or reading and spelling games (Young and Tyre, 1983). Lynda Pearce's resource, *Partners in Literacy*, published by LDA, is a valuable source of ideas on how to ensure that there is variety, and how to structure the regular well-planned meetings with parents that are needed to generate the bursts of enthusiasm and commitment which account for much of the success of parental involvement schemes.

At the level of action plans for the individual child rather than whole school or class parental involvement projects, success in engaging parents will depend on factors surrounding the way in which invitations to parents to discuss their child's progress are given, and how meetings are handled. Many parents are put off by fears based on their own experiences of school, or by meetings where they have no control of the agenda, no sense of being listened to, no privacy, and where all that comes across is apparent criticisms of their child. Much of this can be avoided if there is a whole school context where parents are not just called in when there are problems, but can see meetings about their child's special needs as just one aspect of generally close and friendly contact between home and school.

At a recent meeting between a group of parents of children with special needs and a group of teachers and special needs coordinators in mainstream primary schools, the parents were clear about the factors that help communication between themselves and the school – and those which do not. Top of their list of blocks to communication was a feeling of not being listened to, and of meeting teachers who went on the defensive if they made any comment about how things could be made better in school for the child. They also disliked feeling outnumbered at meetings, and having to be the ones making the running in arranging for follow up and review. What they wanted, they said, was a structure for meetings which:

- involved them early on, when the child's progress first gave cause for concern, rather than when problems had escalated;

- has a clear agenda made known to them beforehand – along with an invitation to add issues and concerns they would like discussed;
- included information about the child's strengths as well as difficulties;
- included opportunities for them to put their views on the best ways to help the child give of his/her best in school;
- included accurate information on the procedures used by the school and local education authority to assess and provide for special needs;
- gave them specific rather than general suggestions on how to help their child at home;
- ended with a clear agreement on the action to be taken, who would take it, and with a plan to meet again to review progress.

These parents valued teachers who were honest, and had evidence of the child's work to show; an approach by the teacher that began with, 'I don't feel I'm doing a very good job with . . .' rather than 'He can't . . .' was appreciated.

The way in which an initial invitation to a meeting is given can be off-putting: many parents report nights of worry after a casual invitation to 'pop in and discuss Andrew's learning problems', or after a more formal letter expressing concern and setting a date and time for a meeting with the teachers. The best way to give an invitation for a first discussion about a child's special needs is probably orally, if possible at a regular parent–teacher evening, when it will arise naturally from the general overview of progress and where the purposes of such a meeting can be explained and clarified. Some schools like to add to the verbal invitation a short information sheet, taken from the whole school special needs policy or the school prospectus, which describes the steps that will be taken when a teacher or parent expresses concern about a child's progress, and the ways in which parents will be involved at each stage, on the lines of:

> At X Primary School there will sometimes be times when a teacher feels the school should try harder to help particular children make better progress. When this happens, we would ask you to come into school for a conference with your child's teacher, and perhaps also the headteacher or the teacher with responsibility for special educational needs.
>
> This kind of conference happens very often in school: we find that many children need a little extra help from time to time.
>
> At the conference, you will be asked to tell us more about your child's strengths and interests outside school. We would also like you to help us with your ideas about ways to get the best from him or her. We will use this information, and the information the teacher has gained from observing the child closely in school, to decide on a plan of action – things the teacher can do, things the child can do, things you can do at home which may help sort out any problems.
>
> We will set a date when everyone concerned will meet again to see whether the plan has succeeded. At this meeting, another plan may be agreed, or we may decide to ask for advice from one of the outside support

services available to us – such as the special needs support service, or the psychology service.

For almost all children, this kind of special help will be enough. If not, we may be able to involve the local education authority in making a fuller assessment, jointly with you, of what the child needs in order to ensure progress.

Types of support parents can give include:

- Direct help with specific work at home.
- Taking a checking and monitoring role (for example, checking that homework has been done, or agreeing to spend time each evening playing a favourite game with the child if s/he has not been in trouble at school that day).
- Freeing professional time to work with the child by helping in school with the preparation of materials or supervising groups under the direction of the teacher.

If direct teaching at home is to be used, paired reading and maths, or cued spelling (see Chapter 12) are techniques that have all proved helpful in providing a structure to the work. The teaching-to-targets approach using a learning chart also lends itself well to parental involvement.

Table 6.3 gives an example of a chart developed for David, a 5-year-old experiencing great difficulty in assigning numerals to counted sets. Assessment showed that he had not mastered an essential component skill: he was not only unable to match written numbers to oral number names, but also could not reliably distinguish numerals from each other. He could, however, count sets accurately with one-to-one correspondence. For a week or two, he worked intensively on matching plastic numerals and numerals on cards with each other, as a first step towards matching the numerals with sets of objects: his parents spent a few minutes each day having him match magnetic plastic numerals on the door of the fridge, and recorded progress on the learning chart supplied. He soon reached the success criterion of correctly matching all ten numbers three days in a row, and was able to go on to a new learning chart where he had to recognize and point to the numerals 2 and 3 when asked to pick them out from several alternatives.

CONCLUSION

In this chapter, we have looked at ways of offering support to children on those frequent occasions when there is no extra teaching time available in the school to meet special needs. These are not just stop-gap resources: as we have seen, involving peers and parents can have benefits that extend well beyond the surface value of the academic teaching and learning that takes place.

Table 6.3 Learning chart with parental involvement

Learning Chart	**Child's Name:**
1 **Target for the week:** David will match the numbers 1–10	4 **When to stop:** Not until David gets all 10 right on 3 days in a row.
2 **Instruction:** Find a number just the same as this	5 **Rewards:** Sticker from teacher
Materials: Plastic numbers	6 **Back up resources for independent practice:** Play dominoes with the domino cards with just numbers on them
3 **How many times each day:** 10	**Next pupil target:** We'll try David on recognizing numbers.

Mon	Tues	Wed	Thurs	Fri	Mon	Tues	Wed	Thurs	Fri
•	√	•	√	√	√	√	√		
√	√	√	√	√	√	√	√		
√	•	√	√	√	√	√	√		
•	•	√	√	√	√	√	√		
√	√	√	•	√	√	√	√		
•	√	√	√	√	√	√	√		
•	•	•	•	•	√	√	√		
•	√	√	•	•	√	√	√		
•	•	√	√	√	√	√	√		
•	•	•	√	√	√	√	√		

Key: √ if correct • if help needed

Parents' comment: He muddled 2 and 5 but seems to have got them now.

Nevertheless, managing daily teaching to targets or peer/parent tutoring makes heavy demands on classroom teachers, and it is here that having someone in the school with a specific brief for supporting colleagues in meeting special needs can prove most valuable. In the next chapter, we look at the roles such a person can play, and at the ways in which schools can make use of any actual teaching time that may be earmarked for work with special needs.

FURTHER READING

Topping, K. (1988) *The Peer Tutoring Handbook*. London, Croom Helm.
Topping, K. and Wolfendale, S. (eds) (1985) *Parental Involvement in Children's Reading*. London, Croom Helm.

7

MANAGING ROLES AND RESOURCES

SUPPORT TEACHING TIME

If schools are in the fortunate position of not having to rely entirely on help from parents, peers and volunteers, and have some extra staffing within the school that is used for special needs support, they then have to deal with the difficult question of how best to deploy the limited amount of extra teaching time available. The issue they face – and this applies also to the deployment of support from external agencies – is whether to opt for a system of withdrawal teaching, or whether to choose a system that provides support mainly within the classroom.

Each system has its advantages and its disadvantages. Withdrawal teaching enables focused work on individualized targets to take place in an atmosphere of calm and concentration. It can help to economize on scant support teacher time, when children from different classes but with similar needs are drawn together as a withdrawal group. It can provide a welcome break for both class teacher and pupil where behaviour or the relationship is problematic, and provide the child with experience of a range of teaching styles. On the other hand, it may mean that the child experiences a fragmented curriculum, missing just enough of what is going on in the classroom to make it difficult to catch hold of important new learning. There may be little or no link between the work done in withdrawal sessions and the work in class, so that there are few opportunities to generalize from one situation to another, or to practise skills taught in withdrawal sessions with sufficient frequency to ensure fluency. The child may be stigmatized for going out of class to a special teacher, to an extent where already fragile self-esteem is shattered. Class teachers may feel that it is now no longer their responsibility to cater for the pupil's special needs; thankfully handing over all responsibility to the withdrawal teacher, they may reduce efforts to support the child in class or adapt teaching styles. There may be few opportunities for the class teacher and support teacher to share information and skills; the withdrawal teacher may experience a sense of personal and professional isolation from colleagues.

Advantages of in-class support are the class teacher maintains a sense of ownership of the problems that are arising for the child, and is encouraged to look – at best, in cooperation with the support teacher – at ways of overcoming them through a differentiated curriculum. Pupils other than targeted individuals can benefit from the presence of an extra support teacher in the classroom, and from the strategies for differentiation introduced as a result of teacher teamwork. The support teacher sees the child in context, and is thus better placed to offer advice about needs; the child does not miss work, and – if not obviously the sole client of the support teacher – is less likely to be teased or labelled by peers. On the negative side, however, the small amounts of in-class support that tend to be available may result in help so diluted as to be ineffective in raising pupil attainment; lack of time for liaison between class and support teacher may lead to the kind of situation where support teachers are used as just another pair of hands in class, with scant regard to their particular skills and potential contribution.

Much of the debate about in-class support versus withdrawal centres on the appropriateness of removing children from the curriculum available to their peers, in order to concentrate on particular areas like language or maths skills. Jane Youdan (1991), for example, argues that

> children learn best in situations where they have a clear perception of the purpose of their task and where that purpose matters to them: for example, a child learns to read because he wants to understand a story or find something out – he does not read because he wants to get the words right, therefore formal instruction based on reading accuracy will not be fulfilling the needs of the child, and in consequence is likely to be less effective in teaching the child to read.

But what if the child does, very much, want to read just because other children can? And what of the considerable evidence that some forms of structured withdrawal teaching can be highly effective in accelerating children's progress in basic skills (Engelmann, 1969; Clay, 1981)? As yet, we have little comparable evidence on the effectiveness of approaches that are solely aimed at helping the child to keep up with his or her work in class – an interpretation of in-class support which is dear to many class teachers, who have plans for what the class will achieve and like to see all children fitting in with these expectations.

There is a real risk with in-class support of this kind that it will satisfy teachers' short-term expectations, but seriously disadvantage children for the future, if they end up thoroughly *au fait* with Roman history or the way in which soil is formed, but without the 'tool' skills of literacy and numeracy which they will need in all of their later education. 'Back to basics' may be a deadly and demotivating cry to many teachers and many schools, but we should not forget that there are good reasons why some skills are designated 'basic', and that there are many children (and adults) who subsequently suffer quite badly because no-one has succeeded in helping them to master them.

Prioritizing support towards the core subjects, rather than the whole curriculum, is one way of making sure that all available extra adult help is not poured into propping up children so that they can be seen to keep pace with an inadequate curriculum ill matched to their needs. This does not necessarily, however, mean that we should return to the practice of withdrawing children (often at times when the things they like best are happening in class) year-in year-out to work individually or in small groups on a tedious diet of basic skills worksheets. Instead, it should be possible to use special programmes of work in basic skills on a time-limited basis (for, say, half a term or a term), with clear targets, either in the classroom or out of it depending on whether the programme (or the child) actually requires a non-distracting environment or whether the special work would distract others if pursued in the room. It should also be possible to embed the programmes firmly within the work pursued by the class as a whole: to use a poem the class have studied, for example, as a starting point for work on a letter string for spelling, or base work on telling the time on a class science investigation of shadow lengths throughout the day, or build an individual child's self-esteem by doing some preparatory work with him so that he can take an expert role in a class discussion.

The important point, however, is that in doing this work the aim of the support teacher is to teach the children to spell particular words rather than appreciate the poem, to tell the time rather than measure shadows, to grow in confidence rather than to gain knowledge of the topic under discussion. The class and support teacher can *change* roles: the support teacher can work with the class on measuring shadows in order to free the class teacher to work with a group on telling the time, for example. They need to work together to plan who will do what, and how work on the core targets that individual children are aiming at can be interwoven with the programme of the class as a whole. Nevertheless, the two roles – curriculum manager and target manager – are kept distinct.

Some children *will* need some form of in-class support: these are the children whose need for bypass strategies, enabling them to circumvent areas of difficulty in order to access the curriculum, is greater than their need for help in acquiring core skills. An example might be a child with a coordination difficulty: in-class support would be necessary if s/he is to cope with technology lessons involving the accurate manipulation of tools and materials. Equally, a child with a hearing impairment might need in-class support in the form of someone to repeat and clarify instructions. But such support may not necessarily require professional teaching skills; when resources are limited, bypass strategies may best be implemented by non-teaching assistants, volunteer helpers, or even the peer group.

Other children – those with specific literacy difficulties, for example – may well need bypass strategies and in-class support based on scribing or taping, but may have a greater immediate need for catch-up programmes in English, or maths. Only a clear distinction between bypass strategies and remediation strategies, and a process of determining priorities like the one described in Chapter 5 can help schools decide where to target limited extra adult help. For each child, this will be an individual decision, rather than one based on doctrine.

The decision must be reviewed in the light of the evidence. The children must be asked, at regular intervals, how they feel about any extra support that is given. Do they value the support? Does it make them look obviously different from their peers? Do they prefer to work in or out of the classroom with their extra helper? Measures of progress, again at regular intervals, will also enable the chosen form of support to be evaluated:

> One teacher, faced with a demand to support large numbers of 9-year-olds just starting at a middle school, decided that help should take a form different from the one-to-one weekly withdrawal sessions that had operated in the past. She agreed to provide in-class support for half a term, and then set up and run a peer tutoring project. Children were all given the GAP reading test; better readers were paired with poorer readers for three sessions a week to read to one another in turn from shared books. Over a five-week period, many children had made substantial gains when retested on the GAP. The children who had previously been targeted for in-class support, however, did not make the same kind of progress. The support and class teachers therefore decided that withdrawal techniques were now the most appropriate course of action for these pupils in the next school term.
>
> (Horner, 1990)

Whatever support teaching system is chosen, if it is to work effectively, it will involve careful attention to relationships – not just those between teacher and pupil, but also those between the teachers involved, those being supported and those proffering support. There is no manual that can guide participants through this potential minefield, or prevent the tensions that can arise when either teaching partner feels threatened or de-skilled. Nevertheless, some basic ground rules, worked out ahead of time by the teaching partners, can do much to help things go smoothly.

The ground rules for support within the classroom have to cover who does what, and need to answer such questions as:

- How will the class teacher make sure that the support teacher has prior information about the schemes of work or specific lessons that will be shared?
- How will the class teacher make sure that the support teacher will be in class at times when s/he can actually be useful – for example, not in formal class teaching lessons?
- When will time be found for joint planning?

- Who will make sure that any special resources required are available?
- What expectations hold in the classroom in relation to pupil noise, movement, access to resources?
- Who will be responsible for discipline within the room when both teachers are present?
- When and how will the support given be evaluated?

As well as these general ground rules, specific roles need to be negotiated for each support situation. All too often these roles are restricted to either helping the child or children in a general way to complete tasks set by the class teacher, or withdrawing them to work on basics. Both, as we saw in the last section, can be valid ways of working, but they still represent only a fraction of all the possible ways of using support time. Table 7.1 provides a fuller menu of options, which could be used as a basis for discussions between the class and support teacher, whenever support is requested from within the school's own staffing arrangements or from an outside agency.

THE ROLE OF THE SPECIAL NEEDS COORDINATOR

The Warnock Report suggested, and the 1994 Code of Practice re-affirmed, that every school should have a teacher designated to help and advise colleagues on the provision for children with special needs. Most schools have now complied with the recommendation, but often with difficulty. The HMI survey (1989a) of pupils with SEN in ordinary schools found that only half of the teachers designated as SENCOs had received any specialist training, and in most cases the coordinator was a class teacher with no extra allocation of non-contact time for the duties involved in the post.

Where this is so, the role of the post-holder is necessarily circumscribed, but still extremely useful. In one school, for example, the coordinator was able to lead colleagues in developing a whole school policy for special needs, as well as manage the day-to-day work of liaising with outside agencies for children who had moved on beyond purely within school assessment. A regular slot at staff meetings for discussion of individual children with special needs allowed her to fulfil an advisory role in a way that was economic of her time, by modelling for colleagues the process of setting appropriate targets, and suggesting appropriate strategies and resources.

In another school, where development work on a whole school policy had already been done, the coordinator chose to spend time organizing a central stock of resources which teachers could borrow for use in their classrooms, and working with colleagues on ideas for differentiating their topic plans.

In a third school, a large primary with over 500 pupils and a post-holder who spent all her time on special needs work, it was possible initially for her to mix in-class support and withdrawal teaching for a large number of individual children, as well as coordinate policy development and INSET. When in the early years of local management her timetable was rearranged so that she now

Table 7.1 The role of the support teacher

- Working with a child or group in class for an extended period of time on targeted skills – for example, using concrete materials to teach the concept of place value, or helping a child to learn to concentrate by providing frequent praise when s/he is on task.
- Extracting a child or group for an extended period of time to work on targeted skills – for example, group discussion of a cloze passage as part of a plan to improve the children's use of context and prediction when reading.
- Working with individuals in turn, in class or by extraction, for short periods of 5–10 minutes on particular teaching activities targeted on basic skills – for example, using a learning chart to have the children practise reading clock times from an analogue clock.
- Working with a child or group in class using special materials or resources appropriate to the topic or lesson that the whole class is studying – for example, using cloze and sequencing activities to aid understanding of newly introduced science concepts.
- Preparing a group of pupils to make an oral or written contribution to a topic that the class is studying – for example, helping them use a story planner to get their ideas organized so that they can later write independently.
- Breaking part of a topic down into small steps and working on them with a child or group – for example, following a route using a plan as a step towards understanding and using maps.
- Using the mainstream curriculum as a vehicle for help with particular targeted skills – for example, using a story the class are studying as a vehicle for teaching listening/comprehension skills.
- Using bypass strategies with individuals or groups in class to ensure curriculum access – for example, acting as scribe for children with coordination and handwriting problems.
- Supporting pupils individually or in groups during national curriculum assessment – for example, by clarifying instructions or helping the pupils to record their ideas in the SATs, or helping them use self-assessment or produce evidence of attainment for profiles and records of achievement.
- Teaching or supervising the class so as to free the teacher to observe, assess, prepare materials for or work with particular children with special needs.
- Observing in the classroom and giving feedback to the class teacher on points where some pupils may need differentiated teaching approaches.
- Drawing up teaching to targets programmes for others to implement on a daily basis with the child.
- Looking at schemes of work with the teacher and helping to plan for differentiation.
- Advising on suitable resources – for example, factual books with a controlled vocabulary and simple sentence structure for work on a particular topic.
- Producing suitable resources – for example, a concept keyboard overlay to support topic work.

had responsibility for a class for half her time, with the other half spent on special needs work, she adapted her role, becoming a programme planner and resource organizer: she assembled and managed a team of volunteer helpers, parents and classroom assistants to work with individual children on structured programmes in basic skills, and on in-class support.

The roles that a special needs coordinator might adopt have been described by Gains (1994). Recognizing that they will not be able, without running themselves into the ground, to fulfil all these possible roles, coordinators can nevertheless use them in order to make choices, based on the amount of time available and the school's current priorities. The full list includes:

- *An assessment role* – identifying children with special needs, monitoring and screening, assessing the needs of individual children and identifying strengths and weaknesses in the curriculum in relation to special needs, planning and supporting differentiated assessment procedures, particularly for the SATs.
- *A prescriptive role* – planning support strategies, matching resources to needs, preparing individual education programmes, costing and budgeting.
- *A teaching and pastoral role* – cooperating with colleagues in joint teaching approaches and teaching/supporting individuals and groups.
- *An administrative role* – interpreting the law, overseeing policy, coordinating provision, maintaining the SEN register and other records, coordinating meetings, monitoring budgets.
- *A staff development role* – contributing to the in-service training of staff, arranging and attending courses, disseminating information.
- *A supportive role* – advising colleagues on strategies and techniques for individual children, and on currriculum differentiation.
- *A liaison role* – with parents, external agencies, voluntary bodies, the governing body.
- *A collaborative role* – transferring pupils, working with other school SENCOs.

SETTING UP A RESOURCE BASE

One particular task many special needs coordinators in primary schools have taken on since the 1981 Act is setting up and managing some kind of central resource base, where teachers (and children) can access books, games, workbooks, software and special equipment to meet individual needs. Diane Sparks and Alan Hiley (1989), for example, describe how they set out to decide on the main curricular areas where children required extra help in their junior school, collect and sort existing resources into these areas, identify areas where new materials needed to be bought or made, and finally set up a method of storage and loan.

These authors also report on some of the difficulties they experienced in making sure that the resources were actually used, in a school where teachers were accustomed to a system of withdrawal teaching, and where there were entrenched ideas that a group of children would disappear from the classroom from time to time, then re-appear having 'done their work'. This is a common experience with central resource bases; storing resources on movable trolleys, which spend a block of time in each classroom in the school in order to introduce all the staff to what is available, is one way around the problem.

Another way of making sure that the resources easily slot into class teachers' plans is suggested by Ann Lewis (1995), in her book on special needs and the national curriculum. She proposes that resources should be indexed against national curriculum programmes of study: schemes of work in English, maths, science, and so on, are subdivided into smaller steps and materials linked to each of these steps.

It is important that children, as well as teachers, are able to understand and use the indexing system. Storage could be in labelled trays, box files and ring binders; masters for photocopiable materials should be in clear pockets, and clear plastic bags with zip or clip tops used for games, sets of materials that need to stay together, and work to take home.

Some of the most useful materials will be those which individual teachers have made to support their particular schemes of work or topic webs: the breakdown one teacher might have done, for example, on how to help children understand how soil is formed, or a set of concept keyboard overlays to support work on the Victorians. These will be supplemented, as finances allow, by commercial materials – software, games, taped exercises, workbooks and worksheets. Many schools have been surprised, when staff looked in cupboards of shared resources, to find out how much was already available (and under-used): at the very least, establishing an indexed resource base allows staff to see exactly where the resource gaps lie, and coordinate their own efforts and those of parents and volunteers to make new materials, or to make better use of materials available for loan from local support services and special schools.

Components of a special needs resource base

What should go into a central special needs resource base? It is impossible to be prescriptive, but the following framework may be helpful.

Information for teachers and parents

Many schools choose to subscribe to journals like *Special Children* (Questions Publishing) or *Support for Learning* (NASEN). As well as books and journals, a collection of leaflets and information packs from voluntary organizations dealing with learning disabilities and medical conditions is helpful to parents and teachers alike. ACE (The Advisory Centre for Education) produce an information sheet called *Children with special needs: sources of help* which lists names and addresses of organizations to write to. NES-Arnold's *Signposts to Special Needs* pack is a ready-made reference resource of this type.

Hardware

If the resource base is mobile, and sure to be in constant use, it will be worth considering including a portable computer and concept keyboard amongst the hardware. Other useful equipment would be a cassette player and headphones, a Language Master or ARROW machine if available, and simple electronic spellcheckers like the Franklin Elementary Spellmaster.

Assessment materials
The resource base should include one or more of the small-step breakdowns of national curriculum attainment targets described in Chapter 4, plus a few user-friendly diagnostic assessment packs in key areas such as behaviour (see Chapter 8) and literacy (see Chapter 11). If the maths schemes used within the school do not have in-built assessment, materials for investigating children's mathematical difficulties such as LDA's *Mathsteps* will also be needed.

Materials for developing language skills
For children of nursery and infant age, there should be a language development programme such as *Living Language* (NFER-Nelson) or *Wordplay* (NASEN). *Teaching Talking* (NFER-Nelson) is useful for older children with language difficulties. Listening skills can be practised in the infant years using taped programmes such as LDA's *Listen and Do*, the *Listening Skills Pack* from Questions Publishing and Dee Reid's indispensable short booklet *Some Well Known Tales* from Philip and Tacey. For older pupils, materials include *Did You Hear That?* from LDA, Schofield and Sims' *Oracy* taped materials from their Language Programme, and Learning Materials Limited's *Oral Comprehension* materials. The *Language for Learning Games* from AMS Educational are invaluable for developing expressive language, as is NASEN's *A Rainbow of Words*.

Materials for reading, writing, spelling and handwriting
Real books covering the whole range of reading ability (and coded for reading and interest levels using readability measures and resources such as Hinson and Gains' *A–Z List of Reading Books* from NASEN) should be in classrooms and library rather than a special needs area. The resource base, however, will need to supply materials that provide an added element of structure and reinforcement. There should be games to reinforce sight vocabulary, home grown or commercial: *Games to Improve Reading Levels* from NASEN is a good source of ideas for home made versions, while an attractive set of photocopy masters from Longman's *Reading World* enables the teacher to make up 50 different games of the lotto, jigsaw and board game type. For reinforcement of phonic skills, there is an enormous amount of materials available; LDA's range is popular with teachers and includes *Sound Beginnings* (to develop phonological awareness), the self-correcting *Stile* phonics, Beve Hornsby's *Alpha to Omega*, Michael Thompson's adventure books and the *Beat Dyslexia* worksheets. If a complete scheme is required, the *Fuzzbuzz* books from Oxford University Press are enjoyed by children and have a good range of back-up materials including keyboard overlays (from North West SEMERC); the *Letterland* materials, with their videos, books, software and puppets, are useful for the same reason.

Reading for meaning can be encouraged through materials that use cloze, sequencing, summarizing and similar activities, such as Learning Materials Limited's *Reading for Meaning*, LDA's *False Teeth and Vampires*, Oliver and Boyd's *I See What You Mean* and Oxford University Press' ever-popular *Headwork* series.

For spelling, Charles Cripps' *Hand for Spelling* (LDA) is widely used, along with Holmes McDougall's *Spelling* series, *Stile Spelling* (LDA), and the rhyme-based *Laughing Speller* books from Blackie. Several sets of plastic letters should be included in the spelling resources, so that children can discover the principles of the spelling system through physically making and altering words.

To help children sequence ideas and structure stories, there should be sequential picture cards like those from LDA, materials that provide a ready-made structure like Learning Materials Limited's *Picture Writing*, and aids to planning like Longman *Reading World's Super Writers* copymasters and Scholastic's *Essential English* series.

A range of illustrated word banks, picture dictionaries and supportive dictionaries for the poor speller (such as the *ACE* dictionary from LDA and Christine Maxwell's *Pergamon Perfect Spelling Dictionary* from Nelson) should find a place on the resources trolley. And for some children with reading difficulties, it may be worth including aids such as LDA's *DexFrame* or Taskmaster's *Linetracker* to help with left-to-right sequencing, and a range of coloured acetate overlays to try out over texts.

For teachers rather than children, the literacy section of the resource base should also furnish ideas for parental involvement with reading projects, such as the *Paired Reading Pack* from Kirklees LEA which includes video material and detailed instructions on setting up a project.

Finally, for handwriting, easy-to-hold pencils and pencil grips (both from LDA) should be available, along with non-slip materials and perhaps an angled writing board. For practice in pre-writing patterns LDA's pre-writing skills fun sheets and the first stage of *A Hand For Spelling* are useful; Collins' *Pencil Fun* and Ladybird's *Learn to Write* books are also popular, and LDA's *Rol 'n Write* helps children master correct letter formation. For older children, there are Scholastic's *Essential English Handwriting Patterns* and LDA's resources linking practice in cursive script with work on letter strings for spelling.

Materials for maths
It is in maths that there is most scope for collating and indexing resources from a variety of schemes and materials against small steps within national curriculum programmes. In schools locked into one workbook-based scheme, there will be a particular need for reinforcement materials in order to avoid the disastrous practice of 'putting children back' on an earlier book. Pages from other schemes can be extracted and mounted on card, or a set of boxed cards, such as those from the Cambridge Primary Maths scheme, introduced as a back-up for any child experiencing difficulties at any stage of their maths work. A useful all-in-one resource which allows teachers to assess children's difficulties and create individual teaching programmes is *Mathsteps* from LDA: this covers all aspects of early stages of the primary maths curriculum and is specially designed for those who find the gradient of other maths schemes too steep. *Quest*, from NFER-Nelson, has a more limited focus but is very useful for

assessment and teaching ideas in basic number concepts. LDA's *Stile* materials include sets on money and time, and are popular with many age groups.

Most important in the maths resources are games and puzzles for use in the classroom and for home loan. NASEN produce a collection of good ideas for over 70 games and activities for the reinforcement of basic number facts and skills. For ready-made games, materials to look at include the Cambridge Primary Maths scheme *Games Pack*, Learning Materials Limited's games on topics like money and time, Schofield and Sims' *Maths Quest* games, Ginn's *GEM* games, New Peak and Nelson's maths games and resource packs, Edudu's *Place Value Games* and *Count Me In* from AMS.

Materials for developing thinking skills

Well worth including amongst the more subject-based materials are those which help children learn abstract thinking skills – how to question, how to discuss issues, how to solve problems. The *Primary Thinking Skills Project* (from the Questions Publishing Company) is based on the work of the American philosopher Matthew Lipman, and provides a six-week programme of discussion activities around a story-book theme and around work on a houses and homes topic. *Top Ten Thinking Tactics* is another useful pack from the same publisher.

Materials for topic work, humanities and science

Differentiated materials in science and topic work are disappointingly thin on the ground. Wayland Publishers, however, have broken new ground in producing books with the same content, at two different language levels. Watts Publishing produce information books with simple sentence structure and controlled vocabulary, and there is an increasing range of publications that use pictorial resource material (such as the popular Collins *Primary History* series). LDA are also good for history resources; Learning Materials Limited have their excellent *Support for History Key Stage 2* resources and a good range of easy to read worksheets covering science, geography and common primary topics. For curriculum access to topic work it is also worth investing in some of Ginn's *Sharp-Eye* resources.

Most useful of all, however, are likely to be the home-grown materials (concept keyboard overlays, topic-related worksheets adapted to different reading levels, cassettes, and materials based on the DARTs activities described in Chapter 11) that teachers have made to support their own lessons. Possibly the best investment a school can make is to set up a workshop for the preparation of such materials, followed by time for people to get together to make their own resources.

Materials for personal and social education

SENCOs are increasingly being asked by colleagues for advice and support in helping pupils with emotional and behavioural difficulties, and have a clear role in drawing up IEPs for these children. It is well worth while setting up a resource file of awards, certificates, contracts, behaviour monitoring and self-monitoring sheets. Ready-made award certificates are available (for example in Lame Duck's *Celebrations*), but personalized versions are easy to create on the word processor. Supplies of reward stickers and stamps for colleagues are also useful. Primary children love the self-inking *Xpressions* stamps from NES–Arnold, and the range of stickers from Brainwaves in Cornwall. There should definitely be a range of resources to help develop self-esteem: a good book for teachers such as Jenny Mosley's *Turn Your School Around* (from LDA), plus structured classroom or small group activities for children like Shay McConnon's *My Choice* from Nelson (secondary focused but useful for older juniors too). Also useful are the ideas in Gill Evans' *Child Protection curricular materials* (Avec Designs) or TACADE's *Skills for the Primary School Child*. Together with books on circle time activities (from Lame Duck and NASEN), the ideas in these resources will cover the whole range of work that may be necessary to help children with special needs of an emotional or behavioural kind to understand and manage their feelings. It may also be useful to have on hand books for children (such as those in the *Let's Talk About It* series from Watts, those from Child's Play and Cherry Tree Books, or the Althea books from Dinosaur Publications) which help them to deal with difficult events and issues – divorce, bullying, stepfamilies, bereavement and loss.

USING INFORMATION TECHNOLOGY

When human resources are scarce, the role of IT in supporting special needs work takes on an extra importance. Aside from its enormous potential in enabling curriculum access for pupils with physical and sensory disabilities, IT can play a range of roles for pupils with less severe difficulties – from providing extra reinforcement in palatable form in programmes of the drill-and-practice type, to supporting the writing task, stimulating language development and thinking skills through shared work around adventure programmes and concept keyboard, and providing information for children to explore at varying levels of complexity for science and topic work. The range of software is vast and ever-changing. A useful source of regularly updated information is the single-source catalogue for IT and special needs, covering all the major suppliers, produced by REM.

Much current good practice in IT work with children who have special needs centres on the use of 'a small number of powerful and flexible programmes, together with teacher developed materials' (HMI, 1990b). Regional centres such as the Special Educational Resource Centres (SEMERC) have concentrated on producing open-ended software, which teachers can adapt to the particular content they need. The concept keyboard figures prominently, linked to databases and word-processing packages. More recently, North West SEMERC have been developing exciting special needs materials using CD-ROM technology – talking text, graphics and photographs to support children's exploration of topic work, and on-screen icons to help those with reading difficulties access the material.

The first step for teachers who want to meet the whole range of learning needs is to familiarize themselves with the many ways in which word processing can be used to support children's writing. Further discussed in Chapter 12, developments such as predictive word processors, talking word processors, on-screen and concept keyboard overlays with pictures and words to suit the learner's ability and interests enable children to create complex and technically perfect pieces of work quickly and easily.

Secondly, teachers with an interest in special needs will want to explore software that supports the curriculum in topic work, science and humanities. For children who find it hard to use books for research, animated 'talking' text programmes are proving invaluable – series covering topics from transport to dinosaurs and Ancient Greece are available from Sherston (*Look! Hear! Talking Topics*) and from SEMERC (*Full Phase* and *Optima*). SEMERC's *My World* series, a framework programme that allows children to discover information and create text through picture screens, is also very popular.

Fictional talking books (such as Oxford Reading Tree's *Talking Stories*) are increasingly produced alongside major reading schemes, and have enormous promise for developing literacy skills.

Finally, it will be useful for teachers with an interest in special needs to explore some of the many materials available to support structured programmes of work in basic skills. Useful maths materials are produced by such companies as Sherston, ESM and Northern Micromedia. In Chapters 11 and 12 we will look at software for practising decoding and spelling words. Often unpopular with IT purists, these types of materials nevertheless have a role for pupils who require a lot of reinforcement of new concepts, and who find using a computer to practise skills both more exciting and less anxiety-provoking than work with a human helper.

CONCLUSION

Children can learn from many sources – from computers, games, books as well as people; from parents and peers as well as teachers. Meeting individual and special needs is about finding out – by observation, and by asking – which way works best for each child, and making sure that the system does allow for flexibility and pupil choice in matching resources to learners. In the last two chapters on the management of human and physical resources, we have tried to outline some of the ways in which these flexible forms of support can be offered.

It is now time to move on from the general issues of organizing the school's response to special needs, and focus on teachers' more immediate concerns: to consider the main areas of individual need that they most commonly encounter, and the response they can make. We begin, in the next chapter, with the issue that often generates the most concern of all – behaviour.

FURTHER READING

Balshaw, M. (1991) *Help in the Classroom*. London, David Fulton.

RESOURCES

ACE (Advisory Centre for Education), Unit 1b Aberdeen Studios, 22–24 Highbury Grove, London N5 2EA.

The ARROW Trust, 3 Church Close, East Huntspill, Somerset TA9 3QF.

Avec Designs Ltd, PO Box 709, Bristol BS99 1GE.

Brainwaves, Trewithen Park, Lostwithiel, Cornwall PL2 0BD.

Edudu, Marsden Enterprises Ltd, 30 Oliver Lane, Marsden, Huddersfield HD7 6BZ.

ESM, Duke Street, Wisbech, Cambridgeshire PE13 2AE.

Franklin Spellmasters, from REM, Great Western House, Langport, Somerset TA10 9YU.

Kirklees Psychology Service, Oastler Centre, 103 New Street, Huddersfield HD1 2UA.

Lame Duck Publishing, 10 South Terrace, Redland, Bristol BS6 6TG.

Learning Materials Ltd, Dixon Street, Wolverhampton WV2 2BX.

Letterland – available from Letterland Ltd, Barton, Cambridge CB3 7AY.

LDA (Learning Development Aids), Abbeygate House, East Rd., Cambridge CB1 1DB.

NASEN (National Association for Special Educational Needs), NASEN House, 4/5 Amber Business Village, Amber Close, Amington, Tamworth, Staffs, B77 4RP.

Northern Micromedia, Coach Lane Campus, Coach Lane, Newcastle upon Tyne NE7 7XA.

Questions Publishing, 27 Frederick Street, Hockley, Birmingham B1 3HH.

REM, Great Western House, Langport, Somerset TA10 9YU.

SEMERC, Northwest SEMERC, 1 Broadbent Rd., Watersheddings, Oldham OL1 4LB.

Sherston Software, Swan Barton, Sherston, Malmesbury, Wiltshire SN16 0LH.

Tacade, 1 Hulme Place, The Crescent, Salford M5 4QA.

Taskmaster Ltd., Morris Rd., Leicester LE2 6BR.

Watts Publishing, 96 Leonard St., London EC2 4RH.

Wayland Publishers Ltd, 61 Western Road, Hove, East Sussex BN3 1JD.

8

MANAGING BEHAVIOUR

INTRODUCTION

Because the term 'special needs' has become, for many teachers, a contemporary substitute used when describing children they would once have called 'slow learners', behavioural difficulties are not always seen as part of the special needs continuum. The role ascribed to the special needs coordinator, for example, frequently stops short of supporting colleagues in relation to pupils who may be quick to learn, but who have difficulty in handling social relationships or in conforming to classroom rules. Yet it is these children who often cause most concern to their teachers, and for whom the special needs framework of assessment, action planning, record keeping and putting in additional resources can be particularly helpful.

Special needs in learning and special needs in behaviour are, moreover, inextricably linked. Teacher judgements of whether particular children have learning difficulties, for example, are heavily influenced by whether or not they demonstrate a particular *behaviour* pattern of fidgeting, distraction and inability to work in a group (Moses, 1982), and it has repeatedly been demonstrated (Westwood 1982) that successful integration for children with learning difficulties into mainstream classes depends relatively little on the extent of the learning problem, but a great deal on whether the child behaves well – follows school rules and routines, does not disrupt in the classroom, shows initiative and self-management when learning, and concentrates on the task in hand.

Such research suggests that behavioural needs should often assume primacy when we are planning support for individual children. There is no shortage of advice for teachers on how to go about this: more has been written about behaviour management than any other area of special need. In this chapter we will aim only to provide an overview of some of this work, and describe a framework that will adapt itself to many different behavioural difficulties and many different situations. Two particular areas – aggressive behaviour and poor concentration – will be considered in more detail, since these are amongst the most common problems which teachers meet and to which they most often seek solutions.

THE RULES, REWARDS AND SANCTIONS FRAMEWORK

The starting point in any planning for individual children's behavioural needs has to be an overall school framework that specifies the expectations the school holds about the behaviour of all members of the school community, and the systems that will be used by all staff to encourage positive and discourage negative behaviour. Such whole school behaviour policies have now been developed by many primary schools, with the help of outside consultants from behaviour support services, and of published packages of support materials (Galvin et al., 1990; Luton et al., 1992). The essential steps involve a review of behaviour in school as seen by staff, parents and pupils, an examination of any factors in school layout, curriculum and organization that may be contributing to behaviour problems, followed by work on the rules, rewards and sanctions that will consistently be applied in school.

> Westgate Primary School began the process of developing a whole school behaviour policy by asking pupils to describe the aspects of behaviour that most bothered them in school, and to discuss in small groups what they thought the rules about behaviour should be. Teachers and lunchtime supervisors completed a checklist over several days that helped to identify what behaviour problems they were encountering most often, and in what circumstances. The school had heard about a training programme called Assertive Discipline (Canter and Canter, 1976) and asked their educational psychologist to organize an INSET day based on its video and workshop material. On the day, teachers and supervisors worked together, using the information derived from their review of behaviour in school, to devise some basic rules for the classroom, and some for the playground. This proved easier than expected; by including catch-all rules such as, 'Do as you are asked by teachers and supervisors first time', and 'Do nothing to stop others from working', they were able to keep the list down to a manageable number. There was a good deal of debate about whether and how to use rewards, but in the end everyone agreed a system of special gold certificates presented to children in assembly, to celebrate good behaviour in school – for children who always behaved well, as well as those for whom this was more difficult. A hierarchical system of sanctions for breaking rules in classroom or playground was then worked out: in the playground this involved supervisors showing children a yellow card as a warning and a red 'straight to headteacher' card for repeated or

serious misbehaviour. Parents were invited into school to discuss the proposed new system, which was then formalized in an attractively-produced booklet with illustrations by the children.

Work of this kind can substantially reduce the overall level of behaviour difficulties experienced in a school. Users, like Westgate, of the Assertive Discipline Framework, for example, typically report reduction in behaviour problems of around 80 per cent (Canter and Canter, 1979; Moss, 1992). This will often have immediate benefits for pupils with special needs; Safran and Safran (1985) have shown that teachers' perception of problem behaviour in individuals is much affected by overall patterns of behaviour – in a generally-disordered class, they found, an individual child was more likely to be seen as the source of any trouble and blamed for it than were children with similar problems in classes that were generally quiet and orderly.

Nevertheless, a whole school behaviour management system will not eliminate individual children's behavioural difficulties entirely. For these children, individual action plans, using the same rules, rewards and sanctions framework, but matched more closely to their unique needs, may be required.

ASSESSMENT

As with special needs in learning, the first step in developing an individual action plan is assessment. There is a natural wish in many teachers to see assessment of behaviour difficulties in terms of discovering the deep-seated causes of the child's failure to conform to behavioural expectations: usually these causes are seen as rooted in the home (Croll and Moses, 1985). There is corresponding disappointment when support agencies appear to discount such forms of investigation and assessment, and instead ask the teacher to look closely at what may be happening in school to spark off or maintain pupil misbehaviour. The reasoning behind this approach, however, is simple and persuasive: it is not that factors and stresses in the child's life outside school are unimportant in the genesis of behaviour difficulties, only that these factors are very hard for teachers (and often other helping agencies) to influence, whereas factors in school are easier to address – and teachers have proved both powerful and effective in modifying children's behaviour when they exert their influence on the things they can change, rather than those they cannot.

The most commonly-used tool for assessing the things that might need to be changed is some form of diary observation of targeted behaviour, in which the teacher records incidents as they happen, along with information about the context and subsequent events – otherwise known as antecedents, behaviour and consequences or ABCs (Table 8.1). The behaviour to be observed is one that all those closely involved with the pupil (and preferably also the pupil him or herself) recognize as a priority problem, using the approach to determining priorities and describing behaviour in precise, objective terms that was discussed in Chapter 5. Behaviours can assume priority either because of their

Table 8.1   Behaviour observation diary

Date/ Time	Antecedents Where did it happen? What was the context? What led up to it?	Behaviour What did X actually do?	Consequences What happened afterwards?

frequency (like the child who constantly calls out in class), or because of their consequences for the pupil's well-being or learning, or the well-being or learning of others (as with the child who occasionally has violent outbursts that put others at risk).

The following example of Katy illustrates the application of ABC assessment to a problem that though mild, was happening often enough to jeopardize one child's learning, and also affect the amount of time the teacher was able to give to other children in her class:

> The aspect of Katy's behaviour that most concerned her teacher was her constant tearfulness. Several times a day, Katy would be seen weeping in class, and would be quite unable to get on with her work without a lot of reassurance and individual help. Over the course of a week, the teacher noted occasions when Katy cried, along with details of the type of work she was being asked to do, and of her own immediate reaction and that of other children. She also tried to make a note at least once a day of the context and consequences at times when Katy was showing the kind of behaviour everyone wanted from her – getting on happily with her work. With the help of the special needs coordinator, she used her observations to draw up a chart showing what seemed to be happening (Table 8.2).

This discussion in itself led the teacher to plan ways in which Katy could gain physical contact through appropriate behaviour, and to make sure that she was not inadvertently rewarding Katy's inappropriate behaviour by reducing reasonable work demands whenever she cried.

Along with diary recording using the ABC structure, assessment should include an attempt to gain an understanding of the children's perspective of the situation. Do they know, first of all, exactly what it is that is causing concern or getting them into trouble? Open-ended questions like, 'Tell me some of the things you do that make teachers pleased with you', and 'Now tell me what sort of things you do that bother them most', are useful here. Then instead of the usual questions about *why* they do this, that and the other (which few children

Table 8.2 Katy: ABC behaviour observations

A *Antecedents*	*B* *Behaviour*	*C* *Consequences*
Happens in class (rarely in playground) Seems to happen whatever kind of work I give her – even very simple work she is really sure of	Katy cries	I usually go and put my arm round her, and ask her what's wrong; she either says nothing or 'I can't do it'. Then I go over the work again or suggest she just tackle part of it. The other children generally say 'Miss, Katy's crying', if I haven't noticed
A Often for the last part of the day	*B* Katy does her work happily without crying	*C* Nobody takes any notice of her, I'm afraid!

can answer), the teacher can ask them to describe a situation in which their behaviour caused concern: the things that led up to it, what they were thinking and feeling at the time, what happened afterwards. This kind of exploration will often provide valuable insights; for example, that one child who is often in trouble for hitting and kicking is aggressive without feeling angry, as a way of establishing a 'macho' image and some degree of acceptance in a peer group where he has few friends, whilst another child who also hits and kicks does so in a blind rage, often as a result of being called names.

For Katy, an individual interview established that she herself did not feel her crying was a problem. In her eyes, the problem was that she had to do 'too much hard work' at school. She felt her teacher was generally pleased with her, adding 'I'm never naughty at school'. At home, though, there were quite a lot of things that made her mum and dad cross with her: 'I break cups and hit my brother and tease my big brother'. Her biggest wish was 'for my mum not to tell me what to do', and for teachers 'not to make you do hard work'.

Katy's teacher had previously interpreted her behaviour in class as a sign of lack of confidence. When she listened to Katy's perspective, however, she began to see a quite determined little girl, who did not like demands imposed on her from outside, and used a range of learned coping strategies to re-establish control over the situation. The teacher decided to try out with Katy's group the High Scope 'plan, do, review' system, where children make their own plans for the work that needs doing and the order in which they will do it. Katy was given a good deal of praise at the review stage with the teacher for following the plan she had set herself. The teacher also made a point of asking Katy quite often whether she felt she could handle a particular piece of work, then modelling and praising her for statements, such as 'I can do it', or 'I think it's going to be easy for me'. Katy was sent once a day, when she had finished all her work, to help reception class children with their reading, and thanked for being such a sensible, grown up and capable helper. At the same time, the teacher stood firm on any attempts by Katy to manipulate her by crying and conveying helplessness, and insisted that she would need to make up unfinished work in her own time, either at playtime or at home.

IMPLEMENTING A BEHAVIOUR PLAN

Assessment by observation and probing the child's perspective will sometimes lead to a plan of action that focuses mainly on changing the various 'A's in the ABC equation – the contextual factors that lead up to a particular behaviour. For the boy who hits out in anger when teased, for example, the plan might include work with the other children to stop their name-calling, or work with the child on coping strategies – counting slowly to ten, taking three deep breaths, walking away, coming up with a jokey response or making himself laugh by imagining his tormentor in an undignified position (like sitting on the toilet). Sometimes the antecedents that need to be changed will be to do with the curriculum or classroom organization: seating arrangements, pupil groupings, work that is better matched to the pupil's interests and abilities.

In other cases, it may be more important to change the 'C's – the consequences that are applied to both positive and negative behaviour. Here Lee Canter's Assertive Discipline framework is often useful in working out a simple contract between child, parents and teacher:

Jamie was constantly in trouble for a variety of different behaviours. His mother came in to school to meet with Jamie and his teacher. Together, they agreed that the biggest problems were Jamie disturbing other children's work, calling out in class and swearing. There were problems at home, too, and Jamie's mother welcomed the idea of going with Jamie to the family counselling centre to see what could be done to help with the management of his behaviour. Meanwhile, in school he would be asked to observe a *contract*. The contract was that Jamie will:

- use acceptable language in school;
- put his hand up and wait to be asked to speak in class;
- keep his hands, feet and objects to himself.

Each day that he succeeds in doing all these things his teacher will send a 'good behaviour' note home. When he has five 'good behaviour' notes, he will:

- be allowed to go and help in Miss Edwards' class,
- his mother will let him choose a small treat from a list he has drawn up with her (going swimming, doing some baking with her, choosing a video, staying up half an hour later on Saturday, having a friend to stay).

When Jamie does not do these things he will:

- be warned once;
- the second time (in one day), he will be last out to play at break times;
- the third time, he will be asked to sit and work on his own in class for the rest of the day;
- the fourth time, he will miss choosing time on Friday;
- the fifth time, he will be sent to Mrs Abbott, who will notify his mother and note his name in the bad behaviour book. If his name is in the book three times, he will have an in-school suspension (working all day on his own away from the class).

Some children, particularly younger ones, may not be able to go for a whole day or even a whole morning before their positive behaviour is acknowledged under a contract system. For them it is helpful to use some form of chart where a space or square is coloured in, or a sticker/smiley face/star stuck on, every time they succeed in showing a particular desired behaviour. When all the squares are full, the child takes the chart to show an adult of their choice (and receive praise), or – if this is not of itself a sufficient incentive – exchanges the completed chart for an agreed privilege (Table 8.3). The form of the chart can be adapted to the child's particular interests. Drawings of dragons, robots, dolls, football pitches and wizards have all been successfully used – though visuals that divide naturally into segments (like the scales of dinosaurs or mutant hero turtles) make an obvious choice. Ready-made and freely photocopiable charts are available in the *Solution Book* from SRA (Sprick, 1981); many schools have also built up their own banks of copymasters, kept in a ring-binder in the special needs resource centre.

INVOLVING THE PUPIL

Critics of the behavioural approach so far described, with its emphasis on modifying behaviour by altering the consequences that children experience as a result of their actions, have argued that it is manipulative and de-humanizing: treating children like puppets to be controlled by pulling this string or that, and producing superficial behaviour change whilst failing to reach the inner states and feelings that in the long term determine how we relate to others. This is a valid argument; to avoid the risks it described we need to make sure we go beyond pulling the strings from outside, and devise ways in which children can gain in autonomy through the experience of setting their own goals, working out their own action plans, and monitoring their own behaviour.

Table 8.3   Rewards available to primary teachers

- Choice of play activities, e.g. construction equipment
- Game with teacher
- First out to play/first out at hometime
- Taking messages
- Being a monitor
- Cleaning the classroom pets out
- Putting chairs out in the hall
- Being the leader of a group
- Busy boxes: small tubs of interesting things like buttons, magnets, lenses which the child can get out and play with
- Time on computer
- Tidying up an area of the classroom
- Working with a chosen adult
- Ringing the bell at break time
- Helping with the tuck shop
- Taking work (or a note about good behaviour) to show other teachers
- Special praise or an award in assembly
- Classroom quiz or wordsearch
- Going to help in a younger class
- House points
- Merit badges, stickers, having your hand stamped with a special stamp/ink pad
- Choosing where you sit
- Certificates or notes sent home to parents
- Individual merit book for each child in the school, in which staff enter positive comments

---

Such self-monitoring might involve the child in keeping his or her own record of the number of times each week s/he is late for school, or in trouble for fighting. It might mean the teacher providing a signal at regular intervals throughout the day, at which the child notes whether or not s/he is 'on task'. It might, for older children, mean using a self-rating scale like the one in Table 8.4: before morning and afternoon break, at lunchtime and hometime the pupil rates his or her own behaviour against criteria that have been agreed beforehand, and then shows the sheet to the teacher. Teachers will discuss it and add their own rating; each week the pupils set a target of points they aim to earn, pushing the target higher as they feel more in control of their behaviour.

Teachers who want to help children set their own goals and work out their own action plans need to be able to set aside for the moment any kind of blaming response to their negative behaviour, and approach the situation with the neutral message: 'There is something going wrong here; let us look together at what we might do about it.' For example, to a child who constantly shouts out in class they might say: 'There is a problem for both of us here. When you talk loudly in class, I'm not able to concentrate on teaching, and I start to feel irritable. I think it's a problem for you too because it is stopping some children

Table 8.4 Self-monitoring behaviour sheet (adapted from Long, 1988)

Name _____

My aim _____

My target for points this week _____

Day _____ Date _____

Period	Self-rating	Teacher rating
1	5	5
	4	4
	3	3
	2	2
	1	1
2	5	5
	4	4
	3	3
	2	2
	1	1
3	5	5
	4	4
	3	3
	2	2
	1	1
4	5	5
	4	4
	3	3
	2	2
	1	1
		Total for day

I will rate myself and be rated for _____

_____

_____

_____

5 = wonderful
4 = very good
3 = OK
2 = very poor
1 = terrible

from wanting to be friends with you. I would like us both to spend some time trying to think of all the things we might do to solve the problem.'

From this point, with the pupil's agreement, both parties can work through a problem-solving process. In this approach (Spivack and Shure, 1974; Thacker,

1983), the child is asked to brainstorm all the possible solutions to the problem, consider the consequences of each, and then choose the one that looks most likely to succeed. This is the process that the teacher encouraged in the following example:

> Robert, aged 10, was often in trouble in the playground. He was over-weight, and frequently picked on by other children. With the help of his teacher, he identified the problem he would like to work on: being teased by Paul about being too fat and no good at football. Brainstorming solutions, he came up with the idea of ignoring Paul, teasing him back or losing weight. Ignoring Paul, he thought, would be a good idea because it would mean he didn't get angry, but a bad idea because it wouldn't stop Paul teasing him in the long run. Teasing back had the advantage of helping him feel he was getting his own back, but might make Paul hit him. Andrew finally chose his third idea: losing weight would make him able to run faster and get better at football, and though it would be hard to stick to a diet he might manage it with help. He drew up an agreement with his teacher which specified weekly weigh-ins, and a half hour of individual football coaching for every pound lost. In one term he managed to lose half a stone, and began to get on better not only with Paul but also with other boys in his class.
>
> (Thacker, 1983)

The teacher's role when pupils set their own goals is to help with recording and review. The child can be encouraged to draw up a self-contract, with headings like 'I want to . . .', 'My plan is . . .', 'My support person will be . . .' and 'I will celebrate success by . . .' (McConnon, 1989). Signed and dated by child and 'witness' (teacher, friend or parent), the plan can be used as a basis for review: the teacher will ask whether the pupil has been able to stick to their plan, praise any successes, and help the child adjust the plan if it is not working.

AGGRESSIVE BEHAVIOUR

Not surprisingly, aggression is the behaviour that worries teachers most (Coleman and Gilliam, 1983), and is a common reason for suspension from school and referral to special educational provision for pupils with emotional and behavioural difficulties. Theories about causes range from styles of discipline at home to exposure to television violence, but whatever outside influences there may be, it is still possible for schools to help children learn non-aggressive ways of relating to others: the ABC model, the charts and contracts and pupil plans are just as valid for aggression as for any other behaviour difficulty.

In addition, however, it may be necessary to work with individuals or groups of children on learning how to control angry feelings and resolve conflicts in non-violent ways. Sometimes it helps to start by making the child more aware of potential trigger situations: by asking them to make a 'boiling point list' of ten things that make them angry, and rank them in order of intensity, or using the traffic light analogy to help them identify the thoughts, feelings and bodily changes that tell them they are moving from a green light, to a warning yellow, to red for danger in situations where they often lose control. Sometimes it may help to model and teach specific strategies to use when the signal changes from green to yellow: muscle relaxation and slow, deep breathing, counting backwards from ten or imagining themselves as a turtle retreating inside its shell, or taking themselves to a cooling-off spot on the fringe of the activity. Children for whom peer wind-ups are a major trigger for aggressive behaviour can be encouraged to develop 'avoiding the hook' imagery, where they picture themselves as fish swimming in a river, while all around them on the banks are fishermen casting their hooks and hoping to catch them. They have to choose; either take the bait and be hooked, or out-smart the fishermen and swim calmly by. Finally, work can be done to involve pupils in considering which responses to conflict situations are likely to escalate the conflict, and which to defuse it, and in practising the negotiation skills of saying what you want and why, listening carefully to the other's point of view, then trying to find a compromise that meets both parties' needs. Good sources for teachers planning such work include Shay McConnon's *Your Choice* materials from Nelson and the *Ways and Means* materials from Kingston Polytechnic.

Any strategies that are taught to pupils need also to be carefully explained to parents, who often see aggression as a necessary tool for children's self-protection; they will need to be convinced that alternative approaches are about giving children power rather than taking it away: power to control their reactions rather than be controlled by them, and power to exercise choice about how they will respond. Parents will also need to be convinced, quite rightly, that the school is able through its policy on bullying to make sure that their children will not end up victims of others' aggression if they succeed in controlling their own.

An example will show how self-control strategies can be combined with more straightforward behavioural approaches to reduce aggressive outbursts:

> Darren was a tall, well-built and active boy who was often involved in fights and arguments. He could be quite overbearing in class and constantly interrupted other children or adults. His teacher's observations showed that other children on his table tended to irritate or tease him, and when this happened he would become increasingly wound-up and explosive. The teacher had tried sending him out for five minutes on his own outside the classroom whenever there were problems, but this only seemed to make matters worse. A system where Darren earned points for good behaviour in school towards rewards at home had not worked either. Darren's teacher believed in negotiated learning and teacher–pupil conferences, and Darren was accustomed to setting his own work targets. The teacher asked him if they could try a similar system for his behaviour, and

discussed with him the strategies that might help. Darren showed a strong preference for sanctions rather than any kind of rewards for good behaviour. He was aware that it was other children's wind-ups that often got him into trouble, but felt that bit by bit they made him so angry that he got to the point where he just could not control himself or get himself out of the situation. Between them, he and his teacher agreed on a signal (the teacher taking his glasses off) that could be given as soon as he could be seen getting 'steamed up'. At this signal, he would take himself and his work to the language room, and come back when he had calmed down. If he called out in class and interrupted others, he would – at his own request – have to miss five minutes of the next playtime. He kept a diary of the times he had to stay in, and the times he managed to control his temper by taking himself out of trigger situations; once a week, he met with the teacher to review the diary and agree the content of a note home which would let his parents know how he was getting on. His parents were asked to give him a lot of praise and encouragement for even small successes. Darren responded well to this approach, and though still not the calmest of children began, over the next few months, to exercise much more control over his angry reactions.

POOR CONCENTRATION AND RESTLESSNESS

The best predictor of children's academic success is the amount of time they spend on a task without distraction (Keogh, 1982). For children with learning difficulties, the relationship between concentration and progress is particularly critical; Moses (1982), for example, found that the slow learners she observed were on task for only about half their time, whereas children of average ability concentrated on their work on average for 70 per cent of their time.

On these grounds alone, helping children to concentrate in the classroom is clearly a priority when making plans to meet special needs. It becomes even more important when we consider that things like 'talking out of turn', and 'hindering other children' are the most common behaviour problems in classrooms, and the source of the greatest irritation to teachers (Wheldall and Merrett, 1984).

What can be done to help? To start with, it is useful when a child is described as having poor concentration to probe for a more precise behavioural description of what it is exactly that the child is doing, or not doing, that causes concern. Sometimes the teacher is actually describing a child who constantly distracts him or herself from the task in hand, or is distracted by others, but sometimes there are other meanings. For example, poor concentration may mean that the child is not able to take in instructions, or forgets what s/he is supposed to be doing, or is restless only in listening situations like assembly and story time. Sometimes the teacher may be describing not distraction but a learned pattern of overdependence on adults: children who are always back and forth to the teacher with one query or another – as an extreme example, the little girl who recently came to her teacher to say, 'Shall I have a go at this on my own without asking you?'!

Again, it is important to establish what the distracted child is doing when not on task. Is s/he quietly day-dreaming, talking to friends who also want to chat, or apparently seeking attention by obviously interfering with others? Is s/he actually taking in the information and getting the work done, but seeming not to because s/he is constantly wriggling and fidgeting?

In each of these cases, the strategies adopted will be different: as with all behavioural difficulties, it is important to start with a clear description of the problem.

The extent of children's concentration is heavily dependent on the curriculum – as anyone knows who has watched a child spend 10 minutes finding a pencil, and 20 minutes on the first sentence when asked to write, then watched the same child's intense concentration on making a model or working with friends on an adventure program around the computer. Many children's apparent concentration problems could be very quickly resolved if tasks were better adapted to their needs, and particularly if there was less emphasis on writing as the only means of recording in the classroom (see Chapter 12). Nevertheless, the possibility of 'within-child' influences on concentration should not be discounted. The effects of diet are still controversial, but some children do seem to show increased restlessness and inability to settle to tasks in reaction to particular foodstuffs such as additives and colourings, and parents may want to bear this in mind. Some will also want to investigate the medical diagnosis of attention deficit hyperactivity disorder and the effects, also controversial, of stimulant medication on their child's behaviour. Children with coordination problems often have associated difficulties in focusing attention; they may be unable to screen out irrelevant stimuli, so that everything – from a car going past to the work displayed on the classroom wall – is a potential source of distraction. If this seems to be the case, then it may be worth having the child do some of his or her work in a quiet area of the classroom, facing a plain wall and with a screen placed either side to create a booth (as long as other children also get the chance to take special work they really want to concentrate on to this area too). Children with intermittent hearing loss or language difficulties may find it hard to concentrate when they have to listen closely for long periods, perhaps against a noisy background: they need the kind of help in tuning into important communications that will be discussed in Chapter 10. Problems in short-term memory may mean that the child appears not to concentrate because s/he has forgotten what to do next: a peer assigned to remind them, or teacher willingness to write down instructions on a sticky Post-it is often all that is needed if this is the source of the difficulty.

Another major 'within-child' influence is the child's developmental stage. Children come into school at very different developmental levels: some have the communication and cognitive abilities of the average 6-year-old, and a concentration span to match, while others are still at a pre-school stage. For them it is entirely appropriate for tasks to be short, and a certain amount of flitting from one activity to another to be expected. All reception teachers know this; many teachers of older children persist in setting tasks of the same length for all, without taking into account the wide range of normal individual differences in concentration span that are part of every junior class.

Planning for children who do not concentrate for long will, then, depend in part on developing an understanding of factors within the child that are contributing to the perceived difficulties, and matching strategies to the outcomes of this kind of assessment. Concentration difficulties are also, however, as we will see in the next example, amenable to the kind of ABC analysis that we looked at earlier in this chapter, with its emphasis on factors in the environment that may be causing or maintaining any problem behaviour:

> Duncan, aged 11, was the despair of his teacher: he was, she said, always wandering around the classroom, talking to other children or annoying them by interfering with their things. Her ABC assessment is presented in Table 8.5. She decided that she needed to look at ways of making writing easier for him, by setting shorter tasks and smaller targets, and by having him choose words to complete cloze sheets for some topic work instead of writing independently from scratch. Since in-class support seemed to help him settle to work, she asked the support teacher to change his timetable slightly and come in for an English rather than a topic lesson. She also decided to try and reduce the amount of attention Duncan gained for his wanderings: when she saw him out of his seat she simply put a check on the board, with five checks equalling loss of a playtime. At the same time, Duncan and his friend Andrew agreed to work together on a specific programme which would help Duncan learn to concentrate for longer: twice a day, Andrew would set a kitchen timer to go off after a fixed period (initially 10 minutes, but progressively longer as the weeks went on). If Duncan had managed to stay on task for the whole of that period, Andrew put a tick on a chart. When Duncan had earned ten ticks, the whole class was awarded extra playtime – as their reward for helping him concentrate by ignoring rather than joining in with his attempts to cause a distraction.

The timer method can be used by parents at home, or by children themselves as part of a self-monitoring programme. Self-monitoring need not necessarily be linked to a reward system to be effective; sometimes becoming more aware of how they are using time is all that is needed, as the following whole class example shows:

> A class of 11-year-olds were asked by their teacher to write down at the beginning of every hour of topic work what they planned to do in that hour; at the end of the period they had to make a private note of whether

Table 8.5 Duncan: ABC behaviour observations

A	B	C
Often when task involves writing	Wanders around class: interferes with others	Peer attention. Avoids task. Teacher nags him constantly to sit down
In practical lessons; science, technology. When there is a support teacher in class	Stays in one place and gets on	No attention unless support teacher is there

they had got everything they meant to done. During two separate sessions, the teacher rang a bell every 10 minutes, so that the children could award themselves a tick if they were on task. She did not look at their tick sheets, but asked the children to add up their own as a way they could 'measure their powers of concentration'. The children showed a significant improvement in both quality and quantity of work output as a result of this experimental intervention.

(Merrett and Merrett, 1992)

Setting a kitchen timer to go off at random intervals throughout the day is a way of keeping a self-monitoring system such as this going for an individual child or a class over a longer period. If self-monitoring is difficult, the teacher can plan to praise the child and put a tick or a star on a postcard on the child's table every time s/he passes by and finds that the child is working. A set number of ticks can be exchanged for a reward (such as licensed day-dreaming time, free choice of activity, the chance to do something active like carry a message or do a job for another teacher), and slowly the ticks replaced by praise alone: by then, the teacher will have become accustomed to the idea of praising children when they are concentrating rather than the much less effective nagging them when they are not.

Another way of monitoring groups for concentration is to put a jar on each table, in which the teacher drops a counter or marble when she sees that the children in the group are all on task. The table with the most counters or marbles at the end of the day (or week) will be chosen for a special privilege.

Some young children, whose pre-school experience has been a mix of active outdoor play and indoor television and video, may never have had the opportunity to learn to sit still at a sustained task. If this is the case, concentration will have to be taught, in small steps, like any other skill. The child's parents or carers can be asked, for example, to try to engage the child in a settled activity like Lego, or jigsaws, or listening to a story tape for a short (but slowly increasing) period two or three times a week: at first they will need to join in with the activity, but later they should try to stand back and offer praise and encouragement at a distance as long as the child perseveres with the activity. A similar idea can be used for short bursts in class, with the help of a classroom assistant. To start with, the assistant sits near the child and gives continuous attention while s/he is on task; later on the distance between her and the child can be increased and only occasional praise given.

In all of these interventions, it is the various 'C's in the ABC framework which are manipulated in order to encourage concentration. The 'A's, however, should not be forgotten. Extensive research (Wheldall, 1988) shows that the most common source of distraction in classrooms is seating pupils in a way that invites social interaction when they are for most of the time working on individual tasks. Few, if any, adults would choose to go and sit in a group with their close friends if they had a report to write or some serious planning to do. Yet this is what we ask children to do, day after day, and then tell them off when they inevitably start to chat. For children whose attention is caught by the least extraneous sight or sound, the busy, active mêlée so beloved of the post-Plowden establishment, and inflexible seating arrangements that group children round tables, are a recipe for low work rate. Philip Waterhouse (1990) suggests we turn to the modern office for ideas on alternatives: furniture can be organized as work stations, with four children on a table that has a removable screen down the middle, and resources grouped on wheeled trolleys in the centre of the classroom so that children can access them without walking past (or through) others' work spaces. When children are genuinely engaged in collaborative group work, the screens are taken away; when it is time for individual seat work they go up, and all the children are expected to work without disturbing others.

CONCLUSION

Children differ, like adults, in temperament: some have a shorter concentration span than others, some are less confident, some are more aggressive. To accept such individual differences, however, does not mean accepting that there is nothing teachers can do to modify behaviours that are causing distress, or are stopping the child or others from learning – at least, to modify those aspects of their behaviour that the children themselves have chosen to work on. In this chapter, we have seen how altering the immediate context and consequences can prove helpful, even where nothing more is done to probe causes and stresses in the child's life that may be prompting a behaviour difficulty. This does *not* mean, however, that schools should see helping children to cope with stress and learn to manage inner feelings as outside their role. There is much excellent work being done in primary schools which falls into this category: it is to this more humanist approach, the necessary complement to the behaviourist strategies we have looked at so far, that we turn in the next chapter.

FURTHER READING

Westmacott, E. and Cameron, R. (1981) *Behaviour Can Change*. London, Globe Education.

RESOURCES

Bowers, S. (1987) *Ways and Means: an Approach to Problem Solving*. Kingston, Kingston Friends Workshop and Kingston Polytechnic. Available from Quaker Meeting House, 76 Eden Street, Kingston upon Thames, KT1 1DJ.
McConnon, S. (1989) *Your Choice*. London, Nelson.

· 9 ·

COMMUNICATION AND CLASSROOM RELATIONSHIPS

INTRODUCTION

It is a common experience to find primary schools where behaviour problems are few, and where children and adults consistently get on well together. Not all of these schools are in leafy suburbs or country villages: some are in inner city areas with high levels of social deprivation. Home life, for many of the pupils, may be stormy or strained, but the school manages to provide a haven and a refuge. Within the school, the children learn to deal with their own often chaotic feelings, to care for one another and – most important, to care for themselves. Their special needs for understanding, tolerance, help in expressing and resolving anger and anxiety and sadness, are met.

What is the secret of schools like these? In this chapter, we look at some of the organizational factors that help to explain their success, and at the range of specific responses they are able to make when children are experiencing stress.

THE CARING CLASSROOM

Arncliffe Down Primary

Arncliffe Down Primary is a large school on a run-down housing estate with high levels of unemployment and a pattern of poor community relationships. Within the school, however, there has been a deliberate attempt to create an ethos of caring and cooperation. Older classes are placed next door to younger groups, and each older child takes responsibility for a younger partner on occasions like school trips and assemblies. The older ones have been involved in a project to teach the younger children some of the playground rhymes and games they have collected from parents, grandparents and neighbours. This was part of a wider plan to improve the quality of playtimes, by designating quiet areas and providing a range of play equipment from soft balls to dressing-up clothes. In class, all the children are involved in a planned programme of personal and social education lessons: they learn how to recognize and express feelings, how to listen to others, how to resolve conflicts, how to be a good friend, how to keep themselves safe. In addition, there are many informal opportunities for children to express feelings and worries to people who will listen. They are all encouraged to keep a journal, which they can use if they wish for private messages to the teacher. Most classes use 'circle time': a time when everyone comes together to talk about the feeling side of their experiences – good and bad things that have happened to them recently, how they are getting on together as a group, how they could sort out arguments and tensions that are cropping up, what they have appreciated in one another. Each class has devised its own classroom charter, listing the rights (such as being listened to, or allowed to work without disturbance) to which everyone in the room should be entitled. When there are behaviour problems, children as well as teachers will draw attention to the charter. There is a lot of emphasis on mutual support: children are encouraged to nominate one another for special awards if they have managed to overcome a behaviour problem, or been especially helpful to others.

This particular school also has well-developed schemes of work for the national curriculum, and high academic expectations for all of its pupils. Like many other schools with a caring ethos, it is not in the business of devaluing the *content* of children's learning, only of recognizing the affective context in which all learning takes place, and using that context as a vital tool for educating the whole child.

The common features of schools which, like Arncliffe, succeed in creating an emotionally supportive framework for children could be described as follows:

- Classrooms are organized in a way that allows pupil autonomy and builds self-esteem: children can access the resources they need, set themselves goals for both work and behaviour, and assess their own progress with the help of other children and adults.
- Adults try to give children the confidence to handle their own difficulties, either in work or relationships: they help children think out their own solutions rather than sorting everything out for them, and reinforce successful problem-solving with generous praise.
- Discipline – through classroom charters and circle time – is seen as something which is shared with the pupils, rather than handed down by the teacher.
- Adults provide models of respect and empathy. Teachers find something to value in every child, and emphasize effort and progress rather than absolute achievement. They make efforts to listen to children's perspective on school, how they like to be taught, and what they think of the work they are asked to do.

- Children's attempts to help and care for one another are explicitly valued, and there is much emphasis on mutual appreciation – children and adults noticing each other's positive qualities, behaviours and achievements.
- Time is allocated to personal and social education, and there is coherent planning to make sure that key themes are visited and revisited in cross-curricular work or special PSE time: making and keeping friends, listening and communicating, awareness of feelings, resolving conflict, coping with loss, self-esteem, assertiveness and self-protection.
- Children are given many opportunities to express feelings – through play, art, drama, puppetry, writing and talk.
- There are resources – information and story books, poems and plays and videos – which cover a range of affective issues from bullying to bereavement to family break-up, and which can be used with individuals or groups when a need arises.
- Staff are alert to the signs of emotional stress in children – both the more obvious signs like fighting or stealing or excessive clinging, and the less intrusive ones like aches and pains, lethargy, social withdrawal and poor concentration.
- Staff know how to listen to children – not just to the content of what they are saying, but to the feelings that lie behind the words.

LISTENING TO FEELINGS

When Gary learned that he was going to have to move house, he told his mum that he did not want to go. His mum said: 'Cheer up; you'll have a lovely bedroom all to yourself, and a nice new school, and you'll soon make some new friends.' Gary felt angry and walked off in a sulk. Later on, he got into trouble for fighting with his brother. Gary told his teacher that he did not want to move house. She just said: 'I see. So you're wishing you could stay here. Could you tell me some more about how you feel about the move?' Gary said he did like the new house, but he wanted to stay with his friends. His teacher said: 'Yes, I understand that you will miss your friends here. It's sad to lose people.' Gary sat quiet for a while, thinking, and then said: 'I'll come and see them, though.'

In responding to Gary, his teacher used some basic counselling skills (Nelson-Jones, 1988) that helped him both to express and come to terms with some difficult feelings. What she did was try to listen very hard to what he was saying – his non-verbal signals as well as his actual words – and acknowledge the feelings he was struggling to convey. She took care not to deny or argue with what he was saying, but to reflect back to him her acceptance and understanding of what he was going through, and provide an open-ended invitation to him to say more. In doing so, she gave him the support of being listened to, and space to sort out some of the things that were on his mind.

These skills are not difficult to learn, and are invaluable in helping children with all kinds of special needs to find their way through the difficulties and stresses that beset them. One essential is using open questions when talking over problems, rather than closed questions that can be answered in a few words: not 'Did you lose your temper?' but 'How did you feel when that happened?'; not 'Have you had a bad day?' but 'Can you tell me how things have been for you at school today?' Another is mastering the art of paraphrasing or reflecting back communications, in order to show understanding and provide scope for the child to build on what s/he has said. To be effective, this relies on a degree of empathy and informed guesswork about what the child might be feeling: 'So your brother has been talking to you about secondary school and now you're feeling a bit worried about it, perhaps?', 'It sounds to me as if you feel whatever you do, it's always wrong', and 'You're feeling very angry about that, I think?'

Most of all, this kind of listening involves teachers in placing a hold on expressing their own opinions for long enough to really hear what the child is saying. Very often, when children talk to us, we block their communication by jumping in with value judgements, instant solutions to their problems, or attempts to smooth over their very real difficulties. Consider this conversation:

Child: My dad's mad at me. I hate him.
Teacher: That's not very nice. What did you do to annoy him?
Child: I dunno – he's just mad.
Teacher: Well I expect he's got a very good reason. Why don't you ask him?
Child: He wouldn't say. He just shouts. He never shouts at Emma.
Teacher: I expect he'll feel better soon. Come on, you go and play with your friends now and forget about it.

Now consider this very different response:

Child: My Dad's mad at me. I hate him.
Teacher: So he's cross and you're feeling very angry with him too at the moment?
Child: Sometimes. But . . . he's . . . I don't know . . . it seems like everything I do . . . he really picks on me. Emma's never in trouble. She starts things but he always says it's me.
Teacher: Mmmmmm.
Child: He lost his job. I suppose . . . but why doesn't he take it out on Emma? Why does it have to be me?
Teacher: You're feeling there may be some good reasons why he's often cross, but that it still isn't fair for you to be the one that gets blamed?
Child: Well . . . he's OK sometimes. He's OK. Maybe I . . . I'll have to see.

The second conversation may feel less satisfactory to the teacher: no neat endings, no advice given, no tidying up of messy feelings. In reality, it is much more likely to be helpful to the child than the first teacher's response. By suspending the normal tendency to offer advice, blame or diversion, the teacher is able to convey that she is really listening, and trying to understand the child's experience and point of view, even if it may be very different from her own.

CREATING OPPORTUNITIES FOR FEELINGS TO BE DISCUSSED

There should not be a need for schools to justify time spent by children in discussing their emotional reactions to their experiences. Helping them to find words for their feelings is a worthwhile educational goal in its own right, that will stand them in good stead throughout their adult lives. It is also the best way of preventing the behavioural difficulties that arise when children's hurt, or anxiety, or anger go unrecognized and unlistened to. Nevertheless, we can if we wish pin attainment targets and cross-curricular themes to this kind of work: such structured situations as circle time, for example, provide an ideal opportunity to address the English programmes of study by working on 'powers of concentration, grasp of turn-taking, ability to gain and hold the attention of their listeners' (DES, 1989c).

Opportunities for individual children to open up to the teacher are created in many schools through bubble time, where each child is guaranteed an uninterrupted few minutes 'inside the magic bubble' with the teacher, and through personal journals (of writing, drawings, cartoons, poems) that children can show the teacher if they wish. They will often make good use of this channel of communication, as the piece of writing in Figure 9.1 shows. The response that this piece evokes – unlocking memories of our own about chaotic mornings, family tensions and big event nerves – reminds us of the power that reading or listening to others' writing can have in helping us all to understand and express our own feelings. Literature is a prompt to self-expression: in the caring classroom teachers make sure that carefully chosen poems and pieces of prose are readily available to help children reflect on recent experiences, or reach feelings they may have suppressed. There is a poem, for example, which never fails to help children let go of some of the feelings they may have been holding on to. The poem, a translation of one by an 8-year-old Turkish girl, starts,

There is a knot inside of me
A knot which cannot be untied
Strong
It feels
As if they have put a stone
Inside of me.

(Ward and Houghton, 1991)

When they identify their own inner knot or stone, children can share the feelings with the teacher, privately, or – more risky but ultimately often more healing – with a supportive group. To help children gain access to this kind of group support, more and more schools are using the idea of circle time (Mosley, 1991). Circle time provides a structure of cooperative activities (games, listening and speaking exercises, drama, puppet and mask work) which get children (and adults) into the habit of talking about feelings and behaviour, and of listening to

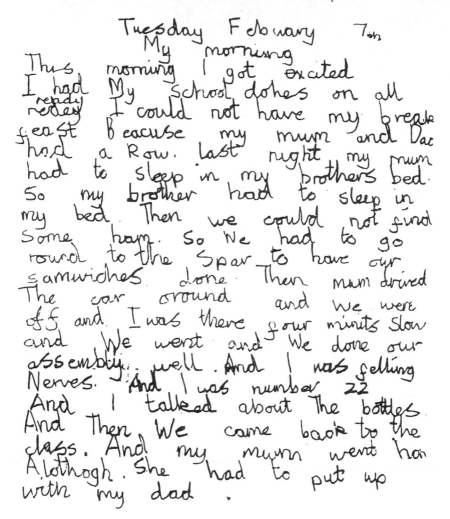

Figure 9.1 Journal writing.

one another with respect. Children sit in a circle, on an equal footing with the teacher, and initially spend time negotiating some ground rules – maybe that people can only speak if holding a particular object that is passed round, that no one is to interrupt, that no one's ideas will be criticized or put down, and that everyone has a right to pass on any activity that feels uncomfortable to them. A session might start with a round, when each child who wants to will complete the same sentence – such as 'I feel happy when . . .', or 'I get fed up when . . .', or 'If I were an animal I'd like to be . . . because . . .'. Then there will be games, on the surface like party games but always with an agenda of helping the children to listen, to trust one another, to develop sensitivity or grow in self-esteem. These may lead to opportunities for the children to discuss the immediate problems that are troubling them: for example, a game in which a blindfolded child has to negotiate obstacles in order to reach some 'treasure' (Mosley, 1992) may allow the children to look at the obstacles (in their own behaviour, or that of others) that prevent them from reaching personal goals in their own lives. Or it may be possible to discuss and tackle a problem (like teasing, or 'breaking friends') that has recently arisen in class.

Sources of ideas for circle time are listed at the end of this chapter. A particularly useful variant (Evans, 1992) is the idea of 'end-of-day' activities, where children spend a few minutes at the end of each school day on rounds such as, 'If you could change places with someone, who would you be . . .', 'You're being bullied; who would you tell?', 'I am good at . . .', 'I've had a good/bad day because . . .'. Any child can pass on any round, but there is an open invitation for children to stay and talk to the teacher afterwards about any item that provoked a strong reaction or made them feel uncomfortable.

HANDLING TRICKY ISSUES

When children are actively encouraged to communicate in school about the things that trouble them, issues will come up that leave staff also uncomfortable, and often unsure about how to respond. For some issues, such as disclosures by children of emotional or physical abuse, there are well-established systems and guidelines in place in most local authorities to help teachers know what to say, what to do, and how to seek support for both the child and for themselves in handling such emotionally charged events. Coping with disclosures about bullying is another area where schools are developing internal guidance on similar lines (Johnstone et al., 1991; Maines and Robinson, 1992). But other difficult and commonly-occurring issues, such as how to help children cope with family break-up, are less well charted.

The principles for these tricky issues are the same as for any other open discussion of feelings with children: listen; do not make judgements or take sides (or if you do, keep them to yourself), provide support if the child is willing in the form of sharing the feelings with other children (who may well have had similar experiences themselves), and in the form of reading or listening to what others have written.

Children going through a family break-up need to know that this happens to many people, and that they should not feel ashamed or different. They should be told that many children feel it is somehow their fault when parents split up, and that it is natural and normal if they feel like this – though almost certainly completely unjustified. It is also natural, but unjustified, to see themselves as unworthy or no good because a parent who has left appears to have rejected them as well as the marriage. They should know that it may take some time before they can get used to the division of their family, and that meanwhile they are likely to feel intense longing for things to be the way they were, mixed perhaps with anger at one or both parents, and perhaps feelings of needing to take sides or look after a parent who once looked after them. They need to be told that the teacher will understand if they find things hard in school for a while, but would want the child to come and talk over how s/he is feeling rather than bottle it up so that it comes out in other ways.

If a step-parent appears on the scene, the feelings that may need acknowledging by the sympathetic teacher could include sadness because this means an end to any hopes that the real parents will get back together again, bitter jealousy if a mother's or father's attention seems to be devoted to a new partner, anger on behalf of the parent who has been replaced, or guilt and split loyalties if the child finds s/he feels positive about the step-parent. Irritation and exhaustion at having to form a whole new set of relationships – often with step-brothers and sisters as well as the step-parent – may also be part of the reaction, as well as relief for the child that s/he is part of a 'normal' family again.

Supporting children after bereavement can prove particularly hard for teachers. There is often a tendency to shy away from mentioning the loss, for fear of upsetting the child or causing embarrassment. Like adults, however, children need to be encouraged to express grief in order to be able to work through it: to say what it was about the person who has died that they most valued, to relive memories, to look at photographs, to cry if they need to. Teachers can help by not avoiding talking about the loss, and by providing a quiet, private place where the child can go when s/he needs to be alone. They need to let the child know that it is normal to experience many bewildering feelings after a loss – not only sadness but also anger (at being abandoned), guilt (about the things s/he feels should have been done or left undone, said or left unsaid), worry (about what might happen to other people the child depends on), or even periods of numbness and no feeling at all.

HELPING CHILDREN COPE WITH ANXIETY

As well as the major stresses of abuse, family break-up and loss we have looked at so far, children can need their teachers' support in coping with anxieties about many lesser events – often school-related, such as worries about moving on to secondary school, speaking in front of a group, going swimming, and so on.

Teachers can help anxious children by mapping out with them a series of small steps that will lead them bit by bit to master particular fears. A child who is worried about giving a talk to the class, for example, might need practice in speaking to a partner, then in threes, then a slightly larger group. Children who are anxious about water might need to spend the first swimming lesson sitting on the edge of the pool splashing with their legs, the next jumping briefly into the arms of a helper in the water, the next spending five minutes in the water. For each step completed, the teacher will praise the child enthusiastically, using words that build up the child's picture of him or herself as a competent person

This tape will help you to practise relaxing. It will show you how to breathe slowly and deeply, and how to relax different parts of your body. You should listen to the tape many times, and practise slow breathing and relaxation over and over again. When you are lying in bed at night is often a good time to listen to the tape and do your practice. If you practise often, you will soon find that wherever you are, and however worried and tense you feel, you will be able to use the breathing and relaxation to make yourself feel calm. This will mean you never have to panic; you will always know what to do to calm yourself down. You will feel in control.

Now let's begin to practise relaxing. Make yourself as comfortable as you can: close your eyes; just let yourself relax. Enjoy the feeling of letting go; breathe in and out, in and out slowly and deeply. Put your hand just above your stomach. Keep breathing in . . . and out. Feel your hand being pushed away from you as you breathe in . . . and out. Slowly and deeply. Now imagine there are lots of little tiny holes in the bottom of your feet. As you breathe in . . . and then out you push all of your worries down through your body and out through the soles of your feet. Breathe in . . . and out, letting all those worries down through your body and out through those holes. Keep breathing in . . . and out, letting all the tensions ease away. Let all the muscles in your face relax completely; let go of all the tightness in your head . . . forehead . . . mouth . . . neck. Let it all go loose and floppy. Keep breathing slowly in . . . and out. Concentrate on your shoulders. Let them go floppy. Now your arms and hands. Tighten all the muscles in your hands; clench your fists . . . now let go, and feel your arms and hands go heavy and floppy. Every time you breathe out feel more and more relaxed. Now your legs . . . tense the muscles in your legs . . . in your feet . . . curl up your toes very tight . . . now let go. Breathe slowly and feel your legs and your feet all heavy and floppy. Let yourself feel more and more floppy and comfortable. Let all your muscles go. Lie still for a while.

Now I'm going to count backwards from seven to one. When I get to one, you will be alert but still relaxed. Seven . . . six . . . you're waking up now . . . five, four, three . . . ready to go now . . . two . . . one.

in control of events: 'You did really well to stick to your plan' or 'You should feel proud of the way you coped with that situation.'

Anxious children also benefit from being taught how they can control their own emotional reactions. Some work in science on the evolutionary significance of the body's physiological response to threat will help children to recognize physical signs, like increased heart rate, sweating, experiencing a dry mouth or knots and butterflies in the stomach, as indications that their bodies are getting ready for swift action (the 'fight-or-flight' response) by shutting down unnecessary systems (such as the digestive system) and pumping energy to muscles. From there, they can be taught how to slow down these physiological responses through slow, deep breathing and progressive muscle relaxation.

They can practise, in PE lessons, tensing and tightening each group of muscles in turn, then letting them go floppy and loose, until they are able to let go of muscle tension quickly and easily. Relaxation tapes, to give extra practice at home for children who are particularly vulnerable to anxiety or anger, can be made by the teacher or parent. An example is shown above.

Children who become so apparently anxious about school that they sometimes refuse to come at all can benefit from both relaxation strategies and a small-steps approach, under the guidance of a psychologist, welfare officer or behaviour support teacher. Often, however, the school and the classroom teacher can prevent such school anxieties from escalating to the point where outside intervention is needed, by the messages they give to the child and to parents. It is necessary to promise that any worries the child may have will be thoroughly listened to in school, and acted upon, but at the same time the message should be that the child must come to school rather than stay at home and have the worries mount up. If the child is reporting morning aches and pains or stomach upset, the parents can be reassured that the teacher will monitor closely, and send him or her home if obviously unwell. If the parents seem unable to get children to come, it can work wonders if someone from school comes firmly once to collect them. The principle is quick intervention before the child gets locked into a pattern of anxious non-attendance, or a belief that whether or not they go to school is under their own control.

HELPING CHILDREN WITH FRIENDSHIPS

Children who are anxious and withdrawn are also very often children who are lonely, and isolated from their peers. So too, very often, are children who are aggressive or disruptive in an attention-seeking way in the classroom: it is surprising how often problems in making and keeping friends lead to behavioural difficulties of all kinds.

Teachers seeking to help children with friendship problems can:

- Involve them in collaborative work with a carefully-chosen group, giving them specific roles and putting in preparation so that they are able to make a success of their contribution.
- Try to raise their status in the class by giving them responsibilities or having them play a key role in a project where they have a special interest, knowledge or skill.
- Involve them in peer tutoring.
- Help them to identify the things they do (like being aggressive, or critical, impatient or fickle) that stop other children from wanting to be friends with them, and making these the subject of a personal plan.
- Identify specific friendship skills they may need to be taught, or praised for using.

A friendship skills course for a group of children is a time consuming but very worthwhile form of intervention, as this example shows:

At St Anne's Primary, a member of staff with a special interest in children's behaviour difficulties decided to run some lunchtime sessions for six children who were a source of concern to their class teachers, because they seemed withdrawn or, in some cases, unpopular and involved in bullying. She started each session with an ice-breaker: for example, a name game where each child had to call out another's name before throwing a soft toy to them, or a game (called untangling the knot) where everyone stood close together and with closed eyes and crossed arms took hold of someone else's hands, then opened their eyes and tried to unscramble themselves into a circle without letting go. The group worked out some ground rules, and reviewed them each week to see if any of them needed to be changed. The theme of Session 1 was, 'What makes a good friend?' The children brainstormed their ideas on a spider diagram. The teacher then put a pile of cards on to the floor, saying things such as, 'I can keep a secret', and the children had to decide whether each card should go into a 'good friend' pile or a 'not good friend' pile. Homework for the week was noting and bringing back to the group examples the children saw of people being 'good friends' to one another in school.

Session 2 began with a round: 'This week I was a good friend because . . .', and 'This week I wasn't a good friend because . . .'. The teacher introduced a game about helping, where all the children had to move around balancing a bean bag on their heads while following instructions to hop, skip, move forwards, backwards, slower, faster. If the bean bag fell off somebody's head, he or she was 'frozen' until another child picked up the bean bag and put it on his or her head. The object of the game was to keep as many people as possible unfrozen. At the end, the children were asked how it felt to help and be helped, and how we should respond when people help us. They went on to watch two children act out a scene where they have been playing a game, and one has lost three times in a row, discussing what the winner might say to help the loser feel better, and how the loser should try to behave.

Session 3 was about listening, with the children working in pairs and taking turns to pretend to be a 'good' listener and a 'bad' listener while the other talked about their interests and hobbies. The teacher collected their ideas about what makes for good and bad listening on a flip chart, and set the children to practise some of their 'good listener' ideas for homework.

In Session 4, the topic was giving and accepting compliments. The children drew round and cut out the shape of their hands. Each 'hand' was passed round, for the children in turn to write something they liked or admired about its owner on one of the fingers. The children spent some time looking at what others had said about them, and could if they wished take their 'hand' away to keep (all but one of them chose to do this).

Sessions 5 and 6 were spent thinking about in group/out group processes, put-downs, name-calling and teasing. The teacher asked the children to talk together in threes in gobbledegook, taking it in turns to be left out by the other two. As a whole group, they discussed how it felt to be left out, and what could have been done to make the outsider feel better. The teacher then said she was going to read them a story about a day in the life of a boy called Paul, who wakes up feeling happy and good about himself. She gave them each a piece of paper, and said this stood for Paul's feelings inside: 'I'm happy, I'm good, I'm OK.' As she told the story of his day, they had to tear off a little piece of paper every time something happened that took away the 'I'm happy, I'm good, I'm OK' feeling. In the story the boy was shouted at by his father, teased by his sister, ignored by a friend, called names at school, and so on. At the end, most of the paper was in bits on the floor. The children were very quiet. The teacher went on to ask them to suggest ways in which people in the story could have helped Paul to feel better about himself, picking up a piece of paper from the floor for each suggestion. The group made a list together of 'put-downs' that children in school use towards one another, and another list of 'build-ups' that could be used instead. They cut up the build-ups and pasted them down one by one over the put-downs. At the last group meeting they shared with the group the put-downs they most often received, and the one taunt or criticism that each felt was guaranteed to hurt or wind them up most. They brainstormed ways of reacting to put-downs and decided together which were most likely to make other children go on teasing, and which might make them stop.

The children finished with a round: 'Something I've liked about being in this group' and a final game of 'untangling the knot'. All of them said they would miss the group and that it had been good fun. Their class teachers felt that it had in small but significant ways helped all of them to get on with others, and asked for the group to be repeated with different children in the next term.

ENHANCING SELF-ESTEEM

A factor that is common to most children with friendship problems, behavioural difficulties, and learning difficulties is low self-esteem – defined as the difference between the way the child would like to be and the way s/he actually perceives him or herself. If the difference is very great, children cannot feel good about themselves. And if they do not feel good about themselves, they approach many situations – both social and academic – with an expectation of failure and a range of negative behaviours that all too often mean that their expectations are confirmed.

What can be done to help children escape this downward spiral? Increasingly, research is showing that it is possible for schools – using relatively simple interventions – to begin to alter pupils' perceptions of themselves, and that the resulting gains in self-esteem are directly linked to improved behaviour and academic achievement. One example is the work on peer tutoring, described in Chapter 6, where very significant improvements in children's rate of progress in learning and classroom behaviour were achieved through no other means than asking them to help teach younger pupils – with all that meant to them in terms of feeling valued and important. Another example is the pioneering work of Dennis Lawrence on the effects on children's reading achievement of providing them with a counselling relationship with a volunteer adult helper, whose job was simply to affirm the child's worth by showing a positive interest in their activities, encouraging them to express feelings and opinions, and showing that those opinions were valued in a non-critical way (Lawrence, 1988). These findings have recently been replicated in a study where the volunteer helpers were older pupils: again, there were very significant improvements in the children's reading and spelling, compared to a control group who also had extra help with literacy skills, but whose self-esteem was not nurtured in the same way (James et al., 1991).

This research involves peers and volunteers; teachers, of course, are an even more potent and ever-present influence on children's self-esteem. Clark and Warlberg (1968), for example, showed that when teachers made a point of praising children with reading difficulties very frequently for their reading, and having the pupils record each positive comment, their rate of progress shot up, as they began to incorporate into their self-image a picture of themselves as 'good readers'.

Sometimes it is apparently casual comments from the teacher which alter self-image: the teacher who says, 'I hear from your mother how grown-up you've been since the new baby came' and finds the child starting to affirm a 'grown-up' image in all sorts of ways in the classroom, or who says of a piece of writing 'You've got a real feeling for words' and finds the child producing better and better poetry as a result. Many teachers can think of a particular child they have taught whose self-image they were able to alter, with spectacular effects; even more so, most parents can think of the special teacher who succeeded in turning a particular key for their child, to unlock whole areas of potential that had previously lain hidden – by nothing more complex than simply making the child feel good about him or herself.

Sometimes the key is not with one teacher, but is turned by a whole school staff working together, as this example shows:

> Brendan was 6, and failing in school. He had a complicated early
> history, with many operations for a series of heart and digestive
> complaints. He showed early developmental delay, particularly in
> language. At 4, he joined a small assessment class in a special school,

but later on at his parents' request moved to a local primary school with a good reputation for 'caring'. When he was in Year 3, he was referred to the educational psychologist: he was not progressing with reading, had great problems with handwriting, and was very easily distracted and unmotivated in the classroom. He said of himself at this time: 'I'm no good at my work and no one wants to play with me.' It was decided to make raising his self-esteem a priority in the school's action plan: a greater priority even than specific help with reading and written work.

Two terms later, the psychologist returned to review Brendan's progress. In the interim, he had been chosen for the part of Joseph in the school nativity play. He had also been selected to serve at mass when it was celebrated in school. He was now sitting between two very able boys in the classroom, and often given responsibilities as the 'oldest boy in the class' (which he was). He had done quite a lot of writing on the computer; this had helped him to produce work that looked good, of which he could feel proud. All the staff made a point of singling him out for special notice; even the headteacher, whenever he went into the classroom, would say, 'Where's that boy who's so good at setting my watch?' and give him the job of doing so.

When she re-assessed his basic attainments, the psychologist found that Brendan had improved at twice his previous rate. Even more important, he was concentrating for much longer periods in the classroom, and mixing indistinguishably with other children in the playground.

As with behaviour management, self-esteem interventions for individual children need to be set in the context of a school-wide framework for enhancing the self-esteem of *all* pupils. This will involve looking at issues of curriculum, discipline and classroom management. Does the curriculum allow opportunities for all to experience success? Does teacher language, marking and display place a value on absolute achievement, or does it instead emphasize the importance of effort and individuality? Is the school one, as some in a recent study in one LEA, where 'a concentration of praise on a small number of high achieving pupils, with consistent negative feedback to others, led to a perception amongst pupils that their contributions to the school were not valued' – with an associated high rate of behavioural difficulties and pupil suspensions (Nottingham County Council, 1990)?

Then there is the balance of rewards and sanctions, and the ways in which these are applied. In the average primary school, pupils receive about four-and-a-half times as many negative comments about their behaviour as positive (Merrett and Wheldall, 1987), leaving them with little chance of developing an image of themselves as well behaved, kind, helpful or hard working. It is, however, quite possible for teachers to reverse the ratio by following the adage 'catch them being good', and explicitly praising pro-social behaviour rather than taking it for granted.

When children do need telling off, this can be done in ways that avoid the humiliation, sarcasm and personal criticism which the Elton Report (DES, 1989b) highlighted as still the most prevalent discipline strategy in many schools. Teachers can use language that shows they reject particular behaviours, without also rejecting the child (Maines and Robinson, 1989a). Saying 'You are a bully' will only reduce self-esteem and provide both teacher and child with a convenient label that will direct much of their future behaviour, while 'Hitting other children is not allowed in this school; you have been hitting, and the consequence will be . . .' leaves the child with the chance to learn from the sanction and change their behaviour next time. Children can sometimes be bullies, liars, spoilsports, cheats or fusspots, but there is nothing at all to be gained from calling them any of these things (even in the privacy of the staffroom). Instead, teachers can make use of the more helpful, 'When you . . . then I . . .' or 'I message' framework (Gordon, 1974): 'When you tell me a lie, I feel let down and also angry that I have to spend a lot of time now sorting this out', 'When you keep coming to ask me questions about work I know you can do, I get irritated because I can't get on with the work I've planned for this group', and 'When you spoil the game the others get angry with you and won't want you to play next time'.

The final aspect of a whole school framework for building self-esteem concerns classroom management. Systems that deprive children of the right to exercise choice and independence in the classroom can be very damaging to self-esteem: when the goals and the means to achieve them are always set by others, children never develop the sense of self-direction that is the main characteristic distinguishing those who have high from those that have low self-esteem. Then there is pupil grouping: fixed pupil groupings that make it very clear to the pupils who the teacher views as achievers, and who the no-hopers, are still common in primary classrooms, and are a major source of low self-esteem for many pupils. So are special needs interventions that single children out as obviously different from their peers – having to fetch their reading book from another part of the school, perhaps, having a classroom assistant who works with them and never anyone else, having special equipment that others are not sometimes allowed to try out and share as a special privilege. Yet differentiation can be achieved without such blows to self-esteem: witness the classrooms where resources at different levels are available for topic work, but the children themselves choose which they think are most appropriate for them, or the teacher who covered *all* the children's maths books with wallpaper to avoid the comparisons of who was on which level in the scheme.

Schools that have looked at their overall curriculum, their discipline and classroom management systems in terms of the effects on children's self-image are generally very successful in reducing the frequency of behaviour and learning difficulties. Even the best of them still find, however, that there are children who need a more individual and intensive attempt to boost self-confidence.

These are the children with very low self-esteem, who can be recognized by certain characteristic behaviour patterns: they typically find it hard to concentrate or are apathetic in learning situations, avoid taking part, remain on the fringe of groups, set themselves low goals, continuously ask for help and reassurance, or compensate for poor self-image by trying to appear powerful to other children, exaggerating achievements and possessions, or refusing to conform to classroom norms (Gurney, 1988).

Teachers can explore individual children's self-perceptions using published self-esteem scales (Lawrence, 1988; Maines and Robinson, 1989b), or the discussion format described in Chapter 4: these will identify children whose global self-worth is low, and highlight the particular areas (such as academic achievement, appearance, friendship skills) where they most need help in formulating a more positive self-image.

The strategies that can be used for children low in self-esteem are many, for example:

- Adopting a policy of positive 'noticing' the child by every adult in the school.
- Finding out what the child is good at or knows a lot about, and having him or her share this with the rest of the class or school.
- Helping the child to become an expert, or develop skills in a particular area – which may be extra-curricular: becoming a judo orange belt has worked wonders for some children, as has being given the responsibility of organizing a lunchtime or after-school group, such as a stampbug or nature watch club.
- Drama activities, where the child with low self-esteem is assigned the role of expert who must be consulted by other group members in order to complete a task – such as escaping from a castle or rescuing a group member from danger.
- Choosing the child for special responsibilities.
- Asking the child to tutor another with their work.
- Choosing the child to be part of a group that supports or counsels other children – for example, those who are having problems in the playground, are being bullied, or are new to the school.
- Making much use of praise, stickers, certificates and notes home to highlight achievements in behaviour or learning.
- Giving the whole class a favourite activity or five minutes' extra playtime when the target child has done well in either work or behaviour.
- Having the child set him- or herself small, attainable targets within a special 'success area' they choose to work on.
- Helping the child to keep records of reaching these targets, and dated samples of work so that s/he can clearly see progress and show the evidence to others.

- Asking the child to record one success, however small, in a special praise book at the end of each day.

It is also possible to construct a series of planned activities for a small group of children who share problems of low self-esteem. One teacher, for example, set up what she called the 'I can club', which had a special membership badge; the children took part in a series of affirming activities such as taking photographs of one another, displaying them on posters surrounded by positive comments they had made about each other, completing lists of things they were able to do well, and telling a friend about one special achievement they were proud of. Other children have enjoyed making an 'I can tree', either at home or at school, where they stick paper leaves on a cut-out tree trunk, each leaf recording a skill they have mastered – or some of the everyday things they manage to do well.

Children with low self-esteem will find it hard to think about what they are good at, but can be helped by prompts (in rounds, or on worksheets) such as 'I am liked because . . .', 'The best things about the way I look are . . .', 'Things I've made are . . .', or 'I'm a good friend because . . .'. Or they can finish sentences like these in pairs, then form a group where each child describes some of the positive things they have learned about their partner. Again, using one of Jenny Mosley's ideas, they can be helped to get into the habit of acknowledging positives by choosing a piece of work each week to stick a coloured label on, and present to a small group or to the class at circle time with an explanation of why they are proud of it (Mosley, 1993).

Teacher praise for children with low self-esteem needs to be given with care. If it is to succeed in restructuring the child's self-image in any long-term way, praise for a particular piece of work or behaviour needs to be linked with more general attributes and strengths: not just 'that's a lovely painting' but 'that's a lovely painting; it shows you have good powers of observation'; not just 'good girl for getting that finished' but 'good girl for getting that finished; I can see you are a real hard worker'. It is also important to make it clear that the child has succeeded entirely because of their own efforts or qualities. Research has shown that children with special needs come to believe that while the failure they encounter is the result of their own inadequacies, any success they may experience is due to chance or the actions of others (Dudley-Marling et al., 1982). If I can do a task, the child feels, it must be because the task was easy, or I had help; if I fail, it is because I am stupid or bad.

To challenge successfully this kind of conviction, teachers need to emphasize permanent inner factors in the child when praising success. Conversely, when they have to correct the work or behaviour of a child who is low in self-esteem, they need to stress external and temporary factors. They can convey to the child that if there are mistakes in work it is because the task was too hard, or the teacher had not explained it properly, or even because the child chose, on that particular day, not to try very hard. They can convey that problems in behaviour have arisen because the child chose to react in certain ways to external circumstances – but another time would be able to adopt a different strategy. It is important *not* to let the child feel that you think him permanently slow, or lazy or aggressive, but instead to emphasize factors that are changeable and specific to the situation.

This may call for considerable revision of our own attitudes to children with special educational needs. Despite much evidence to the contrary, there is still a belief in many teachers that some pupils just will not succeed, ever. And if they hold such low expectations of certain pupils, they appear according to research to adopt certain behaviours towards them that actively contribute to these expectations being confirmed – restricting the breadth of curricular experiences, for example (Blatchford et al., 1989). If pupils' self-esteem is to be raised, we need to monitor effects like these very carefully, and reverse them where necessary – as did the teachers in one study (Good and Brophy, 1977), who when they were told that they were offering less praise and more criticism to children they designated as low achievers, immediately altered their responses, and found that the behaviour and performance of the low achieving group improved rapidly as a result.

CONCLUSION

In this chapter, we have looked at ways in which schools can support children's affective development. At a time when teachers are overwhelmed with pressures from the academic curriculum, this may seem inappropriate: time for listening to children's feelings and helping them to relate to one another is hard to come by with so much curriculum content to be covered. The argument has to be, nevertheless, that if we do not pay enough attention to these issues, the time children can spend learning and teachers can spend teaching will be eroded by the resulting behavioural challenges to the teacher's classroom management, and children will continue to underachieve because of feelings of low self-worth. Let children see themselves as valuable, capable of handling stress and sorting out problems, however, and they can get on with their school work – and a good deal more besides.

FURTHER READING

Hall, E. and Hall, C. (1988) *Human Relations in Education*. London, Routledge.

RESOURCES

Bliss, T. and Tetley, J. (1993) *Circle Time*. Lame Duck Publishing.
Bliss, T. and Robinson, G. (1995) *Developing Circle Time*. Lame Duck Publishing. A video (*Coming Round to Circle Time*) is also available.
Bowers, S. (1987) *Ways and Means: an Approach to Problem Solving*. Kingston, Kingston Friends Workshop and Kingston Polytechnic. Available from Quaker Meeting House, 76 Eden Street, Kingston upon Thames, KT1 1DJ. Activities to help children and adults learn to resolve conflict.

Canfield, J. and Wells, H. (1976) *100 Ways to Improve Self Esteem in the Classroom*. Herts, Prentice Hall.

Cox, K. and Desforges, M. (1986) *Children and Divorce*. Sheffield, Sheffield Psychological Service and Methuen. A helpful guide for teachers on supporting children through family break-up.

Evans, G. (1992) *Child Protection: a Whole Curricular Approach*. Bristol, Avec Designs, PO Box 709, Bristol BS99 1GE. Also full of ideas for circle time and PSE activities – especially good on helping children to recognize and convey feelings.

Masheder, M. (1989) *Let's Play Together: Cooperative Games for All Ages*. London, Greenprint. Games without winners and losers, where the emphasis is on interdependency.

Mosley, J. (1993) *Turn Your School Around*. Wisbech, LDA. A good source of ideas for circle time activities.

Prutzman, P. (1978) *The Friendly Classroom for a Small Planet: A Practical Handbook*. New York, Avery Publications. Ways of helping children to get on together.

TACADE (1991) *Skills for the Primary School Child*. Salford, TACADE (1 Hulme Place, The Crescent, Salford M5 4QA). Another complete primary PSE resource.

Ward, B. and Houghton, J. (1991) *Good Grief 2*. Salford, TACADE. A resource to help children cope with loss.

SPECIAL NEEDS IN SPEAKING AND LISTENING

INTRODUCTION

The importance of oral language skills as a vehicle for learning and a means of communicating what has been learned is central to much of the national curriculum documentation. As well as having an attainment target to itself in English, talk is also prominent in programmes of study in other subjects – with children increasingly envisaged working in groups, discussing ideas, reporting back to an audience and learning by listening to one another.

For some children with special educational needs, particularly those with difficulties in writing, the new emphasis on oracy will be immensely helpful. For others, the speaking and listening programmes of study are themselves a stumbling block: these are children who, for whatever reason (whether because of in-built factors or classroom demands ill attuned to their natural language patterns), find it hard to listen and remember, to express their ideas, to ask and answer questions, to recall experiences and describe events.

In this chapter, we consider ways in which teachers can differentiate the national curriculum programmes of work in speaking and listening to meet their needs, and ensure that they can access work in other subjects wherever it relies on well-developed oracy skills.

TWO CHILDREN

David, aged 6, has been with the same teacher throughout his first two years of school. When he started in the reception class, his speech was barely intelligible, and he talked very little: only in a whisper to the teacher, and never in small group or class discussion times. Over the next two years, he became more confident in speaking to one familiar adult in school, and his articulation problems all but disappeared, leaving only slight immaturities such as 'tissors' for 'scissors'. He was making almost no progress with reading and writing, however. He found it hard to follow instructions in class, and would often be found sitting day-dreaming instead of getting going on a task. He still was not consistently participating as a speaker in group activities: he would speak when asked a direct question but not spontaneously relate 'news', or describe something he had done or planned to do in school. The teacher decided to work on this, with the help of David's parents, by keeping a home–school diary: she used the diary to ask David questions at news time (initially closed questions, but becoming more open as he developed confidence). He was also asked to draw pictures in the diary, and use these as a support when talking about his news. Other children in the group were encouraged to ask David questions about his pictures, to promote a less teacher directed exchange.

This plan had some success, but it was slow. David's teacher felt there was enough evidence of language difficulties to ask for a speech and language therapist's assessment: he had some speech therapy in his pre-school years, but had been discharged because his parents failed to keep appointments.

The speech therapist confirmed that David was still a long way behind his peers in many aspects of language. She observed that he had particular difficulties in word-finding: he might know perfectly well what something was called, but be unable at times to recall the name for it. When he looked at a picture of a cup and saucer, for example, he struggled for a long time to name it, saying: 'It's a plate . . . no, it's a teapot . . . a dish.' She felt this might partly explain why he was so reticent in classroom situations where he felt 'on the spot' to produce the right words. He also showed a lot of difficulties in following and processing complex language: he would often pick up only part of a sentence, responding for example to an instruction like 'Before you give me the car, give me the red van', by handing over only the van. Simple mathematical language, such as, 'Find two the same', or 'How many can we have each?' was quite beyond him, but if the instruction was demonstrated by gesture and example he could cope easily with the task.

This assessment helped David's teacher to understand why he often seemed so slow to catch on in the classroom; the speech and language therapist's advice helped her to plan ways of adapting her classroom language to meet his needs.

Emily was 10, and a source of concern to her teacher mainly because of her poor written work. She had been late in talking in her pre-school years, as had her elder sister and brother. She had had consistent, high-quality extra help with reading throughout her primary years and was now a reasonably skilled reader. She had mastered a core spelling vocabulary by learning the words by heart alphabetically, naming each letter to herself over and over until she remembered them. Words outside this vocabulary were often spelled in a bizarre manner – 'pisall' for 'pencil', for example, 'rasey' for 'rice'. Her stories and written work were often disjointed and her teacher could not make sense of them.

She had always tended to jumble her words and substitute one word for another: 'hockeysocks' for 'hollyhocks', 'eiderup' for 'eiderdown', 'beanshooter' for 'peashooter'. If one listened closely to her speech, it was missing little joining words and word endings; when asked to describe what a wheel was in a word game, for example, she said: 'On a car. It black, it round, like a little tube.' She seemed quite unable to understand everyday idioms and metaphors; when her teacher said things like 'Are you with me?' she would always answer 'yes', because she *was* with the teacher, literally at least.

A multidisciplinary assessment of Emily's needs concluded that she had marked specific language difficulties. Her problems with written work were important, but secondary to the wider language problem; commenting on her spelling, for example, the educational psychologist observed: 'Emily finds it hard to discriminate, reproduce and sequence speech sounds in words, and has not as a result been able to reliably map the written symbols on to these patterns of spoken sounds.'

What do these two children need, in terms of help from their teachers? Both require ongoing literacy support, it is clear, but also more fundamental support with spoken language.

First, they need specific programmes of work within the speaking and listening programmes of study, perhaps planned with the help of a speech and language therapist and special needs support teacher. For Emily, this might focus on non-literal uses of language and expressing her ideas grammatically and in sequence; for David, work on processing the complex language he hears in the classroom and on expressing himself fluently in group situations.

Secondly, both children need 'bypass' strategies that make sure they have full access to, and a fair chance to succeed in, the *whole* curriculum despite their communication difficulties. Many of these bypass strategies will relate to teacher language. David's teacher has to make her instructions short and back them up with demonstration and gesture, Emily's teacher to explain and clarify metaphor, jokes, irony, idiom. For David, too, there will be a need to find ways in which he can demonstrate his learning other than by contributing to group discussion.

IDENTIFICATION AND ASSESSMENT

How can teachers become more aware of children, such as Emily and David, with special needs in language? We are not speaking here of bilingual children, for whom English is not the language of the home: these children have traditionally not been considered to come under the special needs umbrella, and this is the convention followed here. The focus here is, rather, on children who have difficulties in acquiring – or using appropriately in the classroom – a single language, and who show one or more of the following behaviours:

- unclear speech;
- difficulty in listening to and understanding what they hear in school;
- inhibited or restricted expressive language.

Such difficulties are common; some years ago, for example, it was estimated that 1 in 20 children started school unable to make themselves understood (Hersov and Berger, 1980); now that more and more four-year olds are in reception classes, the figure is likely to be very much higher. The difficulties can also have long-term consequences for the child's development: the overt signs of language problems may not be so evident when the child is 7, or 17, but there is often a legacy of emotional, behavioural or learning difficulties that persists over many years. In one study (Sheridan and Peckham, 1975), over half the children identified as having language problems at seven still demonstrated residual language problems, learning, social or emotional difficulties at sixteen; difficulties in reading are particularly likely (Aram and Nation, 1980).

Straightforward articulation problems and unclear speech are the easiest form of language difficulty for the teacher to pick up – but at the same time, it seems, the least likely to lead to long-term learning difficulties (Hall and Tomblin, 1978). It is important for the teacher to be able to screen for more subtle forms of language impairment, using a knowledge of the normal course of development of language in young children (Table 10.1).

They should also be aware of some of the behavioural patterns that might be pointers to language difficulties. This will mean watching out for children who may be always one step behind when following instructions (for example, in PE, where they may be watching the other children to see what they have to do), for children who are restless and inattentive in listening situations like story time and assembly, for children who respond at a tangent in conversation or pick up only the last part of things you say to them – such as the child who on being given an instruction on how to hit a shuttlecock ('I'll hold it like this and when I drop it, you have to hit it') responded only to the 'you hit it' part, and gave the adult's hand an almighty bash. If young children are showing possible signs of language difficulty, it is always wise to have their hearing checked, and to refer the child (with the permission of parents or carers) to a speech and language therapist for assessment and advice.

For older children, it can be more difficult to pick up evidence of special needs in language. Children of seven or over who have had an earlier history of

Table 10.1 Screening for language difficulties in the early years*

A 4-year-old should be able to (at a minimum)	A 5-year-old should in addition be able to (at a minimum)
Follow simple directions directed specifically at him or her	Follow general instructions given to class; manage to listen and play/work at the same time
Listen and attend to a short, simple repetitive story with pictures	Listen with interest to a more complex, unfamiliar story with pictures
Repeat correctly a sentence, such as 'We're having a visitor tomorrow' (10 syllables)	Repeat correctly a sentence like 'We're going to visit the market tomorrow' (12 syllables)
Give three objects in order – for example 'Give me the pencil, the book and the scissors'	Give four objects in order – for example 'Give me the book, the crayon, the pencil and the scissors'
Respond correctly to simple sentences with four information carrying words – for example '*Put* the *big balls* in the *box*'	Respond correctly to simple sentences containing five information carrying words – for example '*Open* the *book* and *colour* a *ball red*'
Understand concepts of size (big/little), and prepositions (in, on, under, behind)	Understand comparisons (bigger/heavier) and harder prepositions (in front of, above, between)
Understand and use what, where and who questions	Understand and use when and why questions
Use an average sentence length of 4–7 words	Use an average sentence length of 5 + words, but is often able to use even longer sentences with connectors such as 'and', 'but', 'so that' and 'because'
There may be omissions – for example, 'The boy (is) running fast'	There should no longer be omissions
Can relate events concerning self	Can relate stories; beginning to know the difference between fact and fantasy
Can use speech sounds m, n, p, b, t, d, w, and sometimes f, v, k and g	Can use k, g, f, v and sometimes s, z, sh, l, ch, j, and y but may not, until the age of about 7, use r, th and clusters of consonants (sp, fr, pl, etc.) correctly

* Adapted with kind permission from *Speech and Language Norms*, a guide for teachers produced by The Bath and District Health Authority Speech and Language Service. The full guide includes sections on listening and attention, comprehension, expressive language, speech, fluency and voice. It is available from The Speech and Language Therapy Service at Child Health, Newbridge Hill, Bath.

communication difficulties may still, however, have difficulty in articulating the finer sounds (such as consonant clusters), in sequencing events when re-telling a story, dealing with complex tenses and structures (especially passives, as in 'More roads had to be built'), and making adequate 'how', 'why', 'what if', 'what next' inferences. They may talk or write in a roundabout way, not completing sentences, or repeating themselves. Their writing may contain odd grammatical structures, with little grammatical joining words or word endings missed out – as in 'He go somewhere to get a ladder and try to open the window. He go to his friend house and phone his mum and dad'. They may be puzzled by indirect instructions (saying, for example, 'No thank you', in response to 'Would you like to join the story group now?'), and fail to understand irony, sarcasm and metaphor – so that a request to 'Pull up your socks' is taken literally.

Again, children with very specific language impairments as these are likely to benefit from referral to a speech and language therapist, so that a special programme of work can be drawn up and implemented – perhaps at school – in order to meet their needs. There are also commercially-available resources (such as *Teaching Talking* from NFER-Nelson) which enable schools to assess children's language difficulties themselves, in all but the most serious cases, and use their assessment to set priorities and plan language work to be done in a small group.

For the purposes of differentiating speaking and listening tasks within the national curriculum, the most useful forms of assessment will chart the child's progress on small steps within the five strands that make up the key stages 1 and 2 programmes of study. These are:

1 Participating as speakers and listeners in group discussion and conversation.
2 Listening and responding to stories and poems.
3 Responding to instructions and conveying information.
4 Describing real or imaginary events.
5 Asking and answering questions.

As an example, the small steps within the asking and answering questions strand might look something like this:

- Understands and uses what, where, who questions.
- Can answer a simple direct question requiring the child to tell about his or her own experiences.
- Can answer a simple open question requiring the child to talk about a TV programme or story.
- Understands and uses when, why, how, which questions.
- Uses grammatical inversion, e.g. 'I can go' – 'Can I go?'
- Uses restructuring of sentences, e.g. 'I need my coat' – 'Do I need my coat?'
- Can answer (in turn) a question put to everyone in the group.
- Puts simple questions to peers in order to make contact, or obtain information about immediate events.

- Can ask each person in the group a specific question in order to collect data, e.g. about favourite foods.
- Can role play the teacher, asking questions of others in the group.
- Can ask others for ideas in a group project.
- Uses questions to obtain information about abstract concepts and remote events, e.g. plays twenty questions.
- Can devise questions in order to follow a line of enquiry, e.g. plan an interview.
- Can respond to others' questions in order to guide them in completing an activity, designing or making something.
- Can in response to a question advocate and justify a point of view.

Another strand, listening and responding to stories and poems, might start with listening to simple repetitive picture stories on a one-to-one basis, go on to listening to a picture story in a small group, then in a class, then longer stories without pictures. The responding aspect would begin with joining in familiar rhymes, then go on to answering simple questions about stories and drawing pictures to illustrate them or acting them out. The next step would be contributing to group re-telling or 'finishing off'. At the next level, the child would discuss the characters and events in a story or poem, and say whether they liked it and why.

The response to instructions strand is particularly important in that if they have problems in this area, children are likely to fail right across the curriculum – and sometimes to get into trouble for apparently naughty behaviour as well. Teachers would do well to assess the stage reached in responding to instructions as a matter of course when any child presents learning or behaviour problems, so that they can adapt their classroom language appropriately, and also if necessary plan ways of gradually extending the amount of information the child can take in, remember and act on. A possible sequence of small steps might include:

- Can respond to directions if the adult goes up to the child, turns him or her to face the adult before speaking.
- Can respond to instructions when the teacher gives a preliminary alerting signal, names/looks at the child, and the child is not occupied.
- Responds to instructions containing three key, information carrying words, e.g. 'Put the *book* on *my table*', and to a single instruction, e.g. 'Choose the colours you want'.
- Can give a friend simple one-step instructions in pretend or constructional play.
- Responds to instructions containing four information carrying words, e.g. 'Put the *big balls under* the *table*'.
- Responds to general instructions given to the class when all are asked to stop what they are doing and listen.
- Responds to general instructions given to the class while doing something else at the time.

- Can take a written message to another teacher.
- Responds to complex sentences with five information carrying words, e.g. '*Find* your *book* and *colour* a *teddy red*', and to a two step instruction, e.g. 'Put your book away and then line up'.
- Can pass on the meaning of a simple instruction to another person – child or teacher, e.g. 'Ask her for the register please'.
- Can follow a simple three step instruction, e.g. 'Get out your maths book; find the page with the picture of buttons, and write in the numbers next to each set'.
- Can give two step instructions to another child in pretend or constructional play.
- Can give two step instructions to another child or group, which they follow in order to make something or complete a set task.
- Can respond to complex multi-step instructions such as 'Find a flower you'd like to use for your art work; decide what materials to use and then get to work in the area just outside the classroom'.
- Accurately conveys verbatim messages and telephone messages.
- Gives and follows precise instructions for playing a game, making a model, or conducting an experiment when pursuing a task individually or as part of a group.
- Guides other pupils in designing something.

In making a small-steps assessment of the stage that children have reached in speaking and listening skills, the teacher may choose to observe their response to standard tasks, such as those suggested for teacher assessment within the national curriculum. It is also very important, however, to try to discover from parents more about the range of language the child uses at home, since many children have language capabilities which they do not display in the school setting. It is also useful to gather information about the child as a speaker and listener over time, in a variety of contexts, using the methods suggested by the National Oracy Project (Norman, 1990), such as notepad jottings of verbatim quotations, audio or video taped samples of talk, or having an older child scribe a whole piece of talk about a picture or an artefact the child has made.

DEVELOPING EXPRESSIVE LANGUAGE

The national curriculum programmes of study for Speaking and Listening involve talking confidently in language which increasingly approximates standard English when appropriate, and is adapted to the needs of the listener. The current consensus of view amongst specialists in the education of children with speech and language disorders (Beveridge and Conti-Ramsden, 1987; Webster and McConnell, 1987) is that all these skills are best learned in a meaningful context where the child has a powerful reason to communicate, rather than through any form of drill.

This conclusion is based on research into the factors that seem to promote language development in young children (Wells, 1981; Wood, 1986). This has shown that both at home and in nursery classes, children make most progress when available adults foster real conversational interaction over a shared activity: when they take time to listen to the child's contribution, add something of their own, hand the conversation back to the child and give them space to respond, expand and paraphrase what the child has said in sentences just a little more linguistically complex than they are yet able to use. By contrast, language development is slowest when adults are unresponsive, or control the conversation with a string of closed questions, or with requests to the child to repeat something in correct form.

For children with expressive language difficulties this means that the first element in an action plan should be finding for them a regular, sympathetic adult listener (whether volunteer helper, parent, grandparent or classroom assistant).

The adult helper will foster conversation over all those classroom activities that are the traditional vehicles for talk: making things, finding out, cooking, drawing, role play in the home corner or home corner 'conversion' to hospital, cafe or bank. The helper can also be asked to read to the child, as often as possible, since we know this to be another major contributor to language development (Wells, 1981), and to share books with lots of detailed pictures to talk about, books without text where they can make up a story together, and interesting non-fiction.

There should be good access to story tapes at the listening centre, so that the child can recreate at will the experience of listening to a special story that has been read to them, and have extra repetition of its vocabulary and language structures.

Specific language structures the child may need help with can be practised, usually under the guidance of a speech and language therapist or language support teacher, in the context of turn-taking and games. For example, if the child is learning to use questions with inverted word order, the helper might unveil a complex picture bit by bit while the child has to guess as each new piece is revealed 'Is it a . . .?' Or, for regular and irregular past tenses, the child and helper might take turns to mime an action and ask each other, 'What did I do?'

Another technique that can be used to help the child learn new structures is the technique of forced alternatives. Here the helper or teacher asks questions which offer the child a choice of responses and an appropriate adult model. A child learning to describe future actions using 'going to' might, for instance, be asked, 'Are you going to draw now or are you going to play with the sand?'; if s/he produces only 'play sand' the adult can still expand this into correct form – 'Oh, I see; you're going to play with the sand', so that the child will have heard the correct model not just once, but three times. Similarly, a child learning vocabulary of 'bigger' and 'smaller', say, can be offered two pieces of paper and asked not 'Which one do you want?', but 'Do you want the bigger piece or the smaller piece?': the possibilities of the technique for expanding children's language skills in naturally-occurring classroom situations are endless.

Children with difficulties in word finding (retrieving words they know) – like David, whom we met earlier in the chapter – need to be encouraged to express themselves in whatever way they can: the emphasis should be on getting meaning across, even if in a roundabout manner. If, for example, the child should say 'You know . . . the place where . . . where you do the cooking and all that', the sympathetic listener will say 'Oh yes, in the kitchen, go on . . .', rather than build up tension and anxiety by waiting for the child to find the right word. These children can also practise, on other occasions, the skill of explaining word meanings – perhaps by giving a partner clues in a guessing game: 'It's an animal. You see it in the zoo. It has a hump and lives in desert.' If they have to be asked for the name of something in class, they should be cued in with an associated word or phrase ('needle and . . .', 'we cut wood with a . . .') if they are struggling to respond.

For most children, however, difficulties in expressing themselves fluently in school are more likely to be due to the lack of an appropriate vocabulary rather than to word-finding problems. The teacher's role is then one of helping to expand that vocabulary, most importantly by making sure the child has a chance to *listen* to a wide range of taped stories and non-fiction that uses mature vocabulary, and where the meaning of new words can become clear from the context.

For children who read reasonably well, reading itself will be the main means of vocabulary enrichment, but encouragement to make use of a thesaurus and dictionary when re-drafting writing will also help. Setting a daily puzzle ('What would you find in a belfry?') or asking children to research and find alphabetical adjectives (as in the old game 'the parson's cat is an avaricious/boisterous/corpulent cat') or alphabetical things for Podd to do (amble, banquet, canter) will expand vocabulary while providing practice in dictionary use at the same time.

Some children with expressive language difficulties need not so much help in acquiring new vocabulary and structures, as encouragement to use the language they already possess in order to convey meaning more precisely. Activities where one child has to give instructions to another in order to complete a task are helpful here, for example:

- Using software such as *Fantasy That* (from North West SEMERC); one child creates and prints a picture, and then has to give instructions to a partner at the keyboard ('Put a witch on the hill . . . put a dragon under the bridge') so that the partner can recreate the scenario – without showing the other child their picture.
- Using a box of materials varying in colour, texture, pattern, shape and size: one child silently chooses a piece and tries to describe it so the other can pick the right one.

- Having one child make a tape of instructions on how to make a model or how to use a particular piece of equipment, and seeing how successful the instructions are when a partner or group of children try to follow them.

Riddles and word games are another way of helping children to use precise language for particular purposes, and need not descend into drill if they have their own opportunity to invent their own puzzles for one another as well as respond to the teacher. Older children enjoy twenty questions, or games where they pick a pair of objects on the grounds of conceptual similarity and challenge the group to find out why they have put them together. Younger children like making up silly sentences ('water is dry . . . cars have four wings . . .') for others to repeat in correct form, or hiding objects and giving each other clues to help find them ('it's under something that tells the time . . . it's behind something square').

So far we have looked mainly at work that will help children to convey information and ask questions. What about another national curriculum strand, that of describing real and imaginary events? Often this is the area requiring the most careful differentiation of teaching approaches, with some children able early on to construct and tell an elaborate make believe story to a group, and others hardly progressing beyond an 'and then . . . and then . . . and then . . .' account of real experience.

At the earliest stages, children will be able to recount recent events at home or school to a small group, perhaps with the prompt of a set of pictures or photographs, or of direct questions about experiences recorded in a home– school diary. A step on from this, to less immediate but still highly personal story-telling, is the nice idea from the National Oracy Project team (Norman, 1990) of asking each child to bring in a photograph of themselves as toddlers, along with a story told to them by parents about something they did when they were little.

When it comes to talking about *imaginary* events, a small steps way in for some children may be asking them to describe, with support, 'pretend' events that happen to their favourite teddy bear or soft toy. For others, it may be re-telling simple, familiar stories in a round, taking turns with the teacher, then dramatizing the story, and finally re-telling it to a partner or parent with the help of pictures or drawings.

After preparation of this kind, children will be ready to work on story telling in mixed ability groups – the child with language difficulties placed in a small group where the other children are good communicators but also good at making space for others, and listening to them supportively. Children can be assigned roles within the group: those who find speaking and listening difficult asked to re-tell a story the teacher has introduced, others assigned to predict things that might happen after the story ends, others to lead the group in trying to make up their own new twist or version.

Or the children can work in pairs or threes of similar language ability; differentiation here will take the form of supplying less or more structure and props, according to need. One group might work around a concept keyboard overlay which provides a high degree of structure in the form of choices between sets of pictures 'Once upon a time there was . . . a princess/soldier/ mermaid who had a magic . . . finger/ring/box that could . . .?' Another group might be given a title and a set of stimulus pictures to sequence, while another would have the title alone.

RELUCTANT TALKERS

The new emphasis on talk within the national curriculum has made teachers more than ever concerned about children who are quiet in class and hardly talk at all. Some of these children may have specific language difficulties; others may have different reasons for reticence – their language capabilities are as good as other children's, but their personality or experiences make them reluctant to communicate. In extreme cases, this may amount to total refusal to speak to the teacher, or to other children, at all.

Assessing the needs of such children requires careful observation. Do they talk freely in group activities but not to adults? In the playground? At home? To whom do they talk? Is there evidence of real language difficulty in taped or scribed samples of their talk? Are they anxious and inhibited in a variety of situations, with many fears? Or are they strong willed by temperament, withholding speech stubbornly because they hate to give in?

Children who talk to peers but seldom to the teacher will need a slow process of relationship-building, and graded opportunities to communicate in non-threatening situations: talking on behalf of a puppet or from behind a mask, making a regular tape recording for the teacher to listen to in the car on the way to school, talking in a whisper or answering forced-alternative questions as a step towards more spontaneous communication.

Sometimes children fall into a pattern of not talking to adults at school, because they never need to – like this little girl, Charmaine:

> Charmaine was 6, and according to her mother 'a real chatterbox' at
> home. She spoke freely to a small group of friends at school, but
> never to the teacher. If she needed anything, she would send one of
> her friends to ask: 'Charmaine wants to go to the toilet,' 'Charmaine's
> not feeling very well.' Her teacher felt she was anxious and shy, and
> let this go on, hoping that eventually she would be able to win
> Charmaine's confidence. But Charmaine never did speak to the
> teacher, and a year later in a different class was still sending her
> friends to talk for her.

Teachers of children just starting school can often help to avoid later problems by pre-empting, at an early stage, the pattern of silence – like one reception teacher, who decided (successfully) to hold on to one mute little boy at breaktimes and ask him at first to whisper 'Yes' when she asked if he wanted to go out to play, later to speak in a normal voice, and later still to make the request himself.

If the pattern of withholding speech is entrenched, however, it is generally wise to seek advice, usually from an educational psychologist; one of the possibilities that will always need to be investigated is that a child's reluctance to speak is linked to the silence and secrecy that surrounds physical or sexual abuse.

Children who *do* talk freely to the teacher, but are self-conscious and quiet in group situations, require a different set of strategies. They need to have a regular 'talking partner', with whom they regularly share ideas and talk things out. Any group discussion can follow the twos/fours/eights pattern: a friendship pair start off by talking to one another, then join another pair to share their thoughts and conclusions, then another foursome. Becoming an expert on a particular topic, and passing on knowledge to younger classes or other visitors, will often help the reluctant talker to gain in confidence: in one class, for example, that had successfully hatched baby chicks in an incubator (National Oracy Project in Avon, 1991), each Year 9 child joined a partnership infant school as a visiting 'expert' to talk about the project, and had responsibility for giving information and answering questions when the younger children visited to see for themselves. The jigsaw groupwork pattern described in Chapter 3 is another way of casting quiet children in an expert role. And again, opportunities to take part *in role* in a group – behind a puppet or a mask as part of a group-composed story, or in drama – can free a child from the constraints of self-consciousness and allow them to use language with a new freedom.

SPEECH DIFFICULTIES

Speech and language therapists draw a distinction between what they call *language* difficulties (where children have difficulty in understanding spoken language or expressing themselves in appropriate grammatical structures and vocabulary), and difficulties that are confined to *speech* (articulating sound and words). Speech difficulties are in a sense easier for teachers to deal with than language difficulties, in that the problem is immediately evident, and very often short-term: relatively few children who start school with unclear speech are still unintelligible by the time they are six or seven. In another sense, however, speech difficulties are harder for teachers to manage: they feel immediately very concerned if they are unable to grasp what the child is saying, unsure of whether or how to correct the child's speech, and aware that s/he may react to not being understood by withdrawal or frustrated, angry behaviour.

Many of these difficulties can be avoided by using particular strategies:

- Encouraging the child to use gesture, drawings, showing a picture from a display or a book to help with communication.

- Trying to make time to offer several versions of what s/he might be saying.
- Trying not to get into the habit of asking the child questions that can be answered with yes or no. Instead use forced alternatives – for example, 'Did you go by bus or in the car?'
- Correcting speech by repeating back what the child has said. For example, if s/he says 'It lellow', say 'Oh, it's yellow, I see'.
- Keeping a home–school diary so that the teacher knows what the child is trying to say about events at home, and the parents know what the child is saying about events at school.
- Making sure there are opportunities for expressing frustration and communicating non-verbally – sand, water, dough, paint, puppets, hammering toys.
- Making plenty of opportunities for the child to talk to the teacher over a shared experience; when both are doing the same thing the child's meaning will be clearer, and s/he will be able to feel s/he is being 'understood'. Examples are the teacher joining in a pretend game, or joint story composition on the concept keyboard.
- Speaking slowly and clearly to the child, so that s/he will be able to see and hear the sounds being made.

It will be sensible to have the child's hearing checked regularly, particularly if s/he is prone to colds and catarrh. In addition, advice on how to help the child achieve clearer speech should be sought from the speech and language therapist. The therapist is likely to emphasize developing listening and discrimination skills before moving on to work on specific sound production.

Some children with unclear speech may be later in learning to read and write than other children, but not all. As long as they are never put into a situation of failure by being expected to read aloud *to* an anxious or impatient adult before they are ready, however, there is no need to postpone ordinary early literacy activities. Shared or paired reading at home and at school, particularly of familiar and oft-repeated stories, and making books that build on the child's own language in conjunction with photographs and drawings, are likely to be helpful to children with all kinds of expressive language problems. Nor is there necessarily any need to avoid the teaching of sound–symbol relationships: indeed, since many children with speech difficulties have the kind of poor phonological awareness of sound patterns in spoken words that is implicated in many cases of severe and persistent reading difficulty (Bryant and Bradley, 1985), there may be even more need than usual to include in their early teaching a wide range of activities to promote sound awareness and mastery of sound symbol links. Such activities will be described later in this chapter.

DEVELOPING RECEPTIVE LANGUAGE

Children who do not seem able to listen to, understand or remember what is said to them are harder to spot than those with expressive language difficulties, but often even more disadvantaged in making progress within the whole curriculum. Assessing children's progress in the national curriculum language strands of participating as listeners in a group, listening to stories and poems, and responding to instructions is, however, now helping teachers to become more aware of such receptive language difficulties.

Receptive language difficulties can arise because the children are following a normal course of language development, but at a slightly slower rate than their peers – perhaps because of the quality of the language they have experienced in the past, or perhaps because of a family pattern of language delay. Or they may have fallen behind in their language because they have had a period of hearing loss: even minor, fluctuating losses caused by repeated ear infections or intermittent catarrh can have long-lasting effects on the child's developing vocabulary and listening skills. Others again – a very small group – may have a very specific language disorder, which means they are more than just a bit late in understanding complex language: they are actually developing differently and can have major problems in making sense of what they hear.

If a check indicates that the child's difficulties may be due to mild to moderate hearing loss, the teacher can help by making sure that s/he can make maximum use of lipreading as an aid to comprehension: placing the child near her, speaking clearly (but at a normal rate) in a good light, never speaking when turned away from the child – for example, to face the blackboard. Attempts should also be made to reduce background noise as much as possible, especially by using a quiet carpeted area for listening activities. If the loss is greater in one ear than the other, the child will need to be positioned carefully so that the 'good' ear is near the teacher; if a hearing aid is worn, it will be important for the teacher to check regularly that it is working properly, and to remember that aids only function really effectively over a 2–3 metre distance. Other useful strategies for children with any hearing loss include cueing them in carefully to the topic of discussion, avoiding unsignalled changes of topic, using visual supports such as pictures or writing key vocabulary on the blackboard, and making sure they can always turn to a normally hearing peer helper for clarification of information and instructions when required.

Assuming that hearing checks have been done, and for the more severe difficulties a speech and language therapist consulted, the teacher's main task for any child with comprehension difficulties, however caused, is to make sure that messages are getting across in the classroom – so that the children are not at a loss in learning from the start because they do not understand what they are supposed to do, or how they are supposed to go about it. It may help to:

- Get the child's attention – before you speak, call the child's name, make sure s/he is standing still and looking, or give a signal like 'Listen carefully'. Give directions before, not during an activity.
- Avoid speaking out of the blue and out of context: try to establish a background to the conversation, so that the child will be cued in from the start.

- Go up close – go up to the child to speak, rather than talk across a busy classroom.
- Place the child in a position where s/he can pick up what is happening by watching the other children, but also where the teacher can easily keep a look out to see if s/he has understood.
- Say it again – give the child time to respond and then, if necessary, repeat what you said *in the same words* – rephrasing may only confuse.
- Use pictures, demonstration and gesture to help get across a point.
- Break it down – break long and complicated questions or instructions into shorter units, for example 'When you've coloured the stars cut them out and stick them on the black paper' into 'Colour the stars. Cut them out. Then stick them on to the black paper', or 'Show me the long red pencils' into 'Show me the pencils. Show me the long pencils. Now show me the long, red pencils'.
- Put the main message last – make sure that the important parts of a message are at the end: not 'Fetch your PE bags; you'll need to take them with you to the hall straight after our television programme', but 'After the television programme, you're going straight to the hall – so fetch your PE bags now'.
- Check for understanding by asking the child to explain to you what s/he's been asked to do, and watch him or her start any new task. Give praise whenever the child asks for an instruction to be repeated or explained.
- Watch your words. Always ask yourself if the child is actually understanding words you use: for example, in number work does s/he know what 'each side of', 'altogether', 'larger number', 'the number before . . . after . . .' mean? Be consistent with the vocabulary you use – for example always using 'take away' until this is established, before introducing 'minus' and 'subtract'.
- Let the child's friends help. When you are busy, appoint a friend to repeat instructions and if necessary demonstrate the task.
- Be prepared for bad behaviour if the child has to spend a long time listening to language s/he cannot understand. When you can, give him or her another task during long assemblies and stories. When you cannot, warn the child of the need to sit still and be ready with a small reward – like a gold star – if she succeeds. Try if possible to have a helper or parent tell a story to the child by him or herself, or in a small group, before s/he is expected to listen at class story time.

To help develop children's ability to respond to stories and poems, to listen in a group, and follow instructions, teachers might want to consider setting up a small language group, made up of children with receptive language difficulties, who work with a volunteer helper or classroom assistant for a short period each day, as did St. Agnes Primary School:

> The reception teacher described her main difficulty with the class as 'getting them to sit still and listen'. There were several children

whose attention span was short, who seemed oblivious to classroom instructions (despite normal hearing), and unable to participate in group discussion of any kind. With the help of a visiting support teacher, she worked out a programme of listening games and activities, which her very good classroom assistant was able to do for 10–15 minutes most days over an eight-week period. Work started with very simple activities: listening to a tape of sounds the children might hear in the house and identifying them, listening with eyes shut to various musical instruments and picking out the one that was played, playing the game called 'Keys to the Kingdom' where keys are passed round a circle with one child blindfolded in the centre trying to point to where s/he thinks the keys might be. Each session ended with a short story told or read to the group.

Over the next few weeks, games with words were introduced. The children played a shopping game with grocery packets, responding to and giving one another instructions to 'buy' two, three or four items. They played 'Simon Says'; they passed whispered messages around the group, and enjoyed the ever-popular Smarties game: the helper would drop three or four coloured Smarties into a tube, saying each colour as it went in, and the child would have to remember and replicate the order with his or her own tube in order to get to eat the contents. They played 'Eligibility': 'Stand up everyone who is wearing grey socks', 'Stand up everyone who is wearing grey socks and has long hair'. In their special story time, they had now to listen for deliberate mistakes, or spot target names or words whenever they cropped up in the story.

Finally, the group went on to games like Kim's game (with words rather than objects), to following sequences of instructions in order to build a model or complete a drawing, and to listening to each other recount news. At this stage, they were able to listen to some stories without many pictures, and to begin to be able to predict outcomes and discuss events and characters.

For schools that have listening centres, there is a good range of listening skills/language comprehension materials on cassette, from publishers such as Learning Development Aids and Learning Materials Ltd. Teachers can also make their own tape recordings relating to duplicated pictures ('On your picture you will see a row of houses. Colour the first door red. Now find the largest window, and give it some frilly pink curtains'), things to draw ('Draw a round pond. Then put some water lilies on the pond, and some reeds all around the outside'), or constructional materials ('Make a wall two bricks high out of green Lego bricks. At one end add a square tower of red bricks'). There should always be a model ('Here's one I made earlier . . .') so that children can check their success in following the tape.

REMEMBERING INSTRUCTIONS AND INFORMATION:
PROBLEMS IN SHORT-TERM MEMORY

In older children, the most restricting legacy of earlier language difficulties is often poor short-term memory for things they hear. Each of us has only a limited capacity for taking in, and remembering, information while we process it – either by acting on it immediately or transferring it to our more permanent long-term memory. For many children with special educational needs, instructions all too often exceed the limits of what can be remembered; their capacity may be smaller than that of their peers, or their strategies for rehearsing information within the short-term memory to keep it available may be less well developed.

The easiest way to assess short-term memory is to ask the child to repeat either strings of digits (at a rate of about one per second), or short sentences. The average four-year old can recall three digits in correct sequence, or a sentence containing ten syllables. The average 5-year-old can recall four numbers, and a sentence of 12 syllables or longer; the average 6- to 7-year-old recalls five numbers, and the average 8- to 9-year-old six or more numbers.

Children with poor short-term memories can also be spotted by their difficulties in following instructions and organizing themselves for learning. Given an instruction about several tasks they have to complete during the day, they may forget all or part; they may find it hard, too, to hold a sequence of events in mind – so that they constantly forget to bring swimming kit on the right day, or always appear at the wrong place at the wrong time with the wrong equipment. Their written work, relying as it does on the child holding an overall plan and the parts they have already written in short-term memory, may appear disjointed and disorganized. They may seem, often wrongly, like all-round slow learners, because what the teacher says does not stick in their minds for long enough to make the necessary transfer to long-term memory.

With the right bypass strategies, however, many of these difficulties can be overcome. The first essential is for the teacher to adjust the complexity of his or her language when giving instructions. It is surprising how complex, in terms of memory load, is much of the language we use in school. A recent five-minute sample in a Reception/Year 1 class in an infant school, yielded the following examples:

> 'When you come in from washing your hands you should sit at the back not the front because if you sit right at the front all the others have to climb over you to find somewhere to sit.'

> 'Now tomorrow or maybe the day after that depending on whether the weather's good and we have sports day we'll ask the juniors to write some prayers for us to say at our assembly.'

Shorter, simpler instructions are one way round the problem of memory overload; the teacher should be prepared to highlight key points, sequence the items clearly and avoid excess verbiage that will only serve to confuse the issue. When children are able to read reasonably well, key points can be written down on a postcard or sticky Post-it and attached to their desk; for younger children a series of drawings might be substituted. One teacher gives children with poor organizational skills a special diary, with each page divided into sections; to begin with she writes just one task in one section, having them bring the diary and their work back to her when this is complete, so that she can write the next instruction. She then slowly builds up the number of sections she fills in at the start of the day, until within a few weeks the child is using the diary to help them organize and sequence an entire morning's work.

For writing, using a story planner sheet at the planning stage helps get over the problem of the child not being able to hold the whole story in mind as s/he writes; some children have also had success by tape recording their whole story, then playing it back bit by bit in order to write it down.

Short-term memory can be improved, by regular practice in taking messages and playing memory games like 'I went to market and bought . . .', or 'I'm going on a trip; in my suitcase I put . . .', where each child repeats the preceding items and adds one of his/her own. Nevertheless, to some extent, limited memory capacity is something children and teachers have to learn to live with; the challenge is to help children find their own independent ways around the problem – like always carrying a notebook and pen to jot down instructions and make lists of things to do, or learning to repeat instructions to themselves over and over again as they go to carry them out, or being very organized about checking calendars and timetables carefully when sorting out equipment that is needed for school.

CURRICULUM ACCESS FOR CHILDREN WITH COMMUNICATION DIFFICULTIES

So far, we have looked at ways in which teachers can use bypass strategies to help children with difficulties in understanding and remembering complex language to access the curriculum – mainly by adjusting the way they themselves talk to individuals or groups in the class.

The important principle in all this is that children should not be held back by language barriers from getting to grips with the curriculum. For example, in maths they should not be prevented from exploring practical and written division operations because they do not understand the meaning of the word 'each' in problems of the kind 'How many can they have each?'; in science they should not be prevented from exploring the properties of objects because they have not yet mastered negatives and do not understand the question, 'Which ones will *not* float/keep out water/get hot in the sun?'; in history they should not be kept from appreciating a sequence of events because they have not grasped the language of 'before' and 'after'. There are always other ways of getting these concepts across, using language that all of the children will be able to understand.

Similarly, when it comes to expressing their own ideas – particularly in assessment situations – it is important that children are not disadvantaged by linguistic constraints. Often we ask children to use language to 'group' 'compare', 'describe' and 'discuss': all activities which will penalize some children, unless their teachers remember assessment guidelines (SEAC, 1992) that children can 'convey what they know and understand by any means appropriate to them: talk, writing, gesture, pictures, models'. They should be encouraged, whenever possible, to develop an oral response when one is required by using pictures and props to aid their talk, by practising first with a 'talking partner', by being assessed on an individual basis rather than in a group. Sometimes even this will not be enough, and the teacher needs to accept that it is enough for children with language difficulties to complete a task, without also having to explain what they did and why.

PLAYING WITH LANGUAGE: AWARENESS OF SOUNDS IN WORDS

A final aspect of work on special needs in language concerns the auditory skills of awareness of sound patterns in words that underpins successful development in reading and spelling. Many young children with language difficulties have problems in this area. They are uncertain when words sound the same: when they begin (alliteration) or end (rhyme) with the same sound. They may not realize, for example, that a word like 'cat' is made up not of one sound but of several, or that it has something at the beginning that sounds like the start of 'cup', and something at the end in common with 'bat' and 'rat'. Without this kind of awareness, they are unable later on to accurately map written symbols against their spoken equivalents. They go on, as much research has now demonstrated (Share et al., 1984; Bryant and Bradley, 1985), to do less well in literacy development than their peers.

Again, however, this is a pattern that is preventable, given appropriate intervention in the early years of school. Research has shown that even small amounts of special practice with rhyme and alliteration in relation to letter patterns, for children initially assessed as having poor phonological skills, appears to produce substantial and long-lasting gains in later measured literacy skills. In these studies, 5- and 6-year-old children who were initially poor at picking the 'odd one out' of groups of spoken words by rhyme or initial sound were given 6–10 hours of training in these skills, spread out over two years. At the end of this training, they were on average in reading 10 months ahead of children who had had extra individual attention but not specifically rhyme and alliteration work. In spelling they were 17 months ahead. What is more, these initial gains seem to be maintained over long periods: four years after the training ended, the children who had the special teaching were approximately two years ahead of the control group in reading, and at least 14 months in spelling.

To reproduce these effects, teachers can use an informal checklist (Table 10.2)

Table 10.2   Checklist for identifying children with little awareness of alliteration and rhyme

---

1 Can think of a word to complete an unfamiliar rhyme
2 Can identify a part of his/her body that rhymes with

peg   sand   rose

or pick an object from a group supplied that rhymes with an object picked from a feely bag
3 Responds with understanding to wordplay such as deliberate errors in familiar rhymes, e.g.

Little Miss Muffet   *Old King Cole*
Sat on a chair   *Was a merry old* man

4 Can succeed in a group lotto game where each child covers pictures that start the same as the one the teacher holds up
5 Can join in, correctly, a game of initial sound 'I Spy' using objects placed in front of the group
6 Can line up on the basis of alliteration – 'all those whose name starts like *r*hinoceros'

---

to pick out those children in infant classes who have poor awareness of sound patterns in words. These children will need a rich diet of rhymes and word play – everything from alliterative alphabet books to nursery rhymes and counting rhymes and finger rhymes – for sharing at home. Parent workshops might also include sorting or spotting games with objects and pictures, where children are helped to find the ones that start with the same sound, and traditional games like 'I Spy', or 'I'm thinking of something in the room that rhymes with . . .'.

In school, there should be time spent on class projects on rhyme and word play. Children will enjoy creating their own class rhyming slang to baffle visitors, or composing tongue-twisters and limericks. Much exciting work can be built around tape recorded and written compilations of playground rhymes, from other generations as well as current favourites.

Class books can be made based on alliteration of the children's names ('Laura likes lollipops . . . Surinda likes sweets'). Feely bags with collections of objects that start the same, or rhyme, are good to feel and guess at. Many other traditional games, such as snap, or grandmother's footsteps ('Take two steps forward if you can say a word that rhymes with bed') can be adapted to rhyme and alliteration. Children can alter well-known songs and rhymes in the manner of 'Happy Birthday to you, Squashed tomatoes and stew'. They can swap initial sounds around in jokes and riddles (what do you get if you cross a labrador and a poodle – a pabrador and a loodle), and illustrate the results. They can experiment with taking away initial sounds, on a day when everyone has to address each other by name with first sound deleted – 'om' for Tom, 'iss' for Miss. They can work in groups with a set of pictures in the middle: one child says the name of a picture sound by sound, and the others have to guess which one s/he means.

As a result of activities like these, children should be able to analyse the spoken sounds that make up words they hear, tell when words start the same, or when they rhyme, and categorize picture cards accordingly. It only remains to help them make the links with written symbols, in the manner of Bradley and Bryant's original research: the teacher or helper puts out plastic letters to make one of the words in a rhyming or alliterative set, and asks the child to choose another picture and make the word him or herself. Initially the child will sweep away all of the letters of the first word and start afresh; over time they learn, for example, that the plastic letter 'p' can stay in place for a set of words like 'pen', 'pig' or 'pot', or the 'all' letter string stay in place with only the first letter changing in rhyming words such as 'ball', 'fall', 'call'. In this way, the child discovers some of the principles that underly the way written language works: their difficulties in oral language become less likely to spill over into the kind of long-lasting literacy difficulties that are the subject of the next two chapters.

FURTHER READING

Webster, A. and McConnell, C. (1987) *Children with Speech and Language Difficulties*. London, Cassell.

· 11 ·

SPECIAL NEEDS IN READING

INTRODUCTION

Paul and Daniel are both 9-years-old. Both struggle with reading and written recording, though they are both as bright as most children their age, and in some ways (technology, science) more able. They go to different schools. Paul is lucky. In his school, there is a part-time special needs support teacher, funded from the school's own budget, who works with him for half-an-hour each day, four days a week, on a carefully planned programme which mixes reading lots of exciting books with learning letter–sound relationships in a highly structured and cumulative way. The support teacher also works closely with Paul's class teacher to make sure that he has help with texts and written recording in his class work.

Daniel is not so lucky. His teacher feels that he is 'just a slow learner', and that he perhaps has not learned to read because of lack of support from home. She tries very hard to give him extra help, and manages to hear him read for a short time several times a week. There is a shortage of books at his level, however, and he seems to be switching off more and more from any effort to improve his skills. Increasingly, he is unable to participate in ordinary classroom work because he cannot read information books for topic work, or even the instructions in his maths book.

These two children are typical of many with literacy difficulties. The outcome for each of them, in terms of future educational success and post-school opportunities, is likely to be very different: the inequities are stark, but not at all unusual. That they persist is a scandalous indictment of our educational system, which often fails to equip teachers of junior-aged children with the necessary skills and confidence to teach reading to the many children who have not acquired even basic literacy skills at the end of Key Stage 1, and fails to fund the kind of provision that we know could prevent the misery of long-term reading failure, if only we cared enough to supply it.

Reading difficulties are very common. In their report on the teaching and learning of reading in primary schools (HMI, 1990c) HMI observed that of Year 6 children whose reading was assessed, 'approximately a quarter were functioning at a fairly low level for their age, including a very small but significant proportion, approximately one in twenty, who were hardly able to read at all'. One in twenty: enough to mean that most primary teachers will have at least one or two children in their class who are unable to read well enough to cope with curricular demands.

What is more, the great majority of these children are of perfectly ordinary general ability, and not particularly 'backward' or slow learning: they have difficulties that are *specific* to literacy. One survey, for example, found that between 4 and 10 per cent of all school-aged children had such specific reading difficulties, defined as reading at a level 28 months or more below prediction from their age and general intellectual ability (Berger et al., 1975).

What do ordinary classroom teachers need to know about teaching these children? First, it is important that they be aware of the high frequency of specific reading difficulties, and that they take care to avoid any assumption that poor readers necessarily need a slower pace to all their learning than children who pick up reading quickly. Instead, the children may only need access to the kinds of bypass strategies that will be detailed later in this chapter: strategies that will make sure they can still get on with their work and have a chance to succeed despite their problems in coping with texts.

Second, the class teacher needs to be able to work out an action plan for teaching the child to read and write, using a wider range of strategies than just hearing them read more often than others, and using strategies that have some proof of past success attached to them – based on the outcomes of careful evaluative research rather than whatever the current educational fad or orthodoxy may prescribe.

These effective, proven strategies fall into four broad groups, which we will consider in more detail later in the chapter:

- Those aimed at increasing the child's contact with print.
- Those aimed at extending the number of channels through which the child can learn.
- Those aimed at ensuring overlearning of core sight vocabulary and letter–sound relationships.
- Those aimed at increasing the learner's self-esteem and overcoming the anxiety and loss of confidence that often accompanies reading failure.

Finally, the class teacher needs to be able to make a careful assessment of children's literacy skills, and monitor closely the outcomes of any intervention. Such assessment and monitoring has been missing from much recent primary practice, a situation that the pre-Dearing national curriculum, with its emphasis on the *applications* of reading (range, response, study skills) at the expense of the actual *fluency* in reading which is the stumbling block for most children with long-term reading difficulties, did little to remedy.

ASSESSING READING DIFFICULTIES

Miscue analysis, keywords and phonics

One positive thing that the early national curriculum did do for children with reading difficulties was to introduce more and more primary teachers – through the Key Stage 1 SATs – to the miscue analysis approach to the assessment of reading skills. In miscue analysis, the teacher analyses the child's errors or 'miscues' when reading aloud, in order to discover which cueing strategies (visual, phonic, meaning) the child is able to apply when s/he meets an unknown word. The analysis will show whether the child is an 'overpredictive' or an 'underpredictive' reader. Overpredictive readers are good at inventing what they think the words should say (using meaning and grammatical cues), but not at checking their predictions against the graphic cues on the page. They appear fluent, but are often wildly inaccurate. They need to have their attention directed, when reading aloud, to initial and final letters, letter strings, word length – anything that will encourage them to focus on visual detail. Underpredictive readers (a larger group) need the opposite kind of support. They tend to read word by word, with little expression, sounding out words a letter at a time when they come to them and paying little attention to the overall meaning. They need to do a lot of talking about what they are reading; to listen to books on cassette and to tapes of themselves reading; to engage in oral cloze work using context and first letter to predict words the teacher leaves out; to read back passages and always ask 'Did that make sense?'

Miscue analysis needs to be supplemented, for the purpose of establishing appropriate readability levels for texts the child is asked to cope with in class, and for the purpose of monitoring progress, with a norm-referenced assessment that will yield a measure of reading age. Several of the more up-to-date assessment tools (such as NFER's very useful Individual Reading Analysis and New Reading Analysis) incorporate both miscue analysis and an assessment of the child's overall reading level. They take only about 5–15 minutes to administer, and fall comfortably into the province of the classroom teacher rather than the special needs coordinator or reading 'specialist'. They have the additional advantage of providing separate scores for the child's decoding and comprehension skills, enabling the teacher to pick out those children who may be expert at decoding but have no idea of what they are reading about, or those, conversely, who have good enough language skills to get the general gist of texts even though they have a very limited sight vocabulary and stumble over almost every word.

Other straightforward assessment tools available to the classroom teacher include keywords lists (the words children will meet most often in their reading, and need to know; see Table 11.1), and lists of regular words exhibiting the main

Table 11.1 Keywords to literacy (Source: Mcnally and Murray, 1984)

in	was	is	I	he
it	a	the	that	to
and	of	are	for	you
had	so	have	said	as
not	they	with	one	we
on	his	at	him	all
but	old	be	up	do
can	me	came	my	new
get	she	here	has	her
will	an	no	or	now

phonic conventions, from three-letter consonant–vowel–consonant words to consonant blends, vowel blends, silent 'e', silent initial letters and prefixes/ suffixes. Oliver and Boyd's Domain Test of Phonic Skills has word lists that save teachers making up their own, or a convenient assessment pack that includes miscue analysis, concepts of print, sight vocabulary and word lists to assess phonic knowledge (RAT-pack) is available from Wiltshire County Council.

Using tools such as these, the teacher will be able to establish which of the small steps on the road to fluent decoding the child has mastered, and what the next steps in the teaching programme might be – whether improved use of a particular cueing system, or a new set of keywords to be practised, or a new phonic convention introduced.

Diagnostic assessment

Beyond the assessment of reading age, use of cue systems and sight vocabulary/ phonic skills we enter the realms of 'diagnostic' assessment, to which a great deal of (largely unnecessary) mystique has attached itself. The mystique has been based on an earlier assumption in the world of reading remediation that in order to construct an adequate teaching programme for children with read- ing difficulties, it was necessary to establish their profile of strengths and weaknesses in underlying perceptual and memory skills – to diagnose the root cause of the reading failure in order to discover the appropriate remedy. This meant the use of elaborate packages of tests, based on complicated theories of the reading process, which many teachers found daunting.

As we saw in Chapter 4, however, research has failed as yet to support the effectiveness of this model. In its place, we can for the moment put a much simpler notion of 'diagnosis', based on the small-steps idea. If a child seems unable to learn something, we can ask what are the necessary prior skills or sub-steps which make that piece of learning possible, and try to find out where in the chain the point of breakdown for a particular child might be.

As an example, it is no good expecting a child to acquire a sight vocabulary if s/he cannot yet reliably discriminate a word from others that may look quite similar. So if children are having difficulty in remembering words out of context, it would be useful to assess this level of visual discrimination by having them match individual words on cards with those in their reading books (particularly words with visually confusable letters such as i/l, h/n, f/t, b/p/d, r/n and c/o/a), and introduce extra practice if necessary. It will also be useful to look for signs of visual sequencing difficulties: children who constantly lose their place on the page, skip lines, or misread the order of letters in words may benefit from using a linetracker, and a brightly coloured card placed down the left-hand side of any page they are working on, to act as a reference point for the left-to-right sequence. A referral for a full assessment of the child's vision (to include investigation of convergence, accommodation, tracking, binocular control and reference eye as well as the conventional tests of visual acuity) should also be considered.

If visual discrimination and sequencing are not the problem, the point of breakdown in acquiring a sight vocabulary may be further down the chain, at the level where the child has to *remember* what the words look like. Showing single words and asking the child to pick them out on a page from memory is one way of assessing this skill of visual recall, which if weak can sometimes be improved by giving practice in the look–cover–write–check strategy for learning spellings, or by asking the child to try to 'carry a picture' of a word in their head from a word bank or picture dictionary or piece of paper, while they go back to their seat, rather than copy-write it directly.

So far we have looked at visual skills; for many children, however, the point of breakdown may lie elsewhere – in auditory skills. Since learning to decode printed words involves learning to match a pattern of written letters with a pattern of spoken sounds, children need to be able to discriminate and recall what they hear as well as what they see. They need to be able to detect similarities and differences between spoken sounds, to segment spoken words into their constituent parts (so as to be able to work out independently how these parts are represented in print), and to handle the opposite process of blending separate sounds and syllables into whole words.

Tests are available for assessing auditory discrimination (for example, in NFER's well-known Neale Reading Analysis), but more informally the teacher will be able to spot children with difficulties by the errors they make in reading and spelling – confusing similar-sounding pairs like d/t, m/n, k/g, p/b, a/u, and e/i. If a child has very pronounced auditory discrimination problems, a hearing check should be requested – though more often than not the difficulty is one of central processing rather than peripheral 'hearing'. Children with poor auditory discrimination need to be helped to find ways around the problem, by learning for example to articulate the words very clearly to themselves as they write, by using visual mnemonics (like those in the Letterland materials) to help them master the confusable short vowel sounds, or moving on to learning the easier-to-discriminate long vowel sounds even though they may not have fully mastered the short vowels.

Ways of assessing children's ability to segment words into their constituent sounds, and recognize when and how some words sound the same, were described in Chapter 10, along with strategies the teacher can use to help children improve their phonological awareness. For sound blending, the child can be asked to guess a word the teacher says slowly, sound by sound (at a rate of about one sound per second): i-n, u-p, l-i-p, b-a-g, etc. The aim is to find out whether the child can cope with blending two sounds, or three, or four: less than three, there is little chance that they will be able to benefit from phonic teaching (beyond predicting words from their initial letter) without some extra practice. This can be achieved by having the child work with a helper to blend – at a purely oral level – short then longer words they are about to meet in their reading books. Children can also be taught how to circumvent the difficulty by blending not separate sounds when reading but initial letter and final letter string (f-ill, s-eat), or blending no more than two sounds at a time ('frog' as f-fr-fro-frog, for example).

The model of diagnostic assessment that is suggested here (summarized in Figure 11.1) does not pretend to be comprehensive. It is practically oriented, aiming to supply information on only those aspects of prior or underlying skill that are critical to the child's progress, and which we can actually do something about. If the model is applied to every child with a reading difficulty it should, however, enable the class teacher – perhaps with a little help from the special needs coordinator – to develop individualized teaching strategies that are more finely tuned than those required by the child who is making normal progress in reading.

INCREASING CONTACT WITH PRINT

Considering that the average teacher in a top infant class spends only 2–3 per cent of his or her time on the teaching of reading (Tizard et al., 1982), it is surprising that so many children succeed in acquiring the rudiments of literacy at all. For all children, an increase in the time spent on reading would be beneficial; for children with reading difficulties, who need much more exposure to words before they can remember them, increasing reading time is even more important.

For them, the effects of reading failure on exposure to print are cumulative and negative: it has been shown, for example, that children making slow reading progress in their first year at school read only an estimated 5000 words, compared to the 20 000 read by children who were making good progress (Clay, 1979).

Yet classroom or school-wide systems which aim to increase the amount of time spent on reading-related activities – such as USSR (Uninterrupted Sustained Silent Reading), ERIC (Everyone Reading In Class), or book floods –

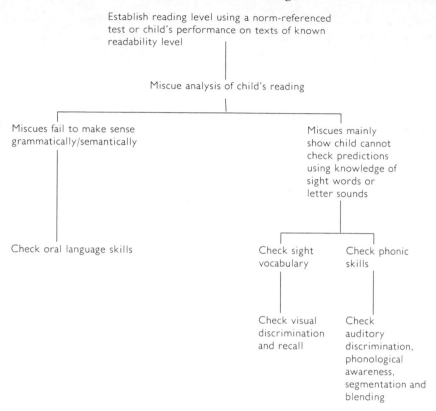

Figure 11.1 A model for assessing reading difficulties.

are unlikely, of themselves, to do much to improve the skills of poor readers, even though they remain vital for fostering interest in, and enjoyment of, books. Poor readers lack sufficient decoding ability to be able to get to grips with texts alone. What they need is some form of regular, frequent *supported* reading practice.

It is unlikely that the class teacher, or even a support teacher, will be able to partner the child in supported reading with sufficient regularity and frequency to be worth while. Reading with children is a time-consuming business, and by and large an individual one: teachers, on the whole, have little time to teach individuals – only groups, or classes. They are just too busy. One group of researchers (Southgate-Booth et al., 1981), for example, found that although children in Years 3 and 4 might be 'heard to read' for three of four minutes at a time now and then, the actual amount of time the teacher was able to concentrate on helping the pupil was on average only 30 seconds in each three- or four-minute period, because his or her attention was constantly required elsewhere.

Given this shortage of teacher time, it makes sense for schools to turn to all possible alternative ways of providing supported reading practice – to peer tutoring, parental involvement, volunteer helper schemes, *group* work on reading with the teacher, and schemes that require no helper present at all, such as taped libraries and computer-aided reading.

Paired reading

One approach that offers children maximum exposure to print, with the chance to learn from a correct model, and read with as much or as little support as they feel they require, is paired reading (Topping and Wolfendale, 1985). Not to be confused with the many other kinds of reading practice called shared, or shared-and-paired reading, paired reading proper follows a particular, tightly structured format:

- Peer, parent or volunteer helper commit themselves to 10 or 15 minutes of reading with the child, preferably daily, for a fixed period (usually of about 6 to 8 weeks).
- The child chooses the reading material, which can be anything at all that they want to read, however difficult.
- The helper and child begin by reading simultaneously, with the helper pointing to the words as s/he goes along.
- When the child feels able to read a little on his/her own, s/he gives an agreed signal – such as a knock or a nudge – and the helper stops reading.
- The child reads alone until s/he makes a mistake or gets stuck. The helper then gives the correct word (not leaving the child to struggle with it for more than about five seconds); the child repeats it and the helper joins in again until the child next signals a wish to read independently.
- The helper praises the child frequently for reading words correctly and for signalling to read alone.

Paired reading has been extensively evaluated (Topping, 1990); typically children make progress in reading over the tutoring period at three or four times the normal classroom rate.

Apprenticeship approaches

Some researchers (e.g. Lindsay et al., 1985) have questioned whether the formal structure of paired reading is a necessary ingredient in successful supported reading, and produced evidence to show that other more 'relaxed' approaches to reading together can be equally effective. Felicity Craig (1990), one of the best recent writers on supporting children with reading difficulties, recommends immersing poor readers in good-quality children's books, with the adult reading *to* the child (preferably daily) for about 15 minutes, encouraging the child to follow the print by running a pencil or finger under the words, then stopping for the child to read back a particularly exciting couple of paragraphs aloud: if the child gets stuck on a word it should be supplied after five seconds or so, with no attempt to make him or her 'work it out'. Again, there is an emphasis on frequent, enthusiastic praise.

In other approaches the child and helper can alternate pages, or paragraphs, or the child can engage in 'repeated reads' (Reason and Boote, 1986): first the peer or helper reads a page or short piece to the child, the child and helper read it simultaneously, then the child reads it with prompts where necessary, and then (if the child would enjoy sharing the book with others), the child reads it to parents, or siblings, or a partner in a younger class, or to a friend.

The essential element in all these approaches is the absence of any possibility of failure, or of any element of performance or being on show – that is, until the child feels really ready for it. The aim is to get through as many exciting books as possible, quickly and enjoyably, rather than struggle painfully through a reading book. Other elements may well be needed in the total reading programme, to provide perhaps more opportunities for over-learning of a key sight vocabulary, or explicit teaching of sound–symbol relationships, but supported reading in one form or another, *in quantity*, is the very first thing to try, and the one essential that must run alongside any other type of programme, so that the child (and teacher) do not lose sight of what real reading is all about.

Taped reading material

Sitting in the book corner or at the listening centre, following text that has been put on to cassette, lacks the interactive element of sharing pleasure in a good book. Nevertheless, when human help is limited, it can be an effective alternative means of providing supported reading practice. In one project (Dring, 1989), for example, pupils who had regular story cassette input (while following the print at the same time) made twice as much progress in reading as children who also had extra small-group language support with a special needs teacher, but without the extra practice with tapes.

Providing a cassette library need not be expensive, or time consuming for the teacher. Having older, more fluent readers work in groups to prepare the tapes will give them practice in reading for a purpose, and in research and design as they experiment with, for example, appropriate reading speeds and end of page pauses. It will also, if some of the tapes they prepare are not story tapes but tapes of reference materials, have the added bonus of increasing curriculum access in science and humanities for children with reading difficulties throughout the school.

An alternative to books on tape that we are likely to see more and more of in the future is books on screen – using a computer to present the text of books, with an associated speech synthesizer to 'say' any word that the child points to with the mouse. The whole page can be read aloud this way, or the child can just ask for help when stuck. Systems that are being developed will also keep a record of which words the child has sought help with, and how often (Davidson et al., 1991).

Group reading strategies

Another way of increasing children's exposure to print, and making the best use of limited adult time, is to build in a daily group text-related activity, such as reading a play with the teacher, or sharing a special large-format book (Holdaway, 1982), or taking part in DARTS or Directed Activities Related to Tests (Lunzer and Gardner, 1979).

Using large format books, children are able to tackle fairly demanding texts by supporting each other in group reading. The teacher can mask individual words or chunks of text for cloze and prediction, and use laminated finishes or acetate overlays for text marking – underlining letter–sound patterns, little words within longer ones, punctuation marks or print conventions such as bullet marks, or highlighting the main idea in paragraphs, or the 'bit that tells you about'.

Many publishers produce large-format books; teachers can make their own by mounting well-loved rhymes or class stories on laminated card.

DARTS activities are a means of both increasing children's understanding of what they read and of improving reading fluency by engaging them repeatedly, in an interesting way, with the same piece of text. Some DARTS activities require text modification and prior preparation:

- A passage is reproduced with blanks in place of some (teacher-chosen) words: the group of children discuss and try to agree what should go in the blank spaces.
- A passage (poem, recipe, historical or scientific account of events or processes) is cut up into sections or strips: the group of children try to re-order them in a way that will make sense.

Other DARTS activities can be done with the text as it stands (a copy per child), and teacher support:

- Underlining categories of information in the text with different coloured pens.
- Labelling key ideas in pages or paragraphs.
- Transferring information from the passage to a chart, hierarchical table, family tree diagram, time line, flow diagram, bar chart or series of labelled pictures.

Once again, evaluation of the use of DARTS techniques suggests that repeated engagements with text is a highly effective form of intervention for children with reading difficulties:

> A learning support teacher, when asked 'to do something' about a group of eleven-year-old children two to four years behind in their reading, decided to use DARTS to support the children's topic work. As part of one term's topic on 'Ceremonies', the group discussed and predicated deleted words from relevant texts – both written, and computer-presented using Developing Tray software. Another term, they researched the big cat

family, taking a book on tigers and underlining, on overlays, facts about tiger size, colouring, food and hunting methods in different coloured pens, then transferring the information to a tabular chart. They labelled a drawing with information about the body of a tiger. They retold, in a series of six pictures, part of a serial story about a boy and a cheetah that the class were studying. Over the nine-month period of support (for two-and-a-half hours a week in a group of four), the children gained on average seventeen months in reading age.

(Pearsall and Wollen, 1991)

Teachers wondering how to fit group reading activities like these into the work of the class when extra support is not available may be interested in the model provided by Thompson (1992). In his school the bulk of children in the younger age groups (Years 2 and 3 children with reading ages over seven) were heard to read by an older (Year 6) partner for 15 minutes three times a week, whilst the children still at the very beginnings of literacy remained with their teacher for small group work. All the children in the scheme made better than average reading progress; those who had the extra time in a small group with their own teacher made progress at twice the usual rate.

EXTENDING THE RANGE OF CHANNELS THROUGH WHICH THE CHILD CAN LEARN TO READ

The debate about the 'best' way to teach reading has often ignored the wealth of evidence that children acquire reading skills in many different ways, using different channels for their learning. Some use their good oral language skills to make maximum use of prediction from context; some apply their good phonological awareness to pick up an early extensive knowledge of letter sound relationships; some have little need of phonic skills because they have such good visual recall that they only have to be told a word once to remember it.

Children with literacy difficulties may have problems in any or all of these areas. Many struggle with the visual memory element: perhaps, it is increasingly thought, because they perceive the words in a shifting, unstable fashion, with the letters of a word arriving at their processing system all at once, instead of in a sequential, stable form. This means that one word – like 'felt', for example – may look like a mixture of 'left', 'flet', 'telf' and so on; many different visual patterns have to be attached to the corresponding spoken word rather than just one. These children may need much more exposure to a word before they remember it than those with neat, sequential, left-hemispheric perceptions.

Very many children with reading difficulties, we know, have poor phonological awareness. They are unable to deduce for themselves, without help, the relationships between written letter strings and spoken sound patterns, because they do not perceive the commonalities of sound that are the foundation of the written code.

Some children appear to have poor phonological awareness *and* an absolute inability to remember what words look like. For them, the outlook can be grim, even with consistent extra help.

In the future it may be possible to accurately assess each individual child's cognitive profile, and match teaching strategies to the learning channels from which they are most able to profit. Some useful work has already been done in this direction (Singleton, 1991). At the moment, our knowledge is too inexact to make such individual programmes really useful to the classroom teacher. What the class teacher *can* do, however, is make sure that the child's reading programme makes use of all available learning channels, so that s/he can make use of strengths and circumvent weaknesses, rather than being constrained by one method that does not suit them. This means going beyond the kind of extensive contact with print that we looked at in the last section (since this relies almost exclusively on visual and sequential channels), to working through the auditory channel on sound–symbol relationships, and even – for the small minority of children with poor auditory *and* poor visual skills, use of the kinaesthetic channel – learning words, via tracing and writing, as patterns of movement.

Using the auditory channel

With the many children whose sight vocabulary grows only very slowly, and who characteristically 'can read a word one minute and forget it the next', it is essential to tap the auditory learning channel, and to teach them to make good use of sound–symbol relationships for cueing unfamiliar or forgotten words. If assessment shows that they have a good auditory awareness of the sound patterns in spoken words, all the more reason to focus on phonic skills; if it shows they have difficulties in auditory perception, then there will need to be work (of the kind described in Chapter 10) on phonological awareness alongside the teaching of letter–sound relationships.

For children with learning difficulties, Felicity Craig's approach (1990) of having a helper run daily through a pack of cards that depict sound on one side and key picture and word on the other until the child knows the whole set is better than the hit-or-miss whole class familiarization with letter sounds that often leaves some children with incomplete mastery. Craig markets her own sets of cards (Sound Spelling Vocabularies), covering letter blends as well as single-letter sounds, and using a special set of words with a high interest value to older, poor readers. The Letterland pictograms can also be used, though only if the child is taught from the start to link sound *and* key word to the written symbol (f-fuh-fireman Fred) rather than just the name of the character (f-fireman Fred). Another useful set of pictograms that help children remember letter–sound associations by making the letters look like relevant pictures is produced by Early Learning Systems.

Using short periods of daily practice and mnemonic cues like these there is no reason why any child cannot learn all the main letter–sound relationships in a relatively short time. As all teachers of reading know, however, mastery of sound–symbol relationships is no guarantee that the child will actually make use of them when reading. There is evidence (Adams, 1990) that children's willingness to use phonetic cues is a direct function of the success they experience with them early on in their learning: if they are exposed to books with a high proportion of phonetically-regular words they are more likely to go on later to apply their phonic knowledge than if they are exposed mainly to phonetically-irregular text. For this reason, it will be worth spending some time on texts with a strong phonetic element. Such texts tended in the past to be stilted and contrived, but with the advent of pattern, rhyme and analogy strands in the new reading schemes from all the major publishers, the teacher now has a wide choice of lively, natural text which stresses sound–symbol regularities.

Structured multisensory approaches

Recognizing that children with literacy problems often need to bring all their senses into play when learning to read, teachers in the specific learning difficulties world have traditionally relied heavily on a range of off-the-peg approaches collectively called 'multisensory'. In these approaches, sound–symbol relationships and irregular sight words are taught in a set order, and learning involves seeing a word or letter, saying it, hearing it, speaking it and – importantly – feeling it either by tracing or writing.

The approaches include the Kathleen Hickey method (Hickey, 1992), the Bangor Teaching Programme (Miles, 1989), Beve Hornsby's *Alpha to Omega* (Hornsby and Shear, 1975), and Keda Cowling's *Toe by Toe*. All ideally require about two hours of individualized (though not necessarily individual) teaching a week, and a teacher who is thoroughly familiar with the materials. Given these conditions, good progress is reported. Whereas children with specific learning difficulties who have only regular classroom teaching and no special help with their reading have been found to fall progressively further and further behind their peers, making on average only five months' progress in reading age in the space of a year (Thomson, 1989), those who do get help in the form of a structured multisensory teaching programme can make better-than-average progress, of the order of 18 to 24 months per year (Thomson, 1989; Hornsby and Farrer, 1990).

The Fernald technique

Even the teacher-intensive structures of multisensory teaching programmes have their failures. Some children, usually those with very poor auditory skills, a poor short-term memory and an inability to recall words visually, find the memory demands and the emphasis on phonics a major stumbling block. For them, a technique that relies on kinaesthetic mastery of words can be useful. In the Fernald method, children begin by choosing words that interest them, and which they would like to learn. A word is written for them on paper or on a card and they trace it with a finger, saying each part as they trace it. This is repeated until the child feels confident s/he can write it from memory. As a bank of words is learned this way, children use them to write sentences and then stories or topic work, always asking for new words as they write and learning them by finger-tracing before putting them in their piece of writing. After each piece of writing is complete, it is typed up and read back by the child.

The Fernald method is slow, because each word had to be learned as a separate unit, but has been recommended by experienced specialist teachers (e.g. Cotterell, 1985) for those who fail to learn by other methods.

ARROW

Another technique that increases the number of channels through which the child can learn is ARROW – an acronym for Aural–Read–Respond–Oral– Written. The ARROW system uses a special two-track tape recorder and headphones, which allows children to listen to pre-recorded material, record their own response, and then listen to their own voice recording. Children use the machine for about 15 minutes a day, three to five sessions a week, with light supervision from the teacher or from a classroom assistant. Pre-recorded materials are available for both reading and spelling, or teachers can make their own. In the reading programmes, the child listens to a piece of text on the tape, following the corresponding text with a finger, tapes him- or herself reading the piece, and then listens to his or her own recorded speech replayed – again following the text at the same time. Tapes can also be made for practising reading comprehension skills.

ARROW is not cheap, but is of proven effectiveness. Children make rapid progress in a short time – as little as five or six weeks (Davies, 1989; Lane, 1990); they find the sophisticated technology motivating, and appear to learn all kinds of material more quickly from listening to their own recorded voice than the voices of others. This may be because ARROW models and establishes a habit of rehearsal (saying things that need to be learned over and over to oneself) which is missing in many children with learning difficulties.

ENSURING OVERLEARNING

As well as increasing contact with print, and making sure that any approach used is multichannel rather than single channel, there is a need with almost all children with reading difficulties to build in an element of 'overlearning' into the reading programme: that is, constantly repeating variations on the same material over and over again so that the knowledge and skills become automatic and resistant to forgetting.

Parents and teachers often find it infuriating that poor readers seem to know a word one minute, but not when they meet it further down the page or the next day. They may blame forgetfulness or laziness, or put it down to inattention;

the myth of 'she could do it if she tried' stems from this characteristic pattern of inconsistent recall. In fact, however, adults can recognize the same pattern of inconsistency in themselves, if they think back to the early stages of learning any new skill — such as learning to drive. When skills are new, and not 'overlearned' to the point of automaticity, performance *is* erratic: competent one minute and chaotic the next. The harder the learner tries, and the more tense s/he becomes, the more likely it is that things will be forgotten and mistakes made.

The remedy is practice, continued well past the point where the child seems to have mastered the new piece of learning. The challenge, for teachers of children with learning difficulties, is how to make the practice sufficiently motivating for them to want to persist.

Traditional reading schemes — especially those developed for the slower learner, such as OUP's *Fuzzbuzz* or Macmillan's *Wellington Square*, rely heavily on the principle of overlearning. A core vocabulary is visited and revisited throughout such schemes, and practised also through a range of supporting materials. Children do not forget earlier words or sound–symbol relationships because they keep on meeting them. Because they recognize the need for such built-in overlearning, many teachers' first step when confronted with a child with reading difficulties is to move them from less-structured reading material on to a scheme or combination of schemes — often with success.

Direct Instruction programmes (such as those marketed by SRA — Reading Mastery for younger pupils, and Corrective Reading for top juniors and the early secondary years) carry the principle of overlearning to its most extreme. These schemes use a short daily group reading lesson of a very formal nature: children chant new words and sounds together and read contrived texts around the group under tightly-controlled conditions. Each new piece of learning builds on the last, and there is constant built-in repetition of every skill taught. A points system ensures pupil motivation. Preparation and planning are minimized; the teacher works to a prescribed script.

The rigidity of Direct Instruction programmes, and their old-fashioned air, mean that most teachers initially approach them with great suspicion. Those who get as far as trying them out often persist, however, when they find that the children enjoy the novel formality of the lessons, and that even the most switched-off do learn to read by these methods after years of failure. There is considerable hard research evidence to back up such these teachers' experiences of success with Direct Instruction (for example, Somerville and Leach, 1988). Schools that are serious about rescuing poor readers — particularly older children in their last years in primary school — and who can staff the necessary three to five 30–40 minute sessions a week of group withdrawal work and fund the initial outlay on teacher and pupil books, would do well to give Direct Instruction some serious consideration.

For younger children, a Direct Instruction scheme of comparable effectiveness comes from Early Learning Systems. This inexpensive scheme calls for individual rather than group teaching, but is designed to be used by parents or classroom helpers working under the supervision of the class teacher. It first teaches initial sounds using a pack of letter–sound cards, based on ingenious pictorial mnemonics, for example as shown in Figure 11.2. When the letter sounds have been mastered through daily practice, the child is taught how to apply them in order to decode a core reading vocabulary of high frequency words.

The advantage of Direct Instruction schemes such as these is that they provide the teacher with a ready-made structure. Overlearning can be achieved without them – but it takes more work. The teacher needs to be prepared to keep an ongoing record of the child's mastery of key sight vocabulary and sound–symbol relationships, and to provide a range of games and worksheet-type activities to reinforce each learning step – such as those suggested in Rea Reason and Rene Boote's excellent *Helping Children with Reading and Writing* (1995). Children can trace or copy word strips from the books they have read and re-read, cut them up, jumble and re-assemble them, if necessary by matching them with the book. They can choose a part they liked from the story book to illustrate, add a caption or speech balloon with words they find and copy from the text, or read and illustrate captions and speech balloons the teacher supplies. They can cover up a word or phrase on a page with Blu-tack, then swap with a friend who has to work out what is underneath, and help each other order photocopied pages of favourite books. They can play board games, happy families, lotto or dominoes based on the core vocabulary or letter–sound links. They can test each other on sentence strips in pairs, trace words or letters on friends' backs for them to guess at, or go through a pack of single sounds or letter blends (with a clue word and picture on the back of each card) together on a daily basis. Or they can create sentences and clue pictures for a small number of hard-to-remember abstract keywords (for example, a picture of an ice cream and the sentence 'I *would* like some ice cream' for the word 'would') then test each other daily in pairs, at first with and then without the clue pictures.

Another way in which children can obtain the necessary repetition and rehearsal is through work on the computer, using a mix of open-ended content-free software and (in small doses) programmes of the drill and practice type. Word processing using a prepared concept keyboard overlay of words to be overlearned (taken from a book the child has enjoyed) will provide repeated practice in reading and using a core vocabulary. Software called *From Pictures to Words*, from Widgit, will support the process of writing on the concept keyboard, and reading back what has been written, by adding pictures from its extensive files to some of the words as they appear on the screen and on print-out. This particular programme also allows for intensive overlearning of sight vocabulary, and for work on initial letter sounds. The Somerset Talking Computer Project materials allow children to use word processing alongside phonics-based practice to achieve substantial, well documented gains in literacy levels.

Most of the drill-and-practice type of programmes are phonically based; they

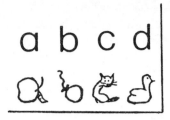

Figure 11.2 Pictorial mnemonics.

aim to increase the speed and fluency with which the child can apply newly-learned decoding skills by providing large amounts of individual, closely monitored practice. *Fun Phonics* from PAVIC, and *HI-Spell* from Xavier provide complete suites covering the whole range of phonic skills from single letter sounds to prefixes and suffixes. Other suitable programmes come from Sherston (especially their *Animated Alphabet*), HS Software (*Read Right Away*) and from Dorset County Council Psychological Service.

Enhancing self-esteem

Wesley, at 7, was a non-reader: the only child of devoted parents, with a mother who ran a successful small business but had herself struggled with reading and writing throughout all her school years. Wesley's teachers found him a nuisance in class; he was restless, unable to work successfully in a group, and always coming to them to ask for one thing or another. His mother was desperately worried about him. He was beginning to show signs of reluctance to come to school, saying that other children called him a thicko and would not play with him. He refused to read with her at home, something he had once loved. One day, she found under the bed a card he had made for his father. It said 'To bad, best wisis from Welsy'. When she asked why he had never given it to his Dad, he said it was because it was all wrong and his writing was no good. He was stupid (had not his teacher told him not to be so stupid that same day, when he refused to go out to play?) and everyone else in the class could read and write except him.

Then Wesley got a new special teacher, who worked with him twice a week on his reading and written work. She could see straight away that his feelings about himself were very negative, and that there was little chance of him learning anything while he felt this way. Instead of asking him to read to her, or write, she worked with him on oral story telling. Using her as a scribe, he began to produce stories that were astonishingly vivid and well thought out. He ought, his teacher told him, to write a proper book, a long story, for others to read. Together they began on a long project. In each session Wesley dictated a new chapter, which the teacher would type up on the computer later. Sometimes Wesley asked to type up some of his story himself. The book was produced, illustrated, and shared around the school. The other children were impressed. The book was sent to publishers; several wrote back to Wesley to say how well he had done. These letters became reading material he would return to again and again. He began to read more, and read more fluently. After talking with his teacher, he also began to be able to say he 'just had a problem with remembering words', but there were many, many things he could do really well. This message was by now getting across to the other children, too. Although he still had a long way to go in mastering the mechanical skills of reading and writing, Wesley was well on the way. He had begun to believe in himself.

Adults who take their own literacy for granted sometimes find it hard to get in touch with the feelings of the child who is struggling with reading, especially the extent to which failure in this one area can come to permeate their whole self-picture. It is because of this pervasive effect, perhaps, that interventions that work *only* at the level of raising the child's self-esteem can contribute significantly to improving reading skills (Lawrence, 1973; Wooster and Leech, 1982).

Combining skills-based approaches with planned work on raising self-esteem seems to work best of all: using interested, sympathetic adult listeners who showed that they valued the child in a series of regular meetings, Lawrence (1988) was able to show enhanced gains in reading age for a group who had regular remedial help plus these extra counselling sessions when compared with a group who had the remedial help only.

Many of the strategies to build self-esteem described in Chapter 9 can be relevant to children with reading difficulties, particularly if used to pave the way for later skills-based interventions. But as with Wesley, the most significant possible boost to the self-esteem of the poor reader (or writer), of course, is being told you are not, as you may have thought, stupid or slow or lazy: that you are, in fact a perfectly able and acceptable person who just happens to have a specific difficulty with written words that is not in any way your own fault. This remains one of the main arguments for using scientifically-inaccurate but emotionally-warming labels like dyslexia with children and their parents, when a child is struggling to acquire literacy.

It remains controversial as to whether there is sufficient commonality in the characteristics and assessment profiles of any one sub-group of children with literacy difficulties to delineate a group who are dyslexic, as opposed to another group of children with reading difficulties who are not. The magical 'test' that will show whether a child is or is not dyslexic does not exist. Nevertheless, there is definitely evidence for a constitutional (often genetic) basis for specific reading difficulties, and a set of loose indicators, all research-based (see Table

Table 11.2 Indicators of specific learning difficulties/dyslexia in the primary school

---

Early warning signs
- Child was a late talker, or speech not fully intelligible on starting school.
- Child had not fully established left- or right-handedness on starting school.
- There is a family history of reading or spelling problems.
- Child has poor ability to analyse or synthesize the sounds in words, e.g. cannot by 6–7 tell when words rhyme, blend three sounds of a word spoken to him/her at one per second, identify first and last sounds in a word s/he wants to write.
- Child has poor short-term memory – for example, for a series of instructions, or for a series of spoken digits (a child of 4 should be able to repeat three digits spoken at one per second; a child of nearly 6 should manage four digits).
- Child has difficulties in remembering the names for objects.
- There is a history of early clumsiness.

Indicators in children over 7–8
- Persisting letter and number reversals, particularly 'b/d' confusion.
- Inability to remember the 'look' of even short, common words; phonetic spelling which persists over 8–9 years – e.g. 'cum' for 'come', 'duw' for 'do', 'hav' for 'have', 'enuf' for 'enough' *or* in children with the most severe difficulties, spelling which bears little relation to either the look or the sound of the word.
- Persisting minor speech (e.g. 'w/r', 'f/th') or auditory discrimination difficulties (e.g. 'e/i' confusion).
- Difficulty in repeating unfamiliar polysyllabic words, e.g. preliminary, statistical, corollary.
- Letter sequence errors in reading of the 'was–saw', 'of–for', 'spot–stop' type.
- Poor auditory short-term memory: the average nine-year old should be able to repeat four digits in reverse order, rising to five digits at 12 years.
- Problems in basic numeracy, though not so severe as in literacy: confusion of $+$, $-$, $\times$, $\div$ signs, poor memory for number bonds and multiplication tables.
- Poor rote memory for sequential information such as the alphabet, days of the week, months of the year.

11.2), which can help the teacher establish whether the child might lie somewhere on a continuum of dyslexic-type specific learning difficulties. And if s/he does appear to show many of these indicators and lie somewhere on the sp.l.d./dyslexia continuum, it seems sensible to try to explain this to both child and parents, so that the child can make a fresh start unburdened by whatever guilt or blame may have accumulated over the years of failure. Using a checklist of indicators of sp.l.d./dyslexia may also be helpful to the teacher when s/he wants to evaluate the need to move towards a somewhat more structured teaching programme, with a strong multisensory element, for a child who seems to be making slower progress in literacy than their oral ability or ability in other subjects would lead one to expect.

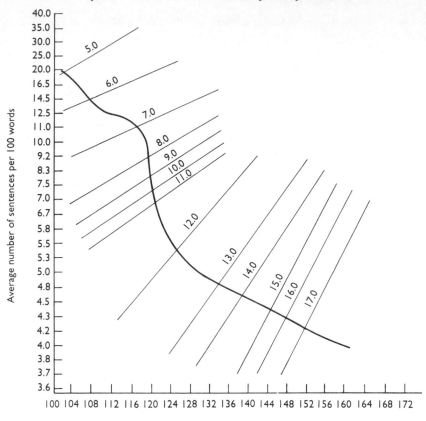

Figure 11.3 Assessing the readability level of text. (1) Choose random samples, each of 100 words. (2) Find average number of syllables, and average number of sentences per 100 words. (3) Plot on graph, and read off the readability level, the minimum reading age needed to understand the text (Fry, 1972).

ACCESSING THE CURRICULUM

The extent to which the teacher is able to raise the self-esteem of children with reading difficulties will often depend on his or her inventiveness in devising bypass strategies, that will make sure the child is able to succeed in the main body of the curriculum even though their performance within English may be problematic. Too many children fall behind in areas they could otherwise do well in, simply because they cannot read instructions, follow worksheets, use information books, cope with classroom notices or read what the teacher has put on the blackboard. Often they are afraid or embarrassed to ask what things say – as with Richard, aged 10, but with the reading skills of a 6-year-old, who said: 'I can't always read what it says in my maths book; I do ask my friends but

Table 11.3 Texts will be easier to read if the following apply

---

- Short sentences are substituted for long and complex ones.
- Short words are substituted for long words.
- There is a word bank giving definitions of difficult words in a box at the end, and all the words in this word bank are underlined or written in bold type when they occur in the text.
- Pictures, diagrams and flow charts are used to clarify the text.
- Instructions are made to stand out clearly from the text – for example, by being put in boxes, or in a different print.
- The layout looks uncluttered, with a wide border round the edge, and not too much print on each page.

An example of text modification might be:

Original text
> Ammonites, aquatic creatures from the distant past, are frequently found as fossils. The fossils were formed when the shell of the ammonite became buried on the sea floor under the mud, which subsequently hardened around it.

Modified text
> Ammonites lived under the sea long ago. When an ammonite died, its shell sank to the bottom of the sea. Mud buried (hid) it. The mud hardened (got hard) into rock around the shell. This made a fossil.

---

they get fed up if I keep on doing it. I ask Gareth most and he's OK but if he wants to get his own work done he tells me to shut up and leave him alone.'

For some children, it works well to quietly appoint a regular 'working partner' for them, who has explicit instructions to read words and supply spellings: it is necessary, though, to rotate the helper role so that no one child is overburdened.

Some really committed schools have used older children (reading for a purpose) to prepare a bank of tapes of the text of maths schemes, and topic information books, for the use of any child who wants support with the reading element. Other schools run regular checks on the readability levels of materials each class is working from: using samples of text and a simple computer formula (Sawyer and Knight, 1991), or a chart as in Figure 11.3, they can assess how well the materials are matched to individual children's needs. Even simpler as a readability measure is the so-called 'five-finger exercise': the child is asked to put a finger on each word on a page that s/he can't read – if the number exceeds the number of fingers, the text is likely to be too difficult to be read without support.

If this is the case, then there are several ways of offering help. The teacher can have the children work in pairs, pairing the child with reading difficulties with a better reader. Alternatively, the child can pair-read the text with a fluent partner before they work on it on their own. Or the text can be modified, ahead of time (see Table 11.3), to make it easier to read.

Materials with several levels of readability can be prepared for the topics or schemes of work regularly used in a school; published materials that will be helpful here include Ginn's *Sharp Eye* high interest level/low reading age information books, anthologies and stories (on common themes such as homes, myself, creatures, school and going places), and information books from Watts Publishing and Wayland. A useful idea that may be taken up by more publishers is supplying, as Kingscourt do with their Literacy Links, books with audio-cassette as well as text versions, and talking books (like Sherston's *Look! Hear!*) with animation and digitized speech.

CHILDREN WITH READING COMPREHENSION DIFFICULTIES

So far, this chapter has mainly concerned itself with strategies the teacher can adopt for children with poor decoding skills – the ones who just do not know what the words say, and cannot seem to remember them when told. Many of these children have an oral language foundation for reading that is at least adequate, and sometimes superior: they are able to use context and their knowledge of language to predict unknown words, and to understand what they have read (if, that is, they are able to decode enough words, rapidly enough, to maintain the overall gist). But there is another group of children with reading difficulties whose needs are very different: they can decode fluently, and at speed, but they do not understand what they read.

For them, work on reading for meaning need not be confined to the traditional type of exercise where children answer oral or written questions on passages they have read. Their reading programme should include:

- Group discussion of the words that should go in text with deletions.
- Correcting deliberate mistakes in a passage.
- Pairing sentences and pictures.
- Pairing sentences of similar meaning.
- Following recipes and written instructions.
- Sequencing sentence strips or longer chunks to make a story, poem or series of events/instructions.
- Discussing and choosing a headline for a newspaper article, or a title for a story.
- Underlining key events, ideas or words on acetate overlays.
- Discussing and choosing appropriate subheadings for paragraphs.
- Composing a telegram of words relating to the main events in a story.
- Discussing and choosing the best of three summaries provided for a piece of text.
- Group SQR3 (Surveying, Questioning, Reading, Reviewing, Reciting). The group is asked to look quickly at illustrations, title, first sentence, last paragraph of a text and then discuss what they think it is all about and what the author's purpose might be. Then the children read the passage silently before completing as a group a review task (which might be underlining

keywords, listing sub-headings, finding out all they can about a particular character). Finally, at the recitation stage the children write a summary, report or book review, or make their own notes on the text.

• Teaching techniques for extracting information from text using a KWL grid, one of the many exciting ideas from the Exeter Literacy project (Lewis et al., 1994):

What I know	What I want to know	What I've learned

Commercial materials to support these activities are available from Learning Materials Ltd (*Reading for Meaning*), Oliver and Boyd (*I See What you Mean* and *Context Reading*), LDA (*Reading Comprehension Workcards*).

CONCLUSION

Without reading skills – both at the mechanical decoding level and at the higher-order level of comprehension – children become increasingly and enormously disadvantaged throughout their school career. It is possible to prevent this; there are plenty of schools and individual teachers with such a strong commitment to each child's right to read, and such confidence in their ability to teach reading, that persistent reading failure is almost unheard of. In this chapter, we have taken a look at the kinds of strategies and materials that contribute to success of this kind.

Many of these strategies involve children learning words as written patterns: reading and writing are, in both multisensory teaching and in the kinds of activities that promote overlearning, often inextricably linked. So too are the children's actual difficulties in both reading and written recording: it is very rare to find children who cannot read well who do not also have writing and spelling difficulties. An action plan for reading must inevitably involve one for writing too. In the next chapter, we will consider how such plans can be made to work.

FURTHER READING

Reason, R. and Boote, R. (1995) *Helping Children with Reading and Spelling*. London, Routledge.

RESOURCES

Dorset County Psychological Service, Purbeck View, 14b Commercial Road, Parkstone, Poole, Dorset BH14 OJW.

Early Learning Systems, Hartley House, Winsley, Bradford on Avon, Wilts. BA15 2JB.

Fun Phonics, PAVIC Publications, Sheffield City Polytechnic.

Letterland, available from Collins Educational.

Sound Spelling Vocabularies, One-to-One Publications, 33 Newcomen Road, South Devon TQ6 9BN.

Toe by Toe, Keda Cowling, 8 Green Lane, Baildon, West Yorkshire BD17 5HL

Widgit Software, 1 The Ryde, Hatfield, Herts. AL9 5DQ.

Other software referred to is available from REM, Great Western House, Langport, Somerset TA10 9BR.

· 12 ·

SPECIAL NEEDS IN WRITING

INTRODUCTION

Ideas about teaching writing in the primary school have come a long way in the past few years. Thanks to the influence of the national writing project and the national curriculum programmes of study, writing in many schools is no longer the tedious chore that once followed every piece of active learning or exploration ('Do we *have* to write about it, Miss?'); it has become a thing of purpose, with children writing letters or stories for a real audience, and using writing as a tool to clarify their own learning, and their own thoughts and feelings. It has also become process, rather than product, oriented; the secretarial aspects of correct spelling, punctuation, and presentation have taken their rightful place as part of the shaping up and editing of initial drafts, so that the dead hand of absolute neatness and correctness no longer lies heavy on the child's initial creative thought.

Yet there is still a tension and an uncertainty about the relative importance of good ideas and correct expression in the teaching and assessment of writing. In the early stages of the introduction of the national curriculum, Key Stage 1 teachers were advised to pay relatively little attention to the presentation aspects in their assessment of pupils' overall performance in the English profile component for writing, because the 80 : 20 per cent split between the creative and presentational ATs meant that the child's level in spelling and handwriting would have little overall influence on the final result. All this has now changed, however, as politicians and the popular press show increasing concern about children's ability to express themselves correctly and present their work neatly. Teachers will have to pay ever more attention to the mastery of spelling, handwriting and punctuation – and to the performance of the many children who find these areas particularly difficult.

It is hard to say whether his new focus will be of benefit to children with special educational needs or not. On the one hand, the focus on ideas rather than presentation did offer some hope to many children with specific literacy difficulties, making them feel they could genuinely be good writers, whose work would be assessed on content even if presentation was very poor. There is a real risk, in a return to an assessment system more heavily weighted towards surface features of written work, that these potential gains in confidence could be lost. On the other hand, the focus on content may have meant that children with spelling or handwriting difficulties did not always get the help they needed. There is also some evidence that the confidence that process writing should give to children with special needs never quite materialized – that no matter how much the teacher showed that s/he valued the content of their writing, these children continued to judge their work harshly if it did not look as good or as prolific as that of others sitting near them, and – more importantly – tended to restrict the range of vocabulary and the complexity of language they used so as to stay within the safe bounds of words they knew how to spell (Mosely, 1989).

Children *are* more surface oriented than adults, and are liable to develop low self-esteem if they cannot spell well or write neatly, such as the little boy, who wrote:

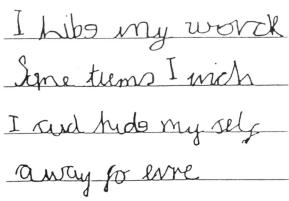

Figure 12.1   Writing by Darrell, aged 10 years (*Dyslexia Institute Annual Review*, 1986).

Acknowledging feelings like these, and making a realistic promise to help children improve their presentation, may be better for them than skirting round problems in spelling and handwriting, or conveying that they are of relatively little importance.

Most of this chapter will be concerned with the ways in which the school can make such realistic action plans to help with the secretarial aspects of writing. We shall however, at the end return to the more creative aspects of writing, and look at ways of supporting children who may be technically competent but are stuck when it comes to generating the initial ideas for a piece of writing, choosing an appropriate vocabulary, and ordering and refining an initial draft.

ASSESSMENT AND TEACHING STRATEGIES

Spelling

As with reading, the assessment of spelling difficulties should include a normative measure (such as the *Vernon Spelling Test* from Hodder and Stoughton) for the purpose of establishing the extent of need and monitoring progress. It should also include either a miscue analysis of the child's own writing, or 'tests' (dictation lists or passages like those in Margaret Peters' *Spelling in Context* from NFER-Nelson, Gill Cotterell's *Diagnostic Spelling Test* from LDA, or Violet Brand's *Spelling Made Easy*), for the purpose of discovering which commonly used keywords and which sound–symbol spelling conventions the child has mastered. The outcomes can be recorded in a small-steps analysis of the national curriculum requirements for spelling, such as the one given in Table 12.1.

Repeated miscue analysis of a child's written work will also provide the teacher with clues about the point of breakdown, for that individual, in acquiring spelling skills. Is it awkward, ill-formed handwriting that prevents them from using kinaesthetic and motor cues to aid spelling recall? If so, they may benefit from practising a fluent cursive script, or from working on spelling materials with a strong handwriting element such as Charles Cripps' *Hand for Spelling* from LDA. Is it poor phonological awareness, so that the letters the child writes bear little relationship to the sound patterns in words? If this seems to be the problem, the child may need to work at an auditory and oral level on 'hearing' correctly when words rhyme, what their constituent sounds are, and how they can be tapped out as chunks or syllables. Or is it a difficulty in visual memory, evident in older children as phonetic misspellings (such as 'duw' for 'do') of short, common irregular keywords? If so, there may be a need for systematic and structured phonic teaching coupled with some activities to improve visual skills – finding small words within larger ones (*Wordscore* from Taskmaster is useful for this), making collections of words with the same visual patterns, using look–cover–write–check on a regular basis, learning new words by linking them in groups and target sentences with words that share the same visual pattern/letter string, and using supporting commercial materials such as LDA's *Stile Spelling*.

As with reading, teaching strategies for children with spelling difficulties do need to be multisensory. Methods that work for the majority of children may not work for those with specific difficulties. Thomson (1991), for example, has showed that while a visual inspection method of learning spellings worked well for children whose reading and spelling was developing normally, poor spellers did much better with a multisensory technique called simultaneous oral spelling (Table 12.2). Classrooms oriented wholly towards a visual approach will fail children who cannot, no matter how hard they try, form accurate visual images of words; classrooms wholly oriented towards phonic approaches will fail those who cannot, no matter how hard they try, analyse the sounds that make up spoken words.

Table 12.1   English AT 3–spelling

- Writes some letters in own name.
- Can play 'I Spy' to identify the initial sound of a word orally.
- Can point to some letters in a book or on a frieze in response to speech sounds and letter names.
- Can match initial sound of some words to letters in a book or on a frieze.
- Writes some letter shapes in response to speech sounds and letter names
- Can write initial sound for some words.
- Writes own first name from memory.
- Can write initial sound for any word.
- Can write first ten keywords: 'I', 'a', 'and', 'was', 'went', 'with', 'me', 'my', 'to', 'the'.
- Uses some invented spellings involving final as well as initial sound.
- Can spell two-letter phonetically-regular words, for example 'is', 'in', 'it', 'of', 'up', 'on', 'an'.
- Can write next twenty keywords: 'this', 'are', 'have', 'he', 'we', 'mummy', 'when', 'some', 'come', 'they', 'do', 'no', 'go', 'see', 'by', 'or', 'her', 'off', 'she', 'said'.
- Uses some medial letters as well as initial and final in invented spellings.
- Can write three-letter phonetically-regular words, for example 'get', 'can', 'big', 'did'.
- Can write the next twenty keywords: 'now', 'how', 'our', 'two', 'look', 'been', 'make', 'over', 'more', 'any', 'many', 'out', 'about', 'same', 'first', 'little', 'new', 'were', 'want', 'only'.
- Can write words with digraphs 'sh', 'th', 'ch', for example 'that', 'then', 'shop', 'chips'.
- Can write words with initial blends, for example 'from', 'stop', 'frog'.
- Can write words with final blends and digraphs, for example 'wish', 'moth', 'much', 'just', 'back', 'black'.
- *Spells correctly simple monosyllabic words* (Level 2)
- Can generalize from one spelling to others that rhyme, for example from 'all' to 'call/ball/fall'.
- Can spell words with common vowel digraphs and patterns: 'ee' 'oo' 'oa' or 'ay'.
- Can write remaining keywords: 'once', 'other', 'their', 'there', 'what', 'where', 'which', 'when', 'who', 'away', 'live', 'very', 'girl', 'next', 'every', 'people'.
- Can spell other common rhyming letter strings: 'and' ('hand', 'stand'), 'ain' ('rain', 'train', 'again'), 'out' ('about', 'shout', 'scout'), 'ame' ('came', 'same', 'shame'), 'ould' ('could', 'would', 'should'), 'ir' ('first', 'bird', 'girl', 'third'), 'ade' ('made', 'spade', 'blade').
- *Can spell common polysyllabic words ('because', 'after', 'open', 'teacher', 'animal', 'together')* (Level 3)
- Can spell prefixes 'pre' ('pretend'), 're' ('remain'), 'de' ('depart'), 'ex' ('express'), 'en' ('enjoy'), 'mis' ('misfire'), 'tele' ('telephone'), 'sub' ('subway'), 'un' ('unless'), 'dis' ('dislike').
- Can spell common suffixes and endings: '-le' ('tremble'), '-ess/less/ness' ('kindness', 'unless', 'express'), '-ment' ('equipment'), '-tion' ('mention'), '-ive' ('active'), '-ily' ('happily'), '-age' ('bandage'), '-ture' ('capture'), '-ous' ('dangerous'), '-ious' ('envious').
- Knows 10 simple spelling rules:
    Q never stands by itself; is always written 'qu'.
    No English word ends in 'v' or 'j'.
    No English word ends in an '-i'; use '-y' instead (except 'spaghetti', 'taxi', 'macaroni' etc. which are Italian).
    A silent 'e' at the end of a word makes the vowel in front of it say its alphabetical name (except for 'done', 'come', 'some', 'give', 'have').

Table 12.1　(*Continued*)

We double 'l', 'f' and 's' after a single short vowel at the end of one syllable words (except 'bus', 'gas', 'if', 'of', 'this', 'yes', 'plus', 'nil', 'pal').

Add '-es' to form plurals of words ending 's', 'x', 'z', 'sh', 'ch'.

Plurals of words ending in '-f': change 'f' to 'v' before adding 'es'.

If a word ends in a single vowel and a single consonant (except 'x'), double the consonant before adding an ending (e.g. 'stop'/'stopped').

If the word ends in '-e' take off the '-e' before adding '-ing'.

When 'all', 'full' and 'till' are joined to a word or syllable they drop an '-l' ('also', 'already', 'hopeful', 'fulfil', 'until').

- *Spelling, including that of polysyllabic words that conform to regular patterns, is generally accurate* (Level 4).

Table 12.2　Simultaneous oral spelling (Bradley, 1985)

1　The word to be learned is written for the child.
2　S/he names the word and writes it, saying the alphabetical name of each letter as it is written.
3　S/he says the word again, and checks to see that it has been written correctly.
4　S/he repeats the look–write–naming each letter–check sequence twice more, covering the word as soon as s/he can manage without it.
5　S/he practises the word this way for six consecutive days.
6　The child learns to generalize from the learned word to words with similar sound and spelling, using plastic letters.

What strategies, then, are likely to be effective for the majority of children with spelling difficulties? These break down into methods of mastering common irregular words, and methods of mastering sound–symbol links. For learning keywords, the child (and parents or peer helper) should be shown how to use a multisensory strategy like simultaneous oral spelling, and should practise two or three new words a week on a daily basis, returning every third or fourth week to a mixed list of the words learned in the preceding weeks to make sure they are not forgotten. They will also benefit from being shown how to highlight the 'tricky bits' in irregular words, and using mnemonic cues to aid recall. This may mean repeatedly re-pronouncing the irregular word phoneti-cally – 'people' as 'pee-o-pull', for example, to help with remembering the 'o' in the middle, or 'Wednesday' as 'Wed-nes-day'. Or it may mean making up a mnemonic like '*B*ig *e*lephants *a*re *u*gly' for the beginning of 'beautiful', or '*We do not eat sweets day*' for 'Wednesday'. Again, it may involve learning a cue sentence ('A *bus* is always *busy*', '*What hat*?', '*You* are *young*', 'A *piece* of *pie*') that links a known spelling with the tricky bit of the new word. Joy Pollock's *Signposts to Spelling* (Heinemann) is a useful source of ideas for such mnemonics, for teachers and children alike.

If the mnemonics are to be home-grown, it works well to pair a poor speller with a peer or parent helper for a short period of daily work on devising cues for a list of words to be learned, and practising saying the cues while writing the word. A video training pack on this approach is available from the Kirklees Paired Learning Project (Oxley and Topping, 1988).

Using mnemonics has been shown (Veit et al., 1986) to be highly effective – more so even than direct instruction and overlearning – in ensuring long-term recall of difficult spellings. Once again, if peer tutoring is used, the experience seems to benefit teacher as well as taught: children in the Kirklees project made highly significant progress in spelling after using the technique three times a week for half-a-term, at a rate of twice the normally expected gains for tutees, and three times for tutors.

Turning now to phonetically regular spellings as opposed to irregular keywords, the same systematic, multisensory approach needs to be applied. The teacher's choice is whether to devise an individualized learning programme, based on mistakes from the child's own written work and/or words s/he really wants to learn, coupled with meticulous record keeping of what has been covered, or whether to use an off-the-peg spelling scheme that will take the child through a set sequence of letter patterns.

An example of the first, tailor-made approach was given in Chapter 6, where the teacher targeted a list of words containing a particular spelling pattern each week, and had a pair of children practise that pattern using a different activity each day. The daily activities can include:

- Using look–cover–write–check or simultaneous oral spelling.
- Making the words with plastic letters.
- Filling them into blanks in sentences made up by their partner.
- Making up and illustrating a silly sentence, rhyme or rap that links as many of the words as possible.
- Using supporting computer software, such as *The Complete Speller* from Northern Micromedia, *Hi-Spell* from Xavier or *Fun Phonics* from Pavic.
- Using worksheet material such as Holmes McDougall's *Spelling* series, Blackie's *The Laughing Speller, Space to Spell* and *More Space to Spell* from the Hornsby Centre.
- Testing each other on the word list.

A tailor-made approach like this is only really possible where the school's special needs resource base has a wide range of worksheet material and software catalogued according to letter strings. It is, however, relatively light on teacher time once this initial organization has been done.

More demanding on teacher input, but useful for those wanting a complete all-in-one scheme, are the structured multisensory approaches listed in Chapter 11. These are as relevant to the teaching of spelling as they are to reading, since they all employ a basic methodology of having the child learn each new sound–symbol relationship by writing it, first on its own and later as part of word lists, then reading back what has been written. Other structured multisensory schemes specific for teaching spelling include Violet Brand's *Spelling Made Easy* and the successful *Word Family* schemes for use with ARROW technology.

Figure 12.2 Eight-year-old's handwriting.

Teaching phonic patterns and keywords is one thing – having children apply this knowledge to their own writing is another. There is so much for them to think about when they write – generating ideas, structuring sentences, remembering punctuation – that the overload means something has to give: often, if new spelling patterns have not reached the point of being automatic, it will be spelling. Fortunately, the process writing approach can help with this. Children can be taught to apply their new learning about how words are spelled at the editing stage – initially by looking for a small, specified number of errors on one or two particular keywords or letter strings targeted by the teacher (ones they should know from previous spelling sessions), later still for an unspecified number of errors on a target pattern chosen by the teacher, later still for errors on a self-chosen spelling pattern or patterns. Ultimately, children should be encouraged to pre-empt the editing process by underlining words they are not sure of as they write, and checking back later using a simple dictionary, word bank or personal word book.

Handwriting

When assessing children's handwriting, it can sometimes be difficult to get away from the global impression of untidiness, and pin down exactly where the difficulties lie. Take the piece of work, from an 8-year-old shown in Figure 12.2. What is it that he is doing, or not doing, that makes his writing so hard to read?

A simple checklist, used by the teacher or by children themselves, can help pin down problem areas. It needs to cover the four 'Ss' of handwriting – shape, spacing, sizing, straights. First, are the letters correctly shaped and formed? Do they start and finish at the correct point – for example, are the circles in the a/o/d/g/q group adequately rounded and closed? For spacing, is a space approximately the width of the child's little finger left between words? Letters should be aligned to a baseline, with correctly positioned ascenders and descenders; all the small letters should be the same size as each other, all the tall and capital letters likewise; the writing should be neither too large nor too small. Straight lines in letters should be vertical or have a slight, even slope towards the right.

This kind of checklist, applied to the piece of writing above, would show that this child had problems in spacing, letter sizing, placing letters relative to a line, and with the formation of the circular shape in some letters.

Assessment should also include watching the child writing, looking for factors such as how s/he holds a pen or pencil and positions the paper, and whether s/he steadies the paper with the non-writing hand. Right-handers should hold a pencil in a tripod grip, with their fingers about three-quarters of an inch or an inch from the point; left-handers need to hold the pencil slightly further from the point – about an inch and a quarter away. For a right-handed child, the paper should be at a $30°$ angle, tilted to the right; for left-handed children (so that they do not cover the work as they write, and develop a 'hooked' grip), the paper should be tilted $30°$ to the left.

It is not easy to alter established habits, but special pencil grips, or for older children who want to appear no different from their peers, three-sided pencils (both from LDA) can help those who hold a pencil wrongly or too tightly, as can placing taped guidelines on the child's table or in the writing corner (clearly marked to show which are for right-handers and which for left-handers) to show how the paper should be positioned and angled. Beyond these simple structural measures, improving children's handwriting is a matter of getting the child to do short periods of regular practice that targets any problem areas

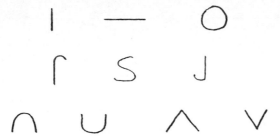

Figure 12.3 Basic shapes of letter formation.

highlighted by the checklist. Young children may need to practise the basic shapes of letter formation as shown in Figure 12.3. The basic shapes should be practised large and small, with eyes open and eyes shut, on the blackboard and on big sheets of paper, with paint and chalk and big felt-tips. To make the practice more interesting, the shapes can be turned into pictures to trace, copy and complete – handles to put on to umbrellas, a picture of waves in the sea to finish, railings on a fence, noses on clowns, dotted lines down the middle of roads. There are many commercially available materials (such as the early stages of the *Hand for Spelling* worksheets and *Prewriting Skills Pencil Fun* sheets, both from LDA, the Collins *Pencil Fun* books, the Schofield and Sims *Early Writing* series) to support this kind of approach.

Once the basic shapes are mastered, children with handwriting difficulties need access to varied worksheets on letter formation, perhaps supplemented by using *Rol 'n Write* from LDA to consolidate their knowledge of where to start letters and which direction to go in. Letters should be taught in groups with a similar pattern of movement – a c d g o q, b f h k l t, i m n r u y, j p, v w. They should be practised in small groups of three of a kind, never a whole line of one letter – it is impossible to sustain a rhythm of correct letter formation along an entire line, and the writing inevitably deteriorates towards the end. Many children find it helpful to have pointed out to them, from the beginning, the difference between the 'giraffe' letters (b, d, l, etc.), the 'turtle' letters (a, c, e, etc.) and the 'monkey' letters (g, j, p, etc.), and to practise placing them relative to the line.

It makes sense, when practising letters together for joined writing, to choose meaningful letter strings rather than random groups. Learning to write, for example, 'an' and then practising it in a list of words like 'can', 'pan' or 'ant' will benefit the child's spelling alongside the handwriting. Charles Cripps' *A Hand for Spelling* adopts this approach, and is increasingly popular with teachers right down to the youngest age groups.

Most children with handwriting difficulties appear to benefit from using lined paper for all their work (Pasternicki, 1986); those with problems in letter sizing or positioning ascenders and descenders may need to use old-fashioned

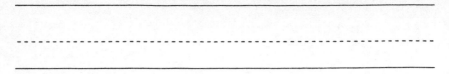

Figure 12.4 Double-lined paper for positioning ascenders/descenders.

double-lined paper for a while, until they sort out where each letter sits in relation to the others (Figure 12.4).

Confusion of b/d (and less commonly, b/p and u/n) is a common problem affecting handwriting. It may lead children to introduce inappropriate upper case B and D in the middle of their work, since they know they can get these the right way round. It also slows them down, and affects the readability of what they write. Many kinds of elaborate schemes, including computer games, have been devised to try to help children with letter reversals, but the most effective intervention is often the simple one of making sure the child can quickly and easily refer to an alphabet frieze on the wall or taped to the desk, and teaching the well-known mnemonic (Figure 12.5), where the 'b' and 'd' form the end of an imaginary bed, and must point in the right direction in order to 'hold the mattress up'.

There are many reasons why children develop handwriting difficulties. Inadequate early teaching or inadequate tools are often to blame – for example, when children learning to write have used a visual model (copying what they see on the page) rather than the necessary correct motor model for letter formation, or when they have not been shown how to position paper and pen, or have been given small pencils and paper when their stage of motor development required something on a larger scale.

Some children, however, do have in-built motor difficulties, affecting their handwriting development no matter how well they are taught and resourced. For these children, like Suresh in the example below, writing can become such an unpleasant – and even physically painful – chore that the whole of their experience of school is coloured by this one difficulty. Not infrequently, they develop such a dislike of the whole business of writing that they more or less down tools and rarely manage more than a few scrappy, stilted lines of written

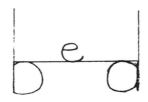

Figure 12.5   b/d mnemonic.

work. The teacher then concludes that they are either lazy or not very bright, and a downward spiral of motivation and behaviour begins.

Suresh was 7: a lively, articulate little boy who read well and impressed his teacher with his mature sense of humour and wide general knowledge. His written work, however, was barely legible. He could not concentrate for long on writing. When his teacher talked to him about the problem, he said: 'I just don't like writing. It's boring. I hate it when we have to copy stuff.' A psychological assessment showed that there was a large discrepancy – of three to four years – between the level at which Suresh was able to reason logically and express himself orally, and his skills in copying shapes with pencil and paper or with coloured bricks. He would often copy shapes in strange ways.

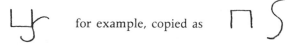

When asked to describe what Suresh was like as a small child, his mother said he talked very clearly early on, but he was late in learning to walk. He seemed to find learning all motor skills difficult – catching and kicking a ball, hopping, doing anything to a rhythm. He was a messy eater, always seemed to have his clothes on askew or back to front, and infuriated the family with his tendency to drop things or knock them over or bump into them. When he started school he used both right and left hand for writing; now he was clearly right-handed.

It was agreed at the meeting between his mother, teacher and psychologist that his motor and spatial difficulties were probably causing him much frustration at school, and that though he needed to work on his handwriting he also, paradoxically, needed much of the pressure taken *off* writing, so that he could get out of what his teacher described as his current 'nose dive in motivation'. Suresh and his teacher struck a bargain. For about half of all classroom recording, she would reduce the writing load by having him use *Stylus* word processing on the computer, dictate his work to her, or work with a partner who would be happy to act as scribe for their joint ideas. For the remainder of recording tasks, Suresh would set himself a target for the amount of writing he would do; if he consistently reached his targets his mother would do something special with him at home – read him an extra story, or do some maths with him, both of which he very much liked (and with three younger brothers and sisters rarely got much of). Suresh would also spend a few minutes each day on 'Hand for Spelling' sheets and cursive writing patterns, and help the reception teacher supervise a group of children in her class who were just learning how to form their letters.

This proved particularly motivating for him: his own handwriting soon improved considerably. Initially, he set himself very low targets for independent writing in class, but over the weeks, as he produced successful dictated and partner work that was read out to the whole class, he began to increase the amount he was willing to write, until after one term he was managing a page or more at a time.

Suresh' pattern of motor coordination and spatial difficulties, sometimes called 'the clumsy child syndrome' (see Table 12.3) is by no means uncommon. Surveys (Gubbay, 1975) have indicated that as many as 5 per cent of children in mainstream schools have significant motor problems of this type. The difficulties can span gross motor coordination, balance, fine manipulative control, spatial and body awareness, visual perception, speech articulation, attention and concentration. The picture presented is of a child who is awkward, uncoordinated, accident prone, disorganized, annoyingly messy and immature in self-help skills such as dressing and eating, and – if their difficulties have gone unrecognized so that people have been impatient and angry with them for their awkwardness – low in self-esteem and lacking in friends. Some (Henderson and Hall, 1982) are academically successful, with only minor handwriting difficulties and some slight difficulties in social integration. Others, however, have widespread academic difficulties, with maths (because of its spatial aspects) as well as written recording showing up as an area of particular concern.

Research has shown that children with coordination problems do not, on the whole, 'grow out of them' as they get older (Losse et al., 1991). As teenagers, children who were identified as clumsy in the primary school were considered by their teachers to be less academically competent than a control group, sat fewer public examinations, had more behaviour problems, were bullied more often and continued to show problems of coordination and personal organization.

Many of these long-term problems are preventable, given appropriate early intervention and support in school – intervention and support that goes beyond the handwriting problem alone. Specific coaching in motor skills, on a programme devised by an occupational or physiotherapist, can do much to improve the child's coordination and self-esteem. In the classroom, helpful strategies include

- Pairing the child with a more coordinated friend for work involving fine motor skills – using scissors, making models, using equipment in science and technology.
- Providing pre-prepared layouts (such as charts or graphs) on which the child can record information.
- Using window markers in different sizes to highlight the area of a busy page that the child needs to work from or on.
- Enlarging parts of busy pages on a photocopy, then spacing them out in the child's book.
- Teaching the child to talk him- or herself through visual and spatial tasks –

Table 12.3 Checklist for coordination difficulties

- Difficulties in learning to do buttons, fastenings, shoelaces, a tie
- Awkward or messy eater
- Immature drawings
- Handwriting problems
- Delayed or impaired speech
- Difficulties in balancing, climbing, throwing, catching, skipping, learning to ride a bicycle
- Tendency to bump into things, drop things, trip up
- Difficulty in organizing personal possessions and organizing self for learning
- Easily distracted
- Difficulties in laying out work on a page
- Difficulties with tasks involving spatial skills such as maps, plans, diagrams, coordinates, telling the time, measurement, shape work, design technology
- Difficulty in locating information on busy pages
- Difficulty in finding way around

---

for example, learning a verbal model like 'start at the top, down, round' for letter formation, or translating visual maths 'sums' into oral problem form (5 × 20 into 'I had five lots of twenty pence').
- Compartmentalizing the child's workspace, and if possible seating the child away from distractions.
- Using alternatives to traditional written recording.
- Providing opportunities for the child to succeed and maintain self-esteem.
- Protecting the child from too public a display of coordination difficulties, for example, at sports day.

CURRICULUM ACCESS FOR CHILDREN WITH SPELLING AND HANDWRITING DIFFICULTIES

Children who find the secretarial aspects of writing difficult have always been at a great disadvantage in school. They are asked to spend long periods doing something they feel bad at. They may be judged by their busy teachers as less competent in many areas of the curriculum than they really are, because they do not succeed in recording what they know and understand. Initially the national curriculum, with its stress on varied modes of pupil response and varied means of assessment, promised them better things; the new focus on short, timed written tests looks like taking them back to square one – if, that is, we are not careful about making full use of the adaptations and concessions available to pupils with special educational needs.

In these circumstances, it becomes very important for all teachers to know about the many ways in which full written recording can be bypassed, in order to enable children to demonstrate, order and reflect on their learning. Such bypass strategies, applied to subjects other than the specific spelling and presentation attainment targets within English, are perfectly legitimate. Some teachers, and many parents, may need reassurance on this point. They may feel that if children are not required to write all the time, in science, history or whatever, then they will never improve their presentation skills, because they will not be getting enough practice. If, this argument goes, they are using a word processor with a spellcheck, or dictating to a scribe, or filling in a cloze sheet the teacher has prepared, then they are somehow getting off lightly, and not learning what they should. The answer to this is that if we try to do everything at once, we are likely to overload children. They will find it hard to practise correct spelling, handwriting and punctuation when they are also struggling to think what to say and how to say it when writing up a scientific investigation, say, or a historical account. There is a place for practising the secretarial skills, but not when the child is having to do all these things at the same time. English lessons are the time to focus on secretarial skills; when the child is working on science or history, it is the science and history we want him or her to learn and anything that gets in the way of the child with special needs accessing those subjects is best either bypassed or modified.

Curriculum access strategies for children with writing difficulties fall into two groups. First, there are the strategies in which the child is not asked to write at all, but to use alternative means of recording. Second, there are strategies that involve *supported* writing in one form or another.

Let us first look at the idea of total writing bypass. If the child is not to be asked to write at all, s/he can instead:

- Do detailed drawings or diagrams.
- Make audio or video tape recordings.
- Use sorting boards and sorting tasks of all kinds.
- Dictate work to a scribe (parent, peer, helper or teacher), or to a tape recorder to be scribed later.
- Work with a partner or small group, where better writers do the recording but the child can contribute his or her ideas.

Supported writing is often easier to manage than total bypass. Here the child can:

- Be provided with pre-prepared cloze sheets (filling in missing words). These sheets may be written by the teacher, or be made by photocopying text and then blanking out some words. Or the child's own work that s/he has dictated to a scribe can have words deleted. The words to go in the spaces can be provided in a box, for the child to choose from: how many words, and whether they are put at the end of a long piece of text, or the end of a paragraph or sentence, will depend on the degree of support the child needs.
- Be provided with sentences to cut out, sequence and illustrate, or with halves of sentences ('tops and tails') to fit together.

- Fill in speech and 'think' bubbles on prepared sheets.
- Fill in information on prepared tables, charts and matrices.
- Colour and label a drawing or diagram – affixing cut-out labels, or drawing lines to match words with the bits they refer to, as in matching descriptive words to the features and clothing of a character from a descriptive passage the children have listened to.
- Write using the magic line idea from the national writing project, with parent, helper or teacher filling in the missing words or parts of words later.
- Be provided with word banks, keyword lists, glossaries of subject vocabulary for easy reference.
- Be provided with dictionaries specially written for children with spelling difficulties, such as the *ACE Spelling Dictionary* from LDA, or the *Pergamon Dictionary of Perfect Spelling* from Nelson.
- Use a small portable electronic spellchecker such as the Franklin *Elementary Spellmaster*, on which the child can enter the word they need 'just as it sounds' and be given several alternative correct spellings to choose from.
- Use word processing software.

Of all these strategies, word processing is probably the most powerful in supporting children with writing difficulties. Using word processing means that the business of editing and producing a published version of an initial draft takes minutes rather than hours. Children are more willing to 'have a go', and write adventurously, because mistakes can so easily be rectified. Davidson (1988), for example, found that the work of a group of children with specific learning difficulties showed a much broader vocabulary and variety of sentence structure, as well as being more technically accurate, when they were using a computer than when they were writing by hand. Word processing also takes the effort out of writing for children who find it difficult to control a pencil and form letters. It means that the child can produce work that always looks good; the problems of handwriting and setting out are overcome. It means that spelling (and, increasingly, grammar) can be checked quickly and easily, in an emotionally neutral way.

Using word processing also means that varying degrees of support can be built into the writing process. At the earliest stages of writing proficiency, children can use concept keyboard overlays that contain important words they will need for their writing, plus lower-case letters, a full stop and a magic line: such overlays will enable them to record their ideas quickly, before they forget what they want to say. Editing will also be quick and easy; they can then print the work out for display, or to take home, or keep in a portfolio or topic folder. They can also use the print-out as a basis for cloze exercises, or for making cloze exercises for one another.

At a slightly more advanced level, software such as *Full Phase* and *Clicker Plus* (both available, like other software mentioned in this chapter, in the REM catalogue), acts like a concept keyboard on the screen: the teacher can display a list of core words for the particular writing topic, or a personal dictionary for each child, from which the child selects using a mouse. Words not on the screen are typed in letter by letter in the normal way.

Another form of supported writing uses predictive word processors, such as *PAL*. These predict, on the basis of the first one or two letters typed in, what the word the child intends to use might be, and offer choices: a single keyboard stroke then enters the word in full. Software like this is particularly helpful for children with motor difficulties who find many keystrokes laborious, and for children with severe spelling difficulties. It can also help with punctuation – *PAL*, for example, automatically puts a capital letter after each full stop.

Older children may need less support than the concept keyboard or predictive systems provide. They may only need to use a word-processing programme with a built-in spellchecker. Such spellcheckers can be very useful for poor spellers – if, that is, they can read well enough to recognize the 'correct' spelling from amongst the several alternatives the spellchecker will suggest. Children with reading difficulties as well as spelling difficulties may do better using a word processor with speech-output device such as *Talking Pendown* and *Full Phase*, so that they can hear what they have written, keep track of where they are up to, and pick up at least some of their more gross spelling errors.

The next example illustrates the successful use of word processing, alongside other alternatives to traditional full written recording. Here a support teacher, working with two Year 6 boys with specific learning difficulties/dyslexia, was asked to work on improving the boys' written language skills, in the context of a class topic on the ancient Egyptians.

> Mark and Paul both had very noticeable spelling problems and had little confidence in their own writing ability. They could read adequately but not with great range or fluency. Both contributed well to class discussion and took a keen interest in most topic work, but rarely got more than a few scrappy lines down on paper. Their support teacher decided that the main target in her work with them should be re-establishing their confidence, by helping them to produce high-quality work for their topic folders. With her help, they brainstormed the words they would need for their writing about the ancient Egyptians, and made an illustrated concept keyboard overlay (Figure 12.6) for use with STYLUS software. The teacher wrote the alphabet sequentially at the bottom of the overlay, rather than in QWERTY form, to provide extra practice in alphabetical order.
>
> Since sequencing events was difficult for both boys, they needed some extra work on certain aspects of the topic – the making of papyrus and the process of mummification – before being able to write about them. The teacher prepared a sentence sequencing worksheet (Figure 12.7), and a tops and tails worksheet (Figure 12.8) for them. They went on to use the prepared keyboard overlay to draft their own piece (Figure 12.9). The teacher edited the first print-out with them,

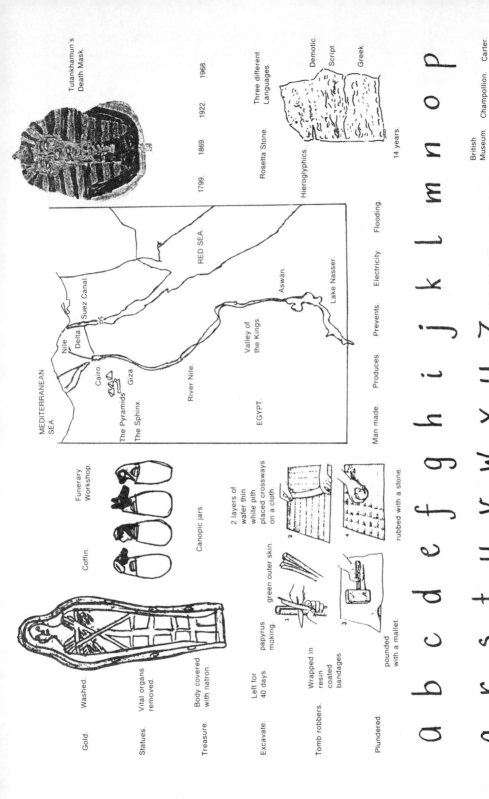

Figure 12.6 Concept keyboard overlay on the Ancient Egyptians.

Making a mummy

> Cut up the strips. Put them in order to tell how papyrus is made. Draw a picture to go with each sentence.

The dead body was washed, and the vital

Then the body was

It was left for

Finally, it was wrapped

forty days

organs removed

covered with natron

in bandages coated in resin

Figure 12.7   Sentence sequencing worksheet.

> Cut up the strips. Put them in order to tell how papyrus is made. Draw a picture to go with each strip.

This was cut into wafer-thin strips, and placed crossways on a cloth.

Finally, a stone was used, like we use sandpaper today, to rub the papyrus smooth.

Its green outer skin was removed, to show the white pith underneath.

First the papyrus was gathered from the banks of the river Nile.

before being pounded to a pulp with a mallet.

Figure 12.8   A tops and tails worksheet.

using this opportunity to do some work on 'ou' and 'oo' sounds. The boys revised the piece on screen, then went on to write in the same manner about the discovery of Tutankhamun's tomb, the Rosetta Stone, the geography of the Nile Delta and the Egyptian gods. They were extremely proud of their final topic book; their class teacher was

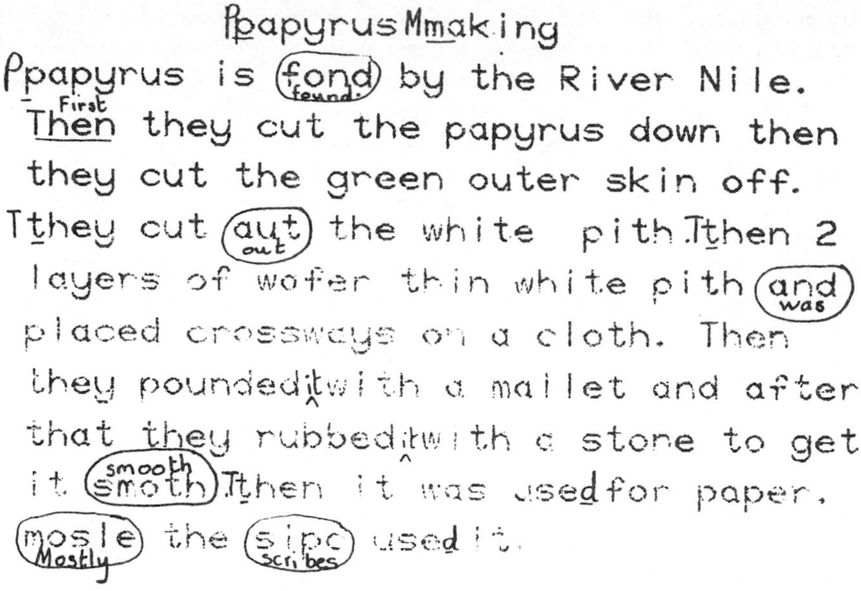

Ppapyrus Mmaking

Ppapyrus is (fond/found) by the River Nile.
Then/First they cut the papyrus down then
they cut the green outer skin off.
Tthey cut (aut/out) the white pith. Tthen 2
layers of wofer thin white pith (and/was)
placed crossways on a cloth. Then
they pounded it with a mallet and after
that they rubbed it with a stone to get
it (smoth/smooth) Tthen it was used for paper.
(mosle/Mostly) the (sipc/scribes) used it.

Figure 12.9 Drafting from a prepared keyboard overlay.

surprised at the quality of the language they had used, and the way they had organized their ideas.

GENERATING IDEAS AND STRUCTURING WRITTEN WORK

Mark and Paul knew what they wanted to say in their writing, and had the spoken vocabulary in which to express their ideas – though this only really became clear when they were provided with appropriate support with the mechanical aspects of spelling and handwriting. Theirs is a common pattern, even if one that is not always readily apparent to the busy teacher. They do not, however, form the only group of children with difficulties in written recording. There are other children, who may or may not have good mechanical skills, but struggle to generate ideas for written work, to find the right words, and to order what they have to say.

These are children who are not, unlike those with specific difficulties in the mechanical aspects of writing, able to improve greatly in the quantity and quality of their work when given the opportunity to dictate pieces to an adult, rather than write them by hand. Support for them needs to take the form of careful preparation before the writing actually begins. The child should be guided through several rehearsals of an idea, story or account at a practical 'doing' level well before s/he puts pen to paper. For example, a child who is to be asked to produce an illustrated booklet retelling a traditional story might need first to take part in dramatizing the story as a class or in a small group, to sequence pictures from the story, to tell the story bit by bit around the group, and to recount it to a parent or younger child. A child who is to write a description of a character might need to answer questions about the character put by a partner, or do a series of drawings and use these to describe what the character is like to a small group. A child who has to make up an adventure story might work with visually exciting computer material that stimulates paired or group discussion, and leads to ideas for writing a story via an adventure game series-of-choices format.

After preparation comes planning: here the ideas of the national writing project are proving a great support to children who have difficulties in ordering their thoughts for writing. If they are supplied with a structure for planning their work, and the teacher or another helper is able to spend a few minutes with them sorting out their plan, they are often then able to write a first draft independently, instead of coming up constantly for help and advice on what to put next.

The structure supplied to children for planning their writing can vary. It may be a sheet folded into small squares, so that they can draw a picture in each, as in cartoon strip; the writing task will then be to write a sentence or paragraph about each picture in the series. Or it may be a series of prompt questions, like those in Figure 12.10. It may be a writing frame, like those devised in the Exeter Literacy Project (Lewis and Wray, 1994), consisting of formats for different genres such as the 'discussion genre', in which arguments are developed for and against particular viewpoints. Or it may be a table with headings – such as those in Longman's *Super Writer Copymasters* – that ask the child to note the type of story (for example, adventure), the time and setting, a description of each main character, ideas for the plot and ending, and so on. The *Writer Copymasters* also include formats for planning book reviews, letters, accounts of investigations and persuasive writing.

Planning tools like these work well with writing on the word processor. The child's plan provides the vocabulary for a concept keyboard overlay or personal on-screen dictionary; the vocabulary can then be used and re-used for multiple versions and drafts.

Further support may be needed at the time of drafting, for children who – even with a prepared plan – find it hard to keep track of where they have got to. These are often children with short-term memory difficulties, who cannot hold a long sentence in mind for long enough to get each part down. It can be helpful to have them use their planner to tape record what they want to say, then play it back a phrase or sentence at a time as they write it.

CONCLUSION

Writing is a public activity, in a way that reading, for example, may not be: what the child commits to paper is open to the scrutiny not only of the teacher, but also of other children. Writing is also permanent: whether the product is

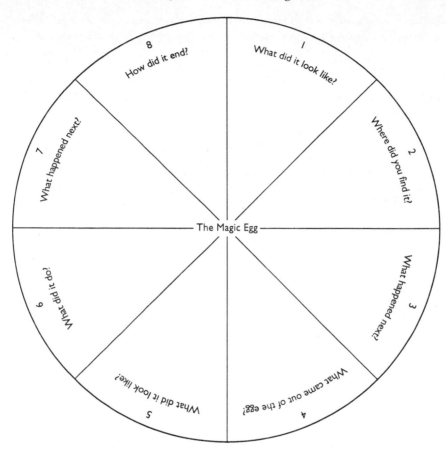

Figure 12.10 Story planner.

good or bad, it does not disappear. Because of this, it is an area where failure is particularly damaging to the child's self-esteem.

We do now have the tools to make sure that this loss of self-esteem is avoided, and that all children are enabled to produce writing that they can feel proud of. What is needed now are whole school systems that will give teachers the confidence, in time, to make full use of these available tools – banks of prepared concept keyboard overlays for schemes of work across the school, for example, readily available spellcheckers and cloze sheets and story planners, adult support deployed to help children plan their writing or scribe for them.

In this chapter we have looked at the strategies for supporting the writing process that might be built into such a whole school plan, and at the equally vital systems used across the school to remediate children's difficulties in basic skill areas of handwriting, spelling and presentation.

It is now time to turn from special needs in the 'tool' language skills that children use across the curriculum to needs in another 'tool' area, where difficulties can also have wide ranging effects – the area of mathematics.

FURTHER READING

Reason, R. and Boote, R. (1995) *Helping Children with Reading and Spelling*. London: Routledge.

RESOURCES

Spelling in Context by Margaret Peters, from NFER–Nelson.
Space to Spell, More Space to Spell, by Frula Shear, from The Hornsby Centre, 71 Wandsworth Common Westside, London SW18 2ED.
Spelling Made Easy, by Violet Brand, from Egon Publishers, Royston Road, Baldock, Herts. SG7 6NW.

· 13 ·

SPECIAL NEEDS IN MATHS

INTRODUCTION

On the whole, primary teachers often feel more confident about working with special needs in maths than they do with special needs in language and literacy. In part this may be because maths schemes based on graded pupil books provide a ready-made structure which assures the teacher that tasks will be matched to the needs of children across the whole range of mathematical ability. The teacher feels confident because s/he knows what work to give to the child; whether it does the child's confidence any good to progress slowly and painfully through a series of books she or he perceives as far 'below' the books classmates are working on is a different matter.

It is debatable, too, whether a slower pace through exactly the same material can meet the needs of all children with mathematical difficulties. A more fine-grained assessment of teaching needs may be required, in order to pinpoint where in particular the child has not succeeded in grasping essential foundation concepts (the small steps approach), and of any underlying reasons for the mathematical difficulties. In this chapter we will look at how such an assessment can lead to individualized action-planning: first of all planning to circumvent identified difficulties – for example, in sequencing, handling abstractions, or handling linguistic or spatial information – and then, later in the chapter, at plans for tackling some of the most common stumbling blocks children encounter along the path of their mathematical development.

ASSESSMENT

Assessment of mathematical difficulties can take place through:

1 Observing children at work – for example, to note patterns of concentration (or lack of it), how often they ask for help, how they go about selecting the

approaches and materials to use for practical tasks, what mathematical language they use, and whether they are able to make generalizations and predictions.

2 Miscue analysis – for example, noting from an addition such as

$$
\begin{array}{r}
36 \\
+\ 1P \\
\hline
91 \\
\hline
5
\end{array}
$$

that the child is experiencing orientation and sequencing difficulties.

3 Using a small steps analysis of national curriculum attainment targets, such as SNIPP or Profiles of Development (see Chapter 4) as a checklist. The aim is to determine which in a series of prior steps leading up to a given concept or skill the child may not have mastered – for example, discovering that a child who cannot add tens and units with carrying cannot manage the conceptually earlier step of identifying in a two-digit numeral which digit represents the number of tens, and which the number of ones.

4 Using an informal interview to probe the child's understanding by asking *how* they arrived at certain conclusions, or as a quick check of the concepts they have mastered. One such interview format is described in Derek Haylock's very helpful book *Teaching Mathematics to Low Attainers* (1991); this allows the teacher to assess, in the space of 15 minutes or so, what the child understands of time, money, measurement, place value, computation and calculator use.

5 Using published tests – for example, those from NFER-Nelson's extensive range. These include, for children of four to eight, the Early Mathematics Diagnostic Kit; this is an expensive resource, but uses inviting and colourful materials to explore systematically, through untimed individual assessment, possible gaps in a child's early mathematical learning. It is particularly useful for assessing understanding of mathematical language (words such as 'smaller', 'longest', 'empty'), the ability to sequence events in time, and early number concepts such as one to one correspondence and conservation of number. For older children (aged six to eleven plus), a good basic resource is the Staffordshire Maths Test; this can be administered to a group, and yields criterion-referenced information on whether a child has reached particular objectives in basic numeracy, fractions, measurement and shape.

A combination of these assessment methods will make it possible for the teacher to do two things. First, s/he should be able to plot precisely the learning objectives for the child: to develop action plans that state, for example, that Michael needs to learn to make up 10 p in different ways using 1 p, 2 p and 5 p coins, or order numbers within 100. Second, the teacher should be able through the assessment process to gather information on where things might be going wrong for the child in maths, so that teaching styles and approaches – the 'how' of teaching, rather than just the 'what' – can be modified accordingly.

COMMON REASONS FOR MATHEMATICAL DIFFICULTIES

Children with specific learning difficulties and maths

Some children have difficulty with maths merely because of the way in which tasks are presented. In classes where most of the work is individual, pupils can fall behind simply because of the reading and writing demands of the textbooks or worksheets. Clement (1980), for example, found that a quarter of twelve-year-olds' errors in written maths tasks arose from difficulties in reading accuracy or comprehension. Using more paired and group investigational and problem-solving work is one way round this problem; giving oral instructions, tape recording the text of worksheets and books, or asking one child to act as regular reading helper to another during maths sessions are others.

Children with reading and spelling difficulties may, however, have reasons for experiencing problems with maths that go deeper than mere text readability. Numbers, like letters and words, are abstract symbols to which the child has to attach meanings; like letters, they have to be written the right way round; as with words, the symbols have to be remembered in a particular order – whether counting to 10, or to 100, or learning a multiplication table. Not surprisingly, in view of these similarities in cognitive demands, two-thirds of children with specific learning difficulties/dyslexia also have problems in basic numeracy (Joffe, 1981). They may have a good understanding of mathematical ideas – may know, for example, what process or operation to apply in relation to a problem, and be good at making generalizations and predictions – but fall down on basic computation. Typically, they will take longer than other children to learn the written form of numbers, to attach reliable meaning to mathematical symbols such as $\langle$ and $\rangle$, $+$, $-$, $\times$ and $\div$, and to master sequences such as counting, days of the week, months of the year, and times tables. They may never develop an automatic knowledge of number bonds, still counting on their fingers for simple sums when other children have long passed this stage. They may show directional difficulties, putting figures in the wrong order (15 for 51, for example), or taking top from bottom instead of bottom from top when doing vertical subtraction.

Children with difficulties like these need a slower pace to their mathematical learning only in some areas – generally in maths AT2. In other areas, what they need are strategies that will enable them to bypass their problems in arithmetical computation in order to access the work on using and applying maths, algebra, shape and space or whatever. The provision of a ruler clearly marked to at least twenty for counting on and back, for example, will help overcome the problem of not knowing number bonds; a tables matrix the problem of poor memory for tables; a calculator the problems of direction and sequence in work with large numbers.

It will be helpful, also, to pupils with specific learning difficulties if the teacher encourages them always to estimate before doing any kind of computation, so that they can apply their often good logical ability as a check on the accuracy of their answers. To overcome the problem of left–right sequencing, they need to be made very sure, conceptually, of the way that numbers in certain positions represent hundreds, tens and ones, and encouraged to talk themselves through computational processes – for example, 'add nine and six, that's fifteen; one ten so I put the one under the tens column, and five ones in the ones column'. To help with the problem of attaching names to symbols, it may be a good idea to have the child accumulate a pack of cards, with symbols such as + on the front, and their meanings (such as add, and, plus, total, sum of, increase by) on the reverse, so that parents or a peer helper can run through them on a regular basis to aid recall.

Finally, with these children it may be necessary to tackle short-term sequential memory problems. Many numerical operations require the ability to hold in mind a series of steps. A problem such as 75 p add 39 p on paper means remembering to add the units, split the result into tens and units, then add all the tens; if done mentally, it means perhaps seeing the 75 as 70 and 5, the 39 as one less than 40, adding the 70 and 40, subtracting one. Some children simply cannot remember where they are in complex multistep operations like these. They should not be expected to manipulate large numbers mentally without a calculator, and may – if they can read well enough – require for written work the support of an *aide-mémoire* for the steps in basic processes: a yellow sticky Post-it for each operation, attached to the inside cover of their maths books – for example,

Subtracting large numbers

1 Round up and estimate.
2 Label columns TU.
3 Take bottom units figure away from top units figure.
4 If it won't go, borrow a ten from the top tens column.
5 Take bottom units figure away from new top units figure.
6 Take bottom tens figure away from new top tens figure.
7 Check your answer is close to estimate.

$$\begin{array}{cc} \mathrm{T} & \mathrm{U} \\ {}^4 5 & {}^1 4 \\ -2 & 9 \\ \hline 2 & 5 \\ \hline \end{array}$$

Thinking in the abstract

Some children with mathematical difficulties have problems that are very different from those of children with specific learning difficulties. These children may be very good at learning things by rote, but find it hard to understand what they are doing. They may cope well with straightforward computation, but be unable to work out whether addition or subtraction or multiplication or division is called for in a given problem – what to do, for example, with things like 'how much less does Mark have than Ben', or 'How many teams of five children will there be in a class of thirty?'

For these children it is the abstract, symbolic nature of maths which causes problems. Other aspects of school experience – such as reading or writing – also involve symbols, but usually the symbols have a fairly straightforward relationship with what is symbolized. In maths, it is different: the numeral '1' may sometimes stand for one, but sometimes – if it is in a different place – for ten, or a hundred, or a thousand; a 5 p coin, the teacher says, is somehow 'the same as' two 2 p pieces and a 1 p piece; the symbol ' – ' stands for take away, minus, decrease, count back, the difference between. The more abstract the concept, the more displaced from what the child can see and hear and touch, the harder it will be to grasp: place value, coin equivalence, and patterns such as the relatedness of addition and subtraction, multiplication and division, are frequent stumbling blocks for children with mathematical difficulties of this kind.

The solution for them is to avoid at all costs presenting disembedded mathematical tasks, devoid of the real-life and concrete context in which the child may in fact function very effectively. If the Ben in the problem given above is Mark's little brother, and is given 40 p to Mark's 30 p by their Dad, Mark will in all probability be acutely aware of the 10 p gap, even if he could not cope with the same problem posed in less personal terms in his maths book; if the children have to organize their own teams of five ahead of time for a PE lesson, and get out a football for each team, they are likely to have no difficulty in understanding that the required operation is division.

Using everyday situations involving the children themselves and their immediate environment, substituting meaningful materials for those with less meaning (using, for example, 1 p and 10 p coins rather than an abacus to teach place value), turning abstract language into concrete ('one per cent' into 'one in a hundred', for example), and using real objects that can be handled before encountering the same experiences with pictures and diagrams, are all essential principles in teaching children who find it hard to deal with abstractions.

If real-life experience cannot easily be achieved in the classroom, then story and role play can help to fill the gap. Diane Montgomery (1990), in her book on teaching children with learning difficulties, gives a vivid example: in some work on measurement, one teacher asked pupils to find out who in the class had the largest and smallest hands, without using any words or sounds to communicate. The two pupils with the smallest hands were chosen to role play the staff serving in a pretend shop; the three pupils with the largest hands were chosen to play customers buying cloth. The rest of the class watched the ensuing argument about whose hand spans should be used to measure the cloth – leaving them able to articulate very clearly the need for standard units of measurement: an abstraction had become real.

As well as work which will translate abstract into concrete, strategies will also be needed to help with the common problem of not knowing which mathematical operation to apply to everyday problems. Research has given us some insights into why this occurs, and what might help. Krutetskii (1976), for example, found that many of the problems of less able children in dealing with verbal phrased questions stem from their inability to pick out essential from non-essential features, or to pay attention to more than one relevant feature at a time.

Simply giving them extra practice does not seem to help; they need a supportive structure, or scaffolding, which can slowly be withdrawn as they become more familiar with the process of turning problems into operations. To begin with, they may need to be taught a list of keywords to look out for: words like altogether, decreased, increased, more, less, difference between, each, heavier / lighter / longer / shorter / older than. They can have the keywords highlighted by the teacher, or practise highlighting them for each other in a range of verbal problems.

Requiring children to use calculators regularly when solving verbal problems is another strategy that is helpful to those with special needs. It takes the focus off how to go about adding, dividing or whatever, and places it on what the teacher actually wants the child to learn – choosing the relevant operation, or key press. Children can overlearn particular formats using calculator sentences (Haylock, 1991): here the teacher writes a sentence in the particular format that is being practised (for example the addition operation in the format 'If the price of £– is increased by £–, the new price will be £–', or '– m is – shorter than – m'). Blank spaces about the size of a calculator are left for the missing numbers. Children work in pairs, turning over cards from two 0–10 packs and placing them in the spaces ('If the price of £10 is increased by £5, the new price will be £   ', '25 m is 5 m shorter than   '). They work out the problem on a calculator and display the calculator with its answer showing, in the empty answer box, before copying the whole sentence into their books.

A particular way of marrying calculator use with the child's common sense understanding of real-life experience is to offer graded problems, which start with small numbers within the pupils' grasp (Haylock, 1991). A child may be able to cope easily with a problem in the form 'Mark has 2 p. The book costs 5 p. Mark needs –p more', but have no idea what operation to enter on the calculator for a problem such as 'Mark has 52 p. The book costs 93 p. Mark needs –p more'. The teacher, however, can help by building in a series of intermediate graded problems: 'Mark has 3 p. The book costs 6 p . . . Mark has 12 p. The book costs 15 p . . . Mark has 14 p. The book costs 24 p . . .' and so on. Using a calculator at the point where the numbers just begin to exceed their mental grasp, but are still within the area where they will have a vague common sense idea of the correct answer, the children can explore the various possibilities for key presses, and discover for themselves the mathematical operations that are needed for problems in this form.

Making up their own verbal problems for 'sums' is a popular activity in many maths books, that will also help children make the links between words and figures. It can be enriched if the children work together, and are given the challenge of tape recording as many 'stories' as they can, set in an ongoing context such as a topic the class are studying, or a story they are reading, for a given sum.

A final need for children with mathematical difficulties in handling abstractions will be to have help in 'closing in' open-ended mathematical tasks. If it is a real life task, like organizing a refreshments stall at a fête, or planning how to spend PTA money on improving the school environment, children with learning difficulties need the teacher there with them at the planning stage; once they have, with help, listed the questions that need to be answered, they will be able to carry on with relatively little support. If it is an investigation, for example explaining what happens when you add pairs of odd and even numbers, they may benefit from being taught, over time, and with many repetitions, a flow chart structure that turns the open-ended task into a series of more manageable steps: 'start with one example ⟡ make up some more examples ⟡ decide what is the same about them ⟡ write down your idea ⟡ use it to predict some more examples ⟡ if it doesn't always work, try another idea.'

Spatial difficulties

So far we have looked at the mathematical needs of children with specific learning difficulties, who have problems with written numbers and with sequencing, and at the needs of children with more general learning difficulties, for whom abstractions and open-ended tasks are the problem. There is another group of children, however, who may have particular teaching needs of a different kind, like Gemma in this example:

> Gemma, though a lively little girl with good language skills, seemed to have a complete block when it came to maths. She made very slow progress through the infant maths books; her numbers were poorly formed and often reversed, and she struggled with the simple adding and taking away picture pages. Later on, her work was always messy, all over the page instead of neatly set out; she could not do the simplest operations without using apparatus; her parents spent many long and unsuccessful hours trying to teach her how to tell the time. She had great trouble with graphs and charts of all kinds. But it was her performance in work on Shape and Space that finally gave the clue to her difficulties; teacher assessment persistently showed her failing throughout the national curriculum areas in this area – for example, in following directional instructions in PE, working with symmetry, constructing nets for shapes, understanding angles and using coordinates. Gemma clearly had major difficulty in perceiving the spatial relationships between objects, or between her own body and the world around her.

For children with spatial difficulties like Gemma's – often children who also present mild coordination problems of the 'clumsy' type – maths can present apparently insurmountable obstacles. The difficulties will go well beyond the obvious shape and space areas to work in many aspects of number. Early on, these children may be slow to acquire any concept of number at all – the threeness of three, the fourness of four – or to handle simple operations of addition and subtraction, because they lose track of groups of objects or pictures they are trying to count. For them, numbers can shift and alter in a way that makes it difficult to attach symbols reliably to the spatial layouts with which they are presented. Later on, they will be confused by the spatial element that runs through more complex number operations: by the fact, for example, that some numbers (1, 2, 3, 4, etc.) increase from left to right, whereas others (in the concept of place value) increase in value from right to left, or by the significance of the way numbers are oriented in space and relative to one another – the differences between the meaning of figures and symbols in these 'sums', for example, are entirely spatial:

$$
\begin{array}{cccc}
14 & 41 & 14 & 14 \\
+6 & +6 & \times 6 & +9 \\
\hline
\end{array}
$$

Spatial skills are also critical in the ability to create and refer at will to a mental map of the number system – the map that places 5 before 6, and after 4, or 90 as ten steps back from 100. Without this mental map, children cannot juggle with numbers, work things out in their heads or check the accuracy of their calculations against an estimate; they have to rely on apparatus and working things out on paper to set rules.

Fortunately, if the teacher is aware that the child has spatial problems (something that is usually fairly obvious from their handwriting and drawings), there is much that can be done to provide appropriate differentiation and support. Early difficulties in counting arrangements can be circumvented if the child is taught to physically move objects from one side of a ruler placed vertically down the table to another while counting, and later to cross out pictures one by one, or map them into a number line, as in Figure 13.1. They should use a number line as much as possible when working with addition and subtraction, since they will find counting on and back easier than manipulating counters or fingers. To introduce them to this, they can physically 'walk' a large floor number line (3 + 2 as 'start at 3, move on 2 steps'), later moving a small toy person along a smaller line, and finally just using their finger. For older children with no mental map of the number system, a pocket number line, or (even more unobtrusive) a long clearly-marked ruler, will be needed for calculations.

To help with writing and recognizing numbers, the young child will need ready reference to a card or frieze showing numerals to ten, with a red dot for the starting point of each numeral and an arrow for the direction of pencil movement. Many children with spatial difficulties will benefit from using squared paper for all their work; this enables them to line up numbers next to and under one another, and leads to clearer, neater work. It may be necessary, too, to highlight mathematical signs in different colours (+ always red, for example, and × always blue), to prevent spatial confusion. Prepared formats for graphs and tables will help with recording; there is some useful software (*MATHS PAGE*, from North West SEMERC) which allows pupils with coordination and spatial difficulties to set out their work on screen, save it and print it using calculating, drawing, table and graph grid facilities.

Other tips include teaching a simple left–right mnemonic (forefinger and thumb on the *left* hand form an L-shape), using a watch or clock face which has

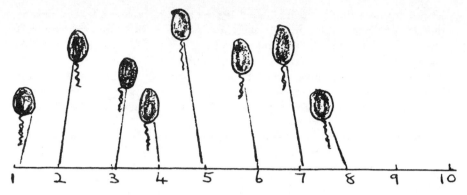

Figure 13.1 Method to circumvent difficulties in counting arrangements.

the 'past' and 'to' halves highlighted in different colours, laying rulers along coordinates when plotting or reading them, and teaching the child to put visual or spatial information into verbal form: 5 × 20, for example, becoming 'five lots of twenty', or 20 ÷ 5 'twenty sweets shared between five children'.

Problems with mathematical language

Maths places heavy demands on children's linguistic understanding. For many children, not knowing the meaning of terms such as 'shorter', 'wide', 'same', 'different', 'more than', 'less than', 'few', 'many together', 'as many as', 'each' or 'either' can prevent them from understanding instructions or sharing a mathematical dialogue with others. Sometimes, too, many different words have to be learned for the same concepts, for example, 'equals', 'makes', 'comes to', 'is the same as' for the '=' sign. At another level, children can be held back by the grammatical complexity and sentence length of problems they are asked to tackle: things like 'How many more cats are there than dogs?', or 'What number between 25 and 30 cannot be divided exactly by 2 or 3?'

Difficulties in understanding the language of maths may be due to lack of pre-school experience in hearing and using mathematical talk, or to specific language delays and disorders of the kind we looked at in Chapter 10. Either way, the result is the same. Unless the teacher uses a checklist to explore the words the child may not understand, and checks regularly for understanding of complex instructions, the child will be stuck and s/he will not know how to help.

If teachers are aware of difficulties for the child in responding to mathematical language, they can plan specific work to remedy the gaps. Small group discussion with the teacher around one of the 'Big Books' from the newer maths schemes, or such resources as LDA's *Talking Maths* posters and photographs may be enough for some children. Others may need daily practice with a parent or helper on particular vocabulary (a 'word for the week'): work with dad's ties or mum's belts to identify the *widest*, for example, or choosing the group or picture that has *the most* in a variety of situations at home or at school. Once the words are understood, materials like LDA's *Stile Maths Language* can be used to reinforce the learning.

For older children there should be mathematical dictionaries and a simple glossary in every classroom, specifying all the possible meanings of mathematical symbols, and the real-life meaning of commonly misunderstood words:

difference　　the result of subtracting one number from another.
equivalent　　equal in value to.
factor　　a number which will divide exactly into another.
fractions　　parts of a whole.

The teacher may also need to simplify instructions and explanations, rewriting them in shorter steps and active rather than passive voice: the 'What number between 25 and 30 . . .' problem above, for example, becoming

You are looking for a number between 25 and 30.
You cannot divide this number exactly by 2 or 3.
What is the number?

The need for overlearning

As we have seen many times in this book a common difficulty for children with special needs is that teaching can expose them to a new concept or idea, but then moves on before they have had a chance to become really fluent and automatic in the new skill. In maths, where learning is often sequential, and one concept or skill builds on earlier ones, this is particularly damaging. It means that maths failure tends to be cumulative; it breeds frustration and irritation in teachers and parents who do not understand why a child seems to have got something one minute, but then forgotten it a few days or weeks later.

Some of the solutions to problems like these were outlined in earlier chapters: building in extra practice (often timed, in order to increase fluency) well beyond the point where the child appears to have grasped the idea, and frequent reviews of earlier learning – in a ratio, some argue, of one-third review to every two-thirds of time spent on new learning.

This need not, when applied to maths, mean a return to what has been called the 'death by worksheet' model of masses of individual written tasks completed day-in day-out by children with special needs (while the others do something more interesting). Overlearning can be achieved in other, more stimulating ways. These include:

1　Investigations, in which pairs or groups of children get repeated practice in a particular skill in the context of a more open-ended task. For example, an investigation like this gives repeated practice in subtraction of two-digit numbers, with or without a calculator:

Take two sets of cards numbered 0 to 9. Turn over a pair, and write down the number – for example, 71. Reverse the pair and write down the number – for example, 17. Now find the difference, 71 − 17. Repeat with more pairs in order to find out which pairs give the biggest difference, and which the smallest difference.

2 Games to play in school. Board games, and games with number cards provide an enjoyable way of practising a wide range of skills. The versatile *Count Me In* games from AMS are an invaluable resource here, not least because the instructions for playing the games are presented in the form of strip cartoons with clear and simple text which can easily be read by children of a wide ability range, and because the accompanying notes give advice on how to adapt the games to meet the needs of children with sensory and physical impairments. Other attractive, inexpensive games are available in most of the newer maths schemes – New Peak, Nelson, Cambridge Primary Maths, Ginn Gem games.

3 Games to play at home. Many traditional board games played at home – like Ludo and Snakes and Ladders – support children's learning of basic mathematical concepts. Some schools (Harrison, 1989) have built on this through 'Paired Maths' schemes, where a stock of games, coded according to the predominant mathematical skill or concept involved, and with an accompanying card to highlight the kinds of mathematical language the game could bring out, are loaned for home use: parents borrow a game or two each week, and record how play went in a home–school book.

4 Puzzles, such as LDA's popular *Puzzle Tables* photocopy masters, which provide intriguing ways of practising addition, subtraction, division or multiplication, or picture puzzles (Haylock, 1991) made by pupils for one another – for dot-to-dot puzzles, for example, pupils place a sheet of tracing paper over an outline drawing and mark significant points with dots; they then write a series of sums or questions under the dot outline, and write the answers to the exercises in order next to the dots, so that their partner can answer the questions and join up the corresponding dots to make the picture.

5 Calculator marking – another Derek Haylock idea – where pupils work in pairs using a calculator to check each other's answers. Instead of written pages of exercises, they can deal each other numbers (to be added, multiplied or whatever it is they need to practise) from packs of cards.

6 Daily challenge sheets, with a set number of problems to be completed: the pupils record their own speed and error rate, and plot these on a weekly or monthly chart.

7 Using computers. Arcade type drill and practice games may not be the best use of limited school computer time, but can be a motivating way of providing extra practice at home. Popular software includes *Fun School 3* from Europress (for Spectrum, Commodore, Atari and Amiga), which includes time, money and database use as well as practice in basic number skills, and *Maths Blaster* from Davidson (for IBM compatibles), covering four rule work and fractions with built in self-assessment and record keeping.

8 Using computers at school. The early infant age range is well covered by software that practises one to one correspondence, counting, ordering and number recognition: *Talking about Numbers* from North West SEMERC, *Getting Ready for Maths* and *Let's Count* from ESM, *Count with Blob* from Widgit, Sherston Software's *Animated Numbers* and *Nuffield Maths* from Longman. Sherston's *Connections* is based on a highly imaginative concept, exemplary in the way it succeeds in providing opportunities for practice in basic skills in an intellectually challenging way; using this software, children have to alter the contents of windows so that they will make the connection of each with a central window 'true', in a variety of maths activities including addition, subtraction, money, fractions, odd and even numbers, graphs. For older children, useful software includes ESM's range, and *Funfair* from Northern Micromedia, which is very popular with children and reinforces basic numeracy through simulated stalls and sideshows, each providing a mathematical problem of a different type.

Motivation, anxiety and dependency

Mathematical difficulties can arise from the interaction of the way in which maths is taught and children's individual characteristics: forgetfulness, spatial confusion, inability to cope with abstractions. Equally, however, difficulties in maths can arise not from cognitive patterns like these but from the way the child *feels* about him- or herself in relation to maths.

Many writers have commented on the extent to which maths arouses complex emotions in children and adults – perhaps because more than any other subject it is open to absolute failure (not just the relative judgements which teachers make about a piece of writing or a drawing or model, but absolute judgements of answers as right or wrong). Common reactions to the possibility of failure of this kind include anxiety and panic, overdependence on the teacher for help in getting everything correct, or avoidance in the form of poor concentration and motivation. It is important that investigation of children's special needs in maths include watching them at work, and asking them how they feel about their work, in order to assess whether any of these behavioural patterns may be contributing to the problems they experience.

Anxiety about maths makes children lose their common sense, grasp at straws for answers, and follow set rules and patterns whether or not they are appropriate to the situation. Children who are anxious need, first of all, active encouragement from their teachers to make 'mistakes'. They need to be told, at regular intervals that if they always got everything right and knew everything there was to know then their teacher would be out of a job, and the school closed. They need to stop doing pages of work that is marked by the teacher, and switch to paired or group investigations or real-life applications of maths that do not have one right answer, to work that they check themselves with a calculator, or to the emotionally-neutral feedback provided by a computer. They need to be helped to make connections between the real world they know and can handle (sharing sweets among friends, giving the right coins in a shop) and the often unreal world of school maths.

Children who are overdependent on the teacher also need these kinds of anxiety-reducing strategy, coupled with challenges to make up their own problems for other children, to take part in maths games in small groups, or help younger children with their maths work. They may need to be set targets for certain amounts of work to be completed within a set period, reinforced regularly with praise or points for tackling new tasks independently, or given time with the teacher to explain how they went about tackling particular problems as a reward *after* they have completed them rather than during the process.

Maths is very vulnerable to the effects of poor concentration. This is often induced by inappropriate teaching methods, such as expecting a child to plough through solitary workbooks in close proximity to his or her best friends, or to work through a series of disembedded tasks that have no obvious relationship with reality. It may be necessary, for children who do not concentrate, to use some of the strategies for increasing concentration suggested in Chapter 8, but not until the teacher has first observed the child's concentration in other situations: using mathematical software on the computer, perhaps, or playing maths games, or engaging in the kinds of active learning implied by the national curriculum programmes of study. If, for example, the child is taking days to complete a sheet asking him to shade in drawings of coins to make certain amounts, will he show the same lack of concentration if the class are set to work in groups of four to find as many ways as they can of making 19 p, and recording their answers as a table? Even better, find the child a real task to do and watch him concentrate – as with the boy described by Derek Haylock, who was given the job of buying the right amount of orange squash for refreshments at a football tournament, and on discovering that he could use repeated addition to find out how many bottles of squash, each providing 26 drinks, were required for 90 children each needing six drinks, said to his teacher in excitement: 'You can use adding for this, Miss. I reckon that's why we learn it, so we can use it for things.'

COMMON PROBLEM AREAS

Conservation and early number concepts

Many young children, who appear to be competent in counting groups and attaching written numerals to them, begin to fail when they move to work on simple addition and subtraction. The reason is often that they have no concept of the stability of numbers attached to groups. If they are shown two lines of counters, and count them to see that they are equal, and then see one line spread out so that it now looks longer than the other, they are likely to say that the longer line now has more counters. If they count a line of objects, then see it spread out and are asked 'How many now?', they will count again rather than know that the number remains unchanged.

In these circumstances, where numbers are seen as shifting things attached to perceptual appearances rather than permanent qualities, what can something like 4 + 2 really mean? If the child has not achieved number conservation, it will be necessary to go back a stage, and offer activities that will help him or her to separate the real meaning of numbers from surface appearances, such as:

- Playing number dominoes – joining cards that have the same number of dots, in different perceptual patterns.
- Dropping a number of small objects (e.g. buttons), and drawing all the different patterns made.
- Colouring on squared paper all the patterns of a given number that the child can think of.
- Provoking what is called 'conservation conflict' – having the child make a line to match another, rearranging one to make it longer (or shorter), whilst simultaneously removing (or adding) one item, and then asking whether the two lines have the same number.
- Using meaningful materials that have real value to the child (e.g. money or sweets) and posing the question 'Which line would you rather have now?' as an alternative to 'Which has more?'

Once conservation is established, the child can be helped to see the meaning and usefulness of numerals, using Martin Hughes' (1986) suggestions for games to play with young children:

- Assembling tins with 0–3 bricks in them for the children to see; putting lids on them, shuffling them around and asking the child to pick, for example 'the tin with three bricks in it'; suggesting the child uses magnetic numerals to help them remember how many were in each tin.
- Adding bricks to a tin and introducing the ' + ' symbol: 'one brick, then another, so 1 + 1 goes on the lid; how many altogether? Now close your eyes ... the lid says 1 + 2; how many have I put in now?'
- Playing a simple board game (where the child moves a counter along a row of squares to reach 'home'), first with a traditional dice marked with dots, then with two dice with dots, then with one dice that has numerals on labels stuck over the relevant number of dots (3 over ∴), then with two dice, one of which has numerals and one with dots.
- Having the child order magnetic numerals then count them (so as to see that the last numeral in the series equals the total number); covering some with your hand, for example, 1, 2 and 3, and asking the child to guess how many are under your hand.

Number bonds

To be seen to be counting on your fingers, or worse still using apparatus when everyone else is doing clever things in their heads, is a source of embarrassment to many children; yet a lack of automatic knowledge of number bonds is a common mathematical difficulty. Endless pages of addition and subtraction sums are not the answer. Investigations and games can do the same job in a much more interesting way; here is a selection of ideas:

1 Clock arithmetic (Womack, 1988). There are several forms of this game, based on the card game clock patience. The game 'Seven-up' requires 35 flash cards on which are written all the addition facts that use numbers 0–7. The child shuffles the cards and deals them face downwards around the 'clock' in positions 1–7 as shown below: two cards at position one, three at position two, four at position three and so on.
The child turns up the last card dealt to position seven, works out the sum, places the card next to the position corresponding to the answer (for example, a card saying 2 + 2 at position four), and turns the top card in that pile over. The game continues until the child places a card next to a position that has no unturned cards left; occasionally, and this is the point that makes the child want to continue playing the game, all the cards get turned over and successfully placed.
   In 'Nine-up', all the subtraction facts involving two-digit numbers less than 20 with answers 1–9 (45 of them) are practised. There are now nine positions around the clock; this time one card is dealt to position one, two to position two, three to position three and so on.

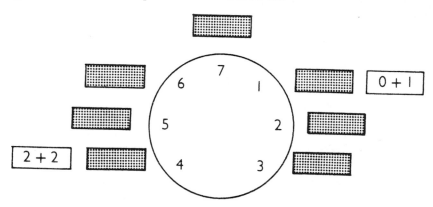

2 The game of WAR (Henderson, 1989). This uses an ordinary pack of cards; face cards are worth ten and an ace worth one. The pack is dealt out to two or more players. All the players in turn put down two cards from the top of their pile, and either add them (in one version of the game), or subtract them in another. Whoever in that round has the highest value collects all the cards. When two players have equal highest, then it is WAR. Each player lines up his of her soldiers – five cards face down – and turns over two more from their main pile. Whoever now has the higher sum wins all 14 cards.

3 Games with two dice – board games, or games with number cards, for example a game from AMS's *Count Me In* where number cards 2–10 are laid out face up

on the table in lines of three. The child rolls both dice, adds up the throw, and turns over the corresponding card (a 4 card for 2 + 2, for example). The next child does the same; the person who succeeds in turning over the third card in a line scores a point. Then all the cards are turned face up again and the game continues until one player reaches a score of five points.

4 The 'One to Twenty' game (Haylock, 1991). Two 1–10 card packs, with tens, elevens and twelves added, are used to produce a pair of numbers to be added. Each player has a strip of card marked off in 20 sequentially numbered squares, and 20 counters to place on the squares. The aim of the game is to cover as many numbers on the strip as possible. The child is dealt his or her cards, totals them, and places counters on the strip in any combination of numbers that make up this total. A player who cannot make up the total is out. The commercially available game *Shut the Box* uses a similar principle for number bonds 0–10.

5 The game 'I Have Who Has' (Haylock, 1991). This game uses a set of cards with addition or subtraction sum questions on one side and answers on the back. The answer to a question is written on the reverse of the card with the next question; the answer to the question on the last card in the set is written on the back of the first card. Each answer should only be used once. The cards are dealt out, and the question side of one remaining card is placed in the centre of the table. If this says, for example, 8 + 3, then the child who has a card with 11 on it places it next to the question card, turned over to show the next question. The child who first gets rid of all his or her cards is the winner.

6 Making up star sums (Womack, 1988), for example

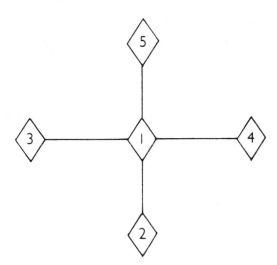

where the numbers in horizontal and vertical lines total the same (given) number.

7 Completing magic squares where rows, columns and diagonals add to a constant number, for example

	2	7
4	6	8
5		3

8 Games with skittles, ringboards, or darts where pairs of numbers have to be added.

9 The password game: a particular number bond (e.g. 8 + 6 = 14) becomes the 'password' for the day; the children have to say the password in order to enter or leave the classroom, use certain equipment, etc.

Understanding the relationship between addition and subtraction, and solving missing number equations

All primary teachers are very familiar with the difficulties of children who can do straightforward addition and subtraction, but do not know where to start when faced with problems like 8 + □ = 12, or 'There were twelve buttons in this box but now there are only eight; how many were taken out?' Games with number cards can help – for example, the game 'Boss Person' from *Count Me In*, where two number cards and the matching total number of counters are placed in a box.

One child takes out one of the cards but does not show it to the other child, who has to guess what it says by finding the difference between the number of counters in the box and the number on the remaining card. This provides a concrete model of the relationship between addition and subtraction. Other ways of showing the relationship include apparatus such as LDA's *Number Bond Investigators*, and trays for interlocking cubes where the action of breaking off three from a strip of seven to leave four can be subsequently seen as four add three making seven. Derek Haylock's (1991) recommendation for helping children see the relationship (and other relationships, such as that between multiplication and division) is short periods of daily class work: the teacher writes an addition fact (such as 8 + 4 = 12) on the board and asks as many questions as possible based on this fact – 'What is eight add four, what is twelve take away four, what is the difference between twelve and four, how many more than eight is twelve, I am eight and my sister is twelve, so how much older is she?' and so on. Making up their own number stories and questions for each other based around a particular number fact is the next step.

Coin recognition and equivalence, making up amounts

Understanding money – recognizing coins, making up amounts, adding amounts and working out change – can be difficult for some children with learning difficulties, because of the abstract nature of the relationship between coins and their value. On the other hand, because of the relevance of money to important everyday experiences, learning how to handle it can prove a good and concrete way into number operations in general: for this reason it is worth spending quite a lot of time making sure that essential money concepts have been grasped.

Coin-recognition activities include games with dice that have 1 p, 2 p, 5 p and so on marked on their sides. The children take turns to throw the dice and pick up the relevant toy (or real) coins to cover a space on a lotto board or a picture (like a 'money man' or 'money cat') made out of coins of various values. The *Money Box* keyboard (from Keyboard Technology) allows real coins of each denomination to be fixed to large keys; the software gives children practice in choosing coins to pay for sweets (and later on adding amounts, giving change, and solving problems of the 'three apples at 12 p each' type).

For work on coin equivalence, exchange games are very useful. Up to four players plus a banker play a game where the winner, for example, is the first to get ten 5 p pieces (or 2 p, or 10 p or whatever). Each player in turn takes a card from a face-down pile of 0–10 number cards; the banker pays them their winnings in 1 p pieces. When they have five they ask the banker to exchange them. A class shop and bank can provide similar experiences of exchange in a role-play context.

For making up amounts, an obvious game is a small group one where one player is banker and children have a supply of coins and draw cards for items and their prices. This can be played at many levels; if there is an additional 1–9 card pack the children will need to work out the cost, for example, of five pens at 11 p each. There are many commercially-available packs on these lines – for example, Learning Materials Ltd's *Money Street*, Cambridge *Primary Maths* money games, *Stile* self-checking money cards from LDA. None is a substitute for the 'real' experience with money – through suggestions for things parents can do at home and in the shops, and through classroom work such as investigating best buys, running a tuck shop, budgeting for a class trip or planning how to spend money on a project to improve the school environment. For children with special needs, however, money games do provide the element of extra structured practice that provides for consolidation and overlearning.

Place value

If children with learning difficulties are to understand the concept of place value, they need a carefully graded series of concrete experiences, leading them from recognition that digits in certain positions represent ones, tens, hundreds and so on, to an eventual ability to group, regroup and exchange both mentally and on paper. One possible teaching sequence might go like this:

Step 1
Learning to count in tens to one hundred, orally.

- Use a number line to 100; 'jump' a man or finger ten steps at a time as the child counts in tens with you.
- Count strips of ten cubes, 10 p pieces and bundles of 10 straws in tens.
- Use a 10 cm strip for measuring, again saying ten, twenty, thirty, etc.

Step 2
Learning that the 1 in numbers 1–19 means one set of ten, and the second digit the number of ones.

- Introduce vocabulary of 'that's a *ten*', and 'that's a *one*', with paper or brick strips.
- Use 1–9 cards with a hole in them so that they can be hung on nails in a board or on the wall. Give the child a brick strip, for example, 13, and have him or her find out by splitting it how many tens and how many ones it has in it. Have the child hang the appropriate cards in labelled 'tens' and 'ones' columns on the wall or board. Draw attention to the fact that there were 13 bricks and s/he has hung up two digits that together show 13.
- Repeat with all the other numbers 10–19.
- Repeat with 1 p coins, 1–19 p.
- Repeat with straws which child puts into bundles of ten with an elastic band.
- Repeat with strips of paper marked into ones that s/he cuts up to establish how many ones, tens.
- Continue until s/he gets the idea that the first digit indicates there will be one ten, and the second the number of 'ones'.

Step 3
Learning that the 2 in numbers 20–29 means two sets of ten, and the second digit the number of ones.

- Repeat the bricks, card strip, money and straws activities as above with numbers 20–29.

Step 4
Learning that the first digit in any two-digit numeral indicates the number of tens.

- Repeat the activities above with numbers 30–99 until the child no longer needs to group physically – can look at the numeral and automatically hang up the right cards in the right places.
- Reinforce regularly by having the child put out apparatus (ten rods and single bricks, card strips, 10 p and 1 p coins) on cards with numerals 1–99, for you to check.

Once children have grasped the way the base 10 number system works, they can play a game where they draw pairs of numbers in turn from a 0–9 pack, and decide whether to put them under a tens or a ones column on a piece of paper: the child who makes the highest number scores a point. They can be asked to add mentally 1 or 10 to a given two-digit number, or to subtract, and complete grids such as the one opposite.

Addition with re-grouping can be introduced through simple exchange games, where children collect winnings generated by turning over 0–9 cards in

Add 10 ⟶

17	27			
15				
				49

Subtract 2 ↓

pennies, but must exchange them for 10 p pieces in order to be 'first to a pound'. Later, the children can play with two packs of cards – one colour for single digits 0–9, another colour for cards where the 0–9 cards represent tens (Haylock, 1991). Each player in a team of two is dealt a card from the tens pack and a card from the ones pack, and asks the banker for the corresponding number of 10 p and 1 p coins. The two players in the team have to combine their winnings, asking the dealer to exchange 1 p for 10 p pieces, and 10 p for £1; the team with the highest total in that round wins a point. When they are comfortable with the game, the children can be given a recording sheet with hundreds, tens and units columns on which to record the way they added their amounts.

For practising exchange in subtraction as well as addition, Derek Haylock has another excellent game called 'Win Some, Lose Some': this uses a pack of 0–10 cards, 1 p and 10 p and £1 coins, and a second pack of 25 cards, of which 10 have the ' + ' sign, and five each have ' − ', ' × ' and ' ÷ ' signs. Each player starts with five £1 coins; the aim is to reach £20. The children turn over cards from the two packs, arranging them in a line, until an ' = ' sign appears. This might, for example, generate $2 + 5 \times 5 - 3 =$. The players use calculators to determine their winnings, and are paid in appropriate coins by the banker. Sometimes the string of numbers and signs will generate a negative answer; in this case the player has to 'take away' from his or her winnings to pay the banker. The banker will not give change, but will allow the players to swap a £1

Table 13.1 Twenty-one table facts

$3 \times 3 = 9$
$4 \times 3 = 12$
$6 \times 3 = 18$
$7 \times 3 = 21$
$8 \times 3 = 24$
$9 \times 3 = 27$
$4 \times 4 = 16$
$6 \times 4 = 24$
$7 \times 4 = 28$
$8 \times 4 = 32$
$9 \times 4 = 36$
$6 \times 6 = 36$
$7 \times 6 = 42$
$8 \times 6 = 48$
$9 \times 6 = 54$
$7 \times 7 = 49$
$8 \times 7 = 56$
$9 \times 7 = 63$
$8 \times 8 = 64$
$9 \times 8 = 72$
$9 \times 9 = 81$

coin for ten 10 p pieces, or a 10 p for ten 1 p pieces. All players must exchange two 1 p pieces for a 10 p and ten 10 p pieces for £1 whenever they can; if they fail to do this and the other children spot it then they miss a turn.

Times tables

The return of the weekly tables test has given knowledge of multiplication facts renewed status with children – not always helpfully to those with special needs, since some (notably those with specific learning difficulties/dyslexia) find learning times tables almost impossible. Some simple teaching tips can, however, go a long way towards making them able at least to get by in this area.

To begin with, the task of learning tables can be reduced to manageable proportions. Most children learn their five and ten times tables easily; if the two times table is taught as doubling, and the principle of reversibility explained, there are only 21 multiplication facts left to be learned (Table 13.1). These can be represented on cards, with a number, such as 27, on one side, and the relevant facts ($3 \times 9 = 27$, $9 \times 3 = 27$, $27 \div 9 = 3$, $27 \div 3 = 9$) on the other, and used for daily practice with a peer or at home. Teaching the patterns in tables will also be helpful: that when the figures in the answers to the three times table are added ($4 \times 3 = 12$ and $1 + 2 = 3$, $5 \times 3 = 15$ and $1 + 5 = 6$, and so on) there is a recurring pattern of 3, 6, 9 throughout the table, and that the figures in the answers to the nine times table always total 9. Or, for the larger multiplication facts, children can be taught how to use lower tables they do know and double the answers, for example, if they do not know 7 × 8, they can use double 7 × 4 instead.

Almost all the games and activities described in the section on number bonds can be used to reinforce multiplication facts as well, for example, the clock patience 'Nine-up' game can be played with 45 cards containing the multiplication facts from 1 × ? = 1 through 1 × ? = 2 and 2 × ? = 4 up to 9 × ? = 81.

DIFFERENTIATING THE MATHS CURRICULUM

So far in this chapter we have looked at developing action plans for children with mathematical difficulties that are based on particular points they have not grasped, or on particular problems with spatial aspects, sequencing, abstract reasoning, and so on. Developing such action plans, though worth while, is clearly time consuming. The busy teacher is still likely to seek a complete scheme of work for the *whole* class, that offers built in differentiation to meet special needs.

Is such a scheme possible? To be sure of meeting special needs in maths, such a scheme would have to have the following qualities.

- Offer activities on a common theme that are simultaneously adaptable to many different levels of learning.
- Offer these adaptations in an unobtrusive way, so that children are not made aware of the level of work to which each child or group is assigned.
- Provide activities that are motivating, meaningful and as close to real life as possible.
- Provide opportunities for both mixed-ability problem-solving, and for smaller groups of comparable ability to work with the teacher on particular teaching points.
- Use language that is adapted to different reading levels, and supported by clear pictorial and graphical clues to meaning.
- Provide alternative ways in which children can record their work.
- Provide for detailed small steps assessment of stumbling blocks for children who are not making satisfactory progress.
- Include parental involvement.
- Provide plenty of opportunities for extra practice of basic skills – preferably in game, puzzle or computer form.

Whatever scheme a school uses, the criteria can be applied, perhaps by special needs coordinator and maths coordinator working together, to identify the major gaps and devise appropriate modifications and supplementary materials. If the text of the scheme is too hard to read, it can be rewritten or taped. If there is an overemphasis on individual tasks or tasks for groups of homogeneous ability, staff can be given ideas for investigations and real-life challenges for mixed-ability groups. If there is insufficient skills practice, extra games can be bought or made.

Properly done, such differentiation should substantially reduce the numbers of children needing any sort of individual action planning for maths difficulties. It will also provide an appropriate focus for the special needs coordinator's work, shifting it towards preventing mathematical casualties – an altogether more satisfactory role than rescuing the casualties after the event.

Further reading

Haylock, D. (1991) *Teaching Mathematics to Low Attainers 8–12*. London, Paul Chapman Publishing.

Womack, D. (1988) *Special Needs in Ordinary Schools: Developing Mathematical and Scientific Thinking in Young Children*. London, Cassell.

BEYOND THE SCHOOL

INTRODUCTION

This book has, for the most part, been about what the primary school can do, from within its own resources, to meet a wide variety of curricular needs. It seems fitting, however, to end by taking a look at the school's role when working in partnership with outside agencies – both on behalf of its 'own' children, and on behalf of others who are at present distanced from the mainstream primary system in special schools and units, but who could, as research and good practice have amply demonstrated, successfully re-integrate if the climate were right.

WORKING WITH OUTSIDE AGENCIES

With the advent of locally-managed schools coinciding with a tight squeeze on local authority budgets, there remains a question mark over the survival of central support services – at least in relation to work that is not under a statutory footing under the 1993 Education Act and 1989 Children Act. For some teachers, in some areas, the issue of how best to work with outside agencies might seem to be becoming largely academic. Nevertheless, two factors make it important for schools to develop clear policies in this area: first, because as customers in a post-LMS market-oriented world, they now have a much greater control over what the central services actually do for them, and second because the cuts to services mean that they need to make the best possible use of the limited amounts of support time that remain.

Well-organized central services should be able to offer a range of interventions, and indicate how costly, in terms of the total budget of time available to the school, each type of intervention would be. The range of interventions might include:

- Direct work at the individual level, for example assessment or teaching of a particular child or group with reading difficulties, individual counselling of a child with behaviour problems, or sessions with a group of children on friendship skills and self-esteem.

- Indirect work, still focused on the needs of individual children, but involving consultation with parents or teachers, for example discussing with parents how to handle their child's anxiety about coming to school, or jointly drawing up an action plan involving daily work in class and a programme at home for a child with a learning difficulty, or discussing with the teacher the implications of a child's special needs for curriculum or SAT access.
- Work at the consultative level that is focused on the curriculum as a whole rather than the individual child, for example looking at schemes of work with the teacher and advising on suitable resources for differentiation.
- Work at the organizational level that is aimed, through INSET and policy development, at increasing the school's ability to respond effectively to individual needs.

It is the task of the school to choose, from a menu of this kind, the services that they feel will have the greatest impact in the time available. Impact need not necessarily be judged by the sheer numbers of children reached (directly or indirectly) by the external support service. It will depend on the gaps identified by the school between what they are aiming to achieve and what they are able to offer from their own resources. There may, for example, be a list of priorities for human resource management in the school's special needs policy, as in this extract:

- Our top priority is for all class teachers to have access to, and time with, someone who can help them plan how to differentiate the curriculum and draw up termly Individual Education Plans for children with special needs.
- If this priority can be met, and further resources are available then we would like to have special classroom assistants available to support the action plans we have drawn up.
- If these two priorities can be met and resources allow we would like to have extra teaching hours from a specialist to work with individual children whose difficulties – either learning or behavioural – have not, after a period of time, responded to the action planning system used so far.

One school, working to a plan like this, might find that it had adequate time available from classroom assistants to support children with special needs, but a gap in advisory expertise, say in the area of mathematical difficulties, that would enable class teachers to draw up differentiated programmes of work. For that year, it might therefore choose to focus limited amounts of input from external support services on INSET and collaborative action planning for individuals in this area.

Another school might feel it was coping well with action planning and in-class support, but was not succeeding in meeting the needs of a handful of children with severe and intractable reading difficulties. That year, it might choose to use the central support service to get this group going with literacy.

Effective work with outside agencies, then, depends in part on matching the customer's audit of needs with the provider's menu of services. This negotiation will result, each year, in a written contract specifying the services that have been agreed, along with the criteria that will be used to judge their quality and effectiveness. This is only fair: support teachers, educational psychologists, education welfare officers and other providers expect, these days, to have their work with the customer evaluated – but evaluated in ways that are specific, agreed beforehand, and which enable them to improve the services they offer in the future. If schools will be judging their support teacher on how easy it is to contact him or her by telephone, on punctuality and the extent to which he or she succeeds in building staff self-esteem, as well as on measured outcomes for INSET or work with individual children, they should say so. In turn, the support teacher should be able to negotiate, for each annual contract, his or her minimum needs for effective work with the school: time to talk to class teachers, for example, a work space that is not subject to constant interruptions, or prior information about the content of a lesson in which he or she will be working in a support capacity.

Sometimes these negotiated agreements will not be between one school and a support agency, but between the agency and a cluster of schools. Increasingly, schools are finding that whereas the small amount of support time available to each of them can do little that is useful on its own, aggregating funding across a group or cluster means that shared support can be bought in, or a shared cluster special needs support teacher appointed.

Finally, in relation to support agencies, schools need to plan how to map the range of support services each class teacher can call on, from outside the education authority as well as in, and the roles they are able to play in schools. The actual roles and services will vary from area to area; Table 14.1, however, provides a blueprint for a possible directory of services that can be adapted to local conditions.

CHILDREN WITH STATEMENTS OF SPECIAL EDUCATIONAL NEED

Children for whom it is particularly important to map and coordinate the work of a range of different support services are those whose special needs are judged sufficiently severe, complex and long-term to warrant the local education authority maintaining a Statement. This Statement will specify their special needs and the provision (all of it – that provided by the school as well as that provided by the LEA) that is required to meet them.

Such Statements were once relatively rare in mainstream primary schools, other than those which had made a conscious effort to integrate children who would otherwise have been in special schooling. Now, however, that

Statements look like the only remaining route to accessing additional resources for *all* children with special needs, not just those with clearly defined disability, they are becoming increasingly commonplace. A few years ago, few class teachers would have experience of working with a child with a Statement: now many have had this experience. They need, therefore, to be sure of their roles and responsibilities in relation to these children, and of how they can get the best out of any support or special resources that come with the child.

First, what does a Statement look like? The quality varies enormously. Some do no more than list the child's difficulties and give a very general description of the extra provision that will be put in ('additional support from a classroom assistant for part of the week', for example). Others, such as the example in Table 14.2, are much more detailed. Government guidance suggests that a Statement should, at a minimum, provide:

- A description of the child's functioning (what s/he can and cannot do), and of his or her learning difficulties.
- The main long-term objectives which the special provision should aim to meet.
- Any modifications to the national curriculum.
- The special educational provision that is required to meet the child's needs – facilities and equipment, staffing arrangements, teaching methods and approaches.
- The arrangements for setting short-term targets and monitoring progress.
- The type and name of school.
- Any non-educational needs and provision as agreed between health or social services and the LEA.

In some local education authorities, a devolved sum of money will be allocated to the school, who will then have the responsibility for providing all the resources and teaching approaches specified on the Statement. In others, additional teaching time or special equipment will come directly from the authority. Either way, the law makes it clear that the school (via its governors) is responsible for making sure that the appropriate provision is made, and the LEA for monitoring its effectiveness.

The main monitoring mechanism is the annual Statement review. The school has the task of coordinating and writing up this review, but the authority may choose to send a representative to review meetings. At such meetings, to which the parents and where possible the child should be invited, the progress made towards meeting the long- and short-term objectives on the child's Statement will be discussed, in specific terms, drawing on evidence gathered by teachers for national curriculum assessment and on assessments carried out by other involved professionals. The review will decide whether the provision on the Statement is proving successful in meeting the child's needs, and whether changes might be needed to make it more effective. It will set targets for the year ahead. Finally, it will consider whether the school placement remains

Table 14.1   Directory of services

School nurse and doctor

How they work with schools:
How to access:
Services provided:

Range of special needs covered:

Family Counselling/Child Guidance

How they work with schools:
How to access:
Services provided:

Range of special needs covered:

Occupational therapists/physiotherapists

How they work with schools:
How to access:
Services provided:

Range of special needs covered:

Speech and language therapists

How they work with schools:
How to access:
Services provided:

Range of special needs covered:

Family Support Centres

How they work with schools:
How to access:
Services provided:

Range of special needs covered:

Social Services

How they work with schools:
How to access:
Services provided:

Range of special needs covered:

Education Welfare Service

How they work with schools:
How to access:
Services provided:

Range of special needs covered:

Advisers and advisory teachers

How they work with schools:
How to access:
Services provided:

Range of special needs covered:

Psychology Service

How they work with schools:
How to access:
Services provided:

Range of special needs covered:

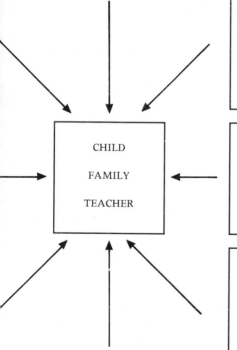

Special Needs Service

How they work with schools:
How to access:
Services provided:

Range of special needs covered:

Advisory teachers for hearing impaired

How they work with schools:
How to access:
Services provided:

Range of special needs covered:

CHILD

FAMILY

TEACHER

Advisory teachers for visually impaired

How they work with schools:
How to access:
Services provided:

Range of special needs covered:

Behaviour Support Services

How they work with schools:
How to access:
Services provided:

Range of special needs covered:

Special school and unit outreach

How they work with schools:
How to access:
Services provided:

Range of special needs covered:

Table 14.2 An example of a Statement of Special Educational Need

Part 2 Special Educational Needs

Simon is a well-liked, responsive child. He is cooperative and determined, and good at making friends. He has strengths in his wide general knowledge, rich imagination, very good reasoning abilities, and use of detailed drawings as an outlet for his ideas. He has difficulties in several areas: spatial perception/motor coordination, listening difficulties associated with catarrhal problems and intermittent hearing loss, difficulties in the control of attention, and difficulties in sequencing and planning skills. He is also quite short-sighted.

Part 3 Special Educational Provisions

Objectives

In the long-term, Simon needs:

- To improve his handwriting skills, and have help to access the curriculum where fine motor skills are involved   not only in written recording, but also in art, technology and science.
- To learn how to locate himself in space and time.
- To learn how to focus his attention, particularly in distracting and less-structured environments.
- To increase his rate of progress in mathematics, particularly those aspects involving spatial and sequencing ability.
- To increase his rate of progress in reading and spelling.
- To improve his listening skills and ability to respond to complex instructions and carry messages.

Educational provision to meet needs and objectives

Simon requires a full curriculum with no exemptions or modifications.

He needs a classroom environment that is orderly, quiet and well structured. He requires frequent praise when he is 'on task'. Teachers should be prepared to simplify and repeat complex instructions, and help him write down or rehearse messages. They should make sure that a range of recording methods are used (drawing, dictation to scribe, paired writing), so that he can make use of his good ideas and oral language skills to access the full curriculum.

He needs special programmes of work on listening skills using taped materials available in school, including ARROW technology.

He requires special programmes of work on handwriting, using such materials as LDA's Handwriting File and Hand for Spelling.

He requires withdrawal teaching for a structured, multisensory programme of work in basic literacy skills: this can be supplied by the school.

In addition, he requires in class general assistant support, provided by the local education authority, for work in maths, technology and science. The role of the assistant would be to implement a small-steps programme of work in mathematics, with plenty of opportunities for overlearning, set up by his class teacher, and to support him in practical work where he has to manipulate equipment.

He should be provided by the LEA with a portable lap-top word processor to use as an alternative to handwriting for much of his written recording.

Monitoring

There should be a meeting in school within one month of the issue of this Statement, involving Simon, his parents, educational psychologist and class teacher, in order to set short-term targets. Progress against these targets will be reviewed termly.

appropriate, and whether any modifications to or exemptions from the national curriculum are necessary.

The extra provision specified in Statements sometimes refers only to physical resources or adaptations to the environment: low vision aids such as closed circuit television, for example, for a child with a visual impairment, lifts or ramps or rails for a child with a physical disability, microtechnology such as speech synthesizers, adapted keyboards with switch access, software such as word or maths processing.

More often, however, extra human resources – such as help from a non-teaching assistant, or consultation or direct teaching from an appropriately qualified visiting advisory teacher – will be part of the provision. It is here that the organizational systems within the school, and the skills of the classroom teacher, are crucially important in determining whether or not the extra support works effectively for the child.

It will work well to the extent that the support personnel and class teacher work towards a jointly determined, regularly-reviewed action plan, and have clearly defined roles and responsibilities within that plan. This is not always the case, as recent reports on pupils with Statements in mainstream schools make clear (HMI 1989c, 1990a). For children with physical disabilities, for example, HMI observed that 'generally the pupil received kindly attention rather than highly effective teaching'. For the broad range of children with Statements, although much good work was seen, and the overall quality of relationships between teachers and the pupils with Statements was good, there were many difficulties in devising and monitoring work for pupils that was part of the overall programme for the class, yet adequately differentiated to meet individual needs.

Provision is least effective in classes where special needs ancillary helpers are just seen as an extra pair of hands, whose role is to help the child accommodate to class tasks that are not matched to individual needs, and where special support teaching takes place in isolation from the work of the class teacher. Most often this kind of situation arises where class teachers lack confidence in their ability to meet very special needs that lie outside their previous experience and knowledge base. It can be prevented if they are aware that a detailed knowledge of the child's particular disability is not actually required of them at all. They need *some* background knowledge, but no more than can be obtained from some basic readings provided by a member of the central support services. Beyond this, their main professional requirement is to know how to make effective use of specialist consultancy, and how to coordinate their own work with that of others. They need to be able to:

- Draw out relevant learning objectives (in both academic and social areas) from the child's Statement and the paperwork that comes with it.
- Develop a termly action plan that will specify who is going to do what (parents, classroom assistants, support teachers, the class teacher) in helping the pupil meet these objectives.

- Provide any classroom helpers, in the light of the negotiated action plan, with a clear description of their roles and responsibilities in relation to those of the class teacher.
- Know who and how to ask for specialist advice on differentiating the overall class schemes of work (including assessment) to meet the child's particular needs, and build any advice given into lesson plans.

The next example will illustrate how one teacher, initially very concerned about how he would cope with a Statemented child in his classroom, succeeded in using his existing skills in special needs work as a whole to coordinate a highly effective programme for a child with a visual impairment:

Alison's Statement said that she was a sociable but rather anxious little girl, with particular strengths in oral language skills. She was partially sighted, but able to use print with the help of magnification. Her support was to come from five hours a week of classroom assistant time, plus fortnightly visits from a teacher from the service for sensory impairment. In addition, she was to be supplied with her own computer, with a specially adapted keyboard and software to enable her to produce large-print text, and with a range of magnifying devices.

Mrs Potter, Alison's special needs assistant, was one of the school's own part-time ancillaries, who had been keen to take on the extra hours attached to the Statement. She had no experience of work of this kind, however, and went to the class teacher to voice her concerns. He arranged a meeting between himself, the visiting specialist teacher and the ancillary, at which it was agreed that Mrs Potter spend some time visiting the authority's unit for primary visually impaired children. The visiting teacher also promised to bring some literature on Alison's particular visual problem for Mrs Potter and the teacher to read. Together, the three looked at the reports which had been compiled for Alison's Statement, and identified some targets they felt they should work on – at least to start with. These included building her confidence by planning ways for her to make a valuable contribution in small group work in speaking and listening, increasing the vocabulary of keywords she could spell correctly, and ensuring full curriculum access – particularly in practical subjects like science and technology, where she had tended to hang back in the past.

Mrs Potter's support time, it was agreed, would be partly spent on preparing materials for Alison – copying, enlarging and spacing parts of the maths scheme in particular. For the remainder of the time, however, she would come into class for science and technology lessons to support Alison directly. The class teacher would, at the start of the week, meet her in assembly time to review any difficulties and outline the practical work that the class would be doing in the week ahead. Mrs Potter's role might sometimes be to give hands-on assistance, but more often would focus on praising Alison for having a try herself, once Mrs Potter had set the scene for her and provided her with large size or tactile materials.

The visiting teacher felt that her role would be observing in the classroom, so as to feed back to the class teacher any information that would help him plan work for Alison. For example, after one visit she advised him that it would help if he always read out anything he put up on the blackboard as he wrote, and made sure the board was really clean so as to provide a good contrast. Another time, she was able to suggest and bring in some electronic measuring devices for Alison to use instead of the regular scales, thermometers and tape measures available in the classroom.

The class teacher also asked the visiting teacher to look at his plan for science and topic work at the start of each term, and make written comments on areas where he would have to take special care to make sure that Alison could participate fully. He requested help, in the Spring Term, in picking out from all the reading he had to do on the forthcoming SATs the adaptations that were allowed for visually-impaired children. Finally, it was agreed that the visiting teacher would be responsible for training Alison and her parents in the use of her low vision aids and specialist technology, and sorting out any hitches that arose in this area.

INTEGRATION

The issues

Alison's presence in his mainstream primary classroom undoubtedly meant more work for her already busy teacher. Hard-pressed as he was, there will have been times when he questioned the effectiveness of the work he was able to do with her, and wondered if she would not have been better off elsewhere, in a special school or unit, taught in small groups by teachers with appropriate specialist expertise.

This kind of self-doubt is very common, and very understandable. The vignettes that follow, taken from a day's visit to two schools and a parents' evening the same day in another, illustrate how widespread the feeling that children should have the chance of a better deal 'somewhere else' can be – extending beyond mainstream education to special schools themselves: to every area, in fact, where committed staff are concerned about the rate of progress that some children are able to make under their care.

Alan, aged 6, was making poor progress in his infant school. He could not write his name or read at all, and could only count to three at school (though at home he could apparently locate the number '8' on the video with ease, and counted as far as ten sometimes when he thought no one was listening). He loved school and had lots of friends, even if they tended, in his teacher's words, to 'look after him' rather than let him participate on an equal level. His teacher was frustrated by her inability to help him learn. 'Surely it would be better for him,' she said, 'to go to —— school' (naming a local school for children with moderate learning difficulties), 'so he could get extra help now, when he needs it. There are 30 children in his class here. I just can't give him the attention he needs.'

Another example. Two mothers were talking at a parents' evening about a child in their sons' class: 'His parents are refusing for him to go to a special school. I don't know their reasons. I can't understand it. Surely it must be better for him to have properly qualified teachers . . . and small classes . . . and then he'd be with other children at his level as well.'

Finally, Samantha, aged 6, had been at a school for moderate learning difficulties since she was four. Unfortunately, her progress had been slow. She could not yet copy shapes or talk in sentences. Soon she would have to move up to the junior department of the school, where class sizes were large and the teachers did not always have ancillary help. 'She'll not be able to cope there,' said her teacher. 'I know her parents want her to stay here but surely she'd be better off at —— school' (a local school with severe learning difficulties) 'where she'd get much smaller groups. We're just not getting anywhere with her and she needs a lot more help.'

Passing the buck, or doing the best for the children involved? The answers are not simple. It may help, however, to look at the facts we have about integration, and examine the widespread belief that small groups and specialist expertise provide the panacea for special needs, to see whether it is or is not well founded.

Research into the relative merits of special versus integrated schooling poses many methodological problems – not least, the probability that children who are integrated into mainstream may have lesser intrinsic difficulties than children who remain in special provision. Nevertheless, enough carefully-controlled large-scale surveys have been done to enable us to draw the following conclusions:

- Children with moderate learning difficulties do equally well academically in mainstream or special schools (Zigler and Hodapp, 1986), though they may in mainstream be more stigmatized and rejected by their peers than children in special schooling (Gottlieb, 1981).
- For children with other special needs, there is again no clear advantage in terms of academic achievement for either special schools or integrated placements (Lindsay, 1989), except in a few studies where the mainstream

teachers involved have had special training and provide individualized teaching programmes (Madden and Slavin, 1983). In these studies, children in mainstream did better. On the whole, however, such individualized teaching programmes are less common in mainstream than in special schools (Zigler and Hodapp, 1986).

- Children with special needs in integrated placements show better social skills than those in special schooling (Zigler and Hodapp, 1986), but tend to have lower levels of self-esteem (Chapman, 1988).

From one perspective, then, the evidence from research does tend to challenge the common assumption that moving a child from mainstream to special schooling will necessarily improve academic achievement, though it may lead to improved self-esteem. From another perspective, however, it could be argued that the case for integration is also unproven – since it leads only to improved social skills, rather than the hoped-for reductions in stigmatization and gains in academic progress.

These statistics, like any others can be read either way, depending on the belief system of the reader. Since this is so, ultimately the teacher's view on integration may have to be a matter of values. These belong to the individual, but should perhaps take into account the fact that the converse of integration, linguistically, is segregation. Children who are not integrated are segregated; it is difficult for this writer, at least, with a daily experience of the shock and sadness faced by parents when told that their child might move to special schooling, to see that this should ever be specified as a necessary condition for learning.

Making it work

If teachers and governors do decide that they see 'the segregation of children and young people outside mainstream institutions on the grounds of disability or other externally defined "difficulties" as a form of discrimination as unacceptable as segregation on the grounds of race or colour would be, whatever the initial motivation may have been' (Newell, 1985), they then need to ask themselves how to make it work effectively, given the evidence that children with special needs in integrated placements can be stigmatized and rejected by their peers, and given the evidence that individualized teaching programmes are effective but relatively uncommon in mainstream schools.

The answer to the problem of individualizing teaching lies, for the most part, in the school's existing arrangements for differentiating the curriculum to meet the needs of *all* their children. As HMI observed (1990a), in some classes 'the fact that a child has a Statement of special educational needs was almost incidental, as the general classwork was carefully matched to children's abilities'. In others, inappropriate work for all but 'average' children in the class meant that a child with very special needs would clearly stand out and fail to achieve. Once again, we are back here to the idea of the whole school policy, of access for staff to consultation with a trained special needs coordinator and outside agencies, of decent action planning for individuals, of differentiated schemes of work, and the availability of teaching resources that have been gathered and developed to meet a range of needs within these planned schemes.

As for reducing stigmatization and peer rejection, there is a great deal that can be done (and is, in many schools), to promote in children, as well as adults, an acceptance of one another's differences, and a commitment to inclusion rather than exclusion for those we perceive as different from ourselves. Circle time and class work in personal and social education can help children think about the effects of name calling, in groups and out groups, and friendship patterns in their class and school. And curricular work – in science, in the humanities, and through literature – can help children gain insight into the experience of others who may not see, or hear, or understand, or be able to use their bodies as they do (Rieser and Mason, 1990). On this can be built an understanding of the ways in which as individuals and as a society we can either choose to 'enable', or 'disable' people with learning difficulties, or physical and sensory impairment.

Schools need to plan, too, how they will encourage social interaction between a particular child with very special needs and his or her peers. Schemes here have been many and imaginative. Children with hearing impairment and Down's Syndrome have, for example, had their social standing raised by being asked to teach a sign language to others. Children with learning difficulties have been taught new games which they then introduce to a selected group in the playground. Peer partners for learning have been appointed, and buddy systems set up outside the classroom. Socially isolated children have been given a key role or key piece of information in small group problem solving work, so that they are actively involved from the start rather than marginalized by other group members.

In the most imaginative projects of all, schools have adopted a model that originated in Canada (Shaw, 1990), where planned strategies are used to prepare peers for the integration of new students into their mainstream classes, and to make sure that things are going well socially as well as academically after the move. Here are two strategies.

'Circle of Friends'

In the first of these strategies, called 'Circle of Friends', a teacher visits the class and briefly describes the new student who is about to be integrated. The teacher helps the children to map, for themselves, the circles that represent the important people in their lives. In Circle 1, the smallest circle, go the people closest to them – family, best friends, those with whom they can be at ease and those whom they can trust. In Circle 2 are people they really like, and see a lot of, but who are not quite close enough to go in the inner circle. In Circle 3 go people they do things with from time to time – people in clubs they belong to, people in their street, people in their class. Circle 4 is for people who are paid to be in their lives and do things for them, such as their doctor or dentist. The teacher then introduces an imaginary person, with a disability, who is the same age as the children in the class. In this person's circles there are parents and perhaps a brother in the centre, but nothing in the other circles except for Circle 4, which is full of people – doctors, physiotherapists, social workers, and so on. The students talk about how they would feel if their circles looked like this. Finally, the teacher again mentions the student who is coming to join them, asks the children why they think they did the activity on circles of friends, and promises to return in a few weeks 'to see what's happening'. This experience alone is usually enough to prompt children in the class to set up their own circle of friends for the new student – to telephone the student before s/he arrives, for example, and to plan ways of including the student in their activities out of school as well as in.

Making action plans

In the second integration strategy, 'making action plans', a team is set up which includes the student with a disability or learning difficulty, family members, and the professionals who work with the child. Importantly, members of the student's Circle of Friends in their class are also included, because they can contribute a unique perception of the social processes that go on in the class, and the student's social needs. The team meet regularly, first to listen to the parents' hopes and fears for the child's future, and build a shared picture of the student's strengths, personality and needs; later to plan the details of how the student will spend his or her time in school. Achieving real social integration is a goal that is given a high priority throughout the planning process, as high a priority as progress in academic areas.

The future

Between 1986 and 1990, the London Borough of Newham succeeded in integrating more than half of their children with Statements of special need into mainstream schools. In Wolverhampton, special school places have declined from over 1200 in 1980, to about one-third of that in 1990, as a team of over 50 teachers together with 40 ancillaries was built up to work in mainstream schools with identified special needs resource bases. A steady stream of books (Booth and Swann, 1987; Moses et al., 1988; Booth et al., 1991) have provided us with compelling examples of successful integration projects across the country. Integration can happen, and still does – in some places.

In others, however, despite the integrationist principles underlying both the 1981 Education Act and the 1989 Children Act, it appears to be becoming harder for schools – overwhelmed by the demands of the national curriculum and the competitive ethos of league tables – to include children with difficulties. This trend seems to be greatest in the primary sector. The Centre for Studies in Integration have reported, for example, an increase in segregation of 2 per cent for children aged 5 to 10 over the period 1988–1991, taken across the country as a whole (CSIE, 1992).

In these circumstances, will it be possible in the future for schools to maintain a commitment to inclusion, and to the idea of neighbourhood schools that serve the *whole* of their local community? Will it be possible for governors, parents, and staff to resist the pressures to up the school's test results by shipping out those who might lower the tone – still less ship in those who are already educated outside the mainstream system?

The answers remain to be seen. Schools can, however, feel justifiably confident that if they have effective systems for assessment, action planning and differentiation for the 18 per cent of their children who will, at some point in their school career, have some kind of special educational need, then they will also be able to work effectively with the more severe, long-term and complex needs of the Warnock Report's 2 per cent.

They can, moreover, take comfort from the considerable evidence that their capacity to meet special needs of all kinds is a reliable indicator of the health of their organization as a whole. Schools that are good at knowing when their system is not working well for an individual child with difficulties in learning, and adjusting the system accordingly, are the same schools that can adapt their system to the needs of the very able, to those who are interested as well as those who seem uninterested, to those who are going through a spurt in learning and those who are going through a slower patch, and to those who can feel neglected because they are neither the best nor the worst.

It is schools like this that parents want for their children. Ultimately, they will choose schools where the teachers seem to know – and care – what makes their individual child tick, and get the best from them as a result, rather than those who work to some mythical idea of the norm.

CONCLUSION

This book has been about the ways in which schools can develop the responsiveness to individuality that parents value. It has been about teachers acquiring confidence in their own very real skills, and very real power to have an intimate and far reaching positive effect on the achievement and self-worth of every child they teach.

The outcomes of such confidence will work for *all* children; meeting special needs and meeting ordinary needs do not, as we have seen, have to be mutually exclusive. But for the children at the margins of our society, the outcome of such confidence will be especially welcome. It means that they will meet teachers who do not have to pass them on to others, who do not have to feel anxious about their ability to cope with everyday problems of behaviour and learning.

And it means, perhaps, that all children with special educational needs can rely on meeting teachers who will say: 'The buck stops here, with me. And in this school, with the support I get, and the resources I can call on, I can do a good job for every single child in my class. *I can do it. I know that I can.*'

REFERENCES

Ackerman, T., Gillett, D., Kenward, P. *et al.* (1983) *Daily Teaching and Assessment –
Primary Aged Children*, in Post-Experience Courses for Educational Psychologists
1983–4. Department of Educational Psychology, University of Birmingham, Birmingham.

Adams, M. (1990) *Beginning to Read*. Boston, MIT Press.

Ainscow, M. (1991) 'Effective schools for all: an alternative approach to special needs in
education', in Ainscow, M. (ed.) *Effective Schools For All*. London, David Fulton.

Ainscow, M. and Muncey, J. (1986) *Small Steps: Module 2, SNAP Materials*. Cardiff,
Drake Educational Associates.

Ainscow, M. and Muncey, J. (1989) *Meeting Individual Needs in the Primary School*.
London, David Fulton.

Ainscow, M. and Tweddle, D. (1984) *Early Learning Skills Analysis*. London, David
Fulton.

Aram, D. and Nation, J. (1980) 'Preschool language disorders and subsequent language
and academic difficulties'. *Journal of Communication Disorders*, 13.

Arora, T. and Bamford, J. (1989) *Paired Maths*. Kirklees, Kirklees Psychological Service.

Bennett, N. (1991) 'Cooperative learning in classrooms'. *Journal of Child Psychology and
Psychiatry*, 32, 4.

Bennett, N., Desforges, C., Cockburn, A. and Wilkinson, B. (1984) *The Quality of Pupil
Learning Experiences*. London, Lawrence Erlbaum.

Bentote, P., Norgate, R. and Thornton, D. (1990) 'Special needs: spelling – some
problems solved?' *Educational Psychology in Practice*, 6, 2.

Berger, M., Yule, W. and Rutter, M. (1975) 'Attainment and adjustment in two
geographical areas: II'. *British Journal of Psychiatry*, 126.

Beveridge, M. and Conti-Ramsden, G. (1987) *Children with Language Disabilities*. Milton
Keynes, Open University Press.

Blatchford, P., Burke, J., Farquahar, C. et al. (1989) 'Teacher expectations in the infant
school'. *British Journal of Educational Psychology*, 59, 1.

Booth, T. and Swann, S. (eds) (1987) *Including Pupils with Disabilities*. Milton Keynes,
Open University Press.

Booth, T., Swann, S., Masterton, M. and Potts, P. (1991) (eds) *Curricula for Diversity in Education*. London, Routledge.

Bradley, L. (1985) *Poor Spellers, Poor Readers: Understanding the Problem*. University of Reading, Centre for the Teaching of Reading.

Bruner, J. and Haste, H. (1987) *Making Sense: The Child's Construction of the World*. London, Methuen.

Bryant, P. and Bradley, L. (1985) *Children's Reading Difficulties*. Oxford, Blackwell.

Cameron, R. and Stratford, R. (1987) 'A problem-centred approach to applied psychology practice'. *Educational Psychology in Practice*, 2, 4.

Canter, L. and Canter, M. (1976) *Assertive Discipline*. Santa Monica, CA, Lee Canter Associates.

Canter, L. and Canter, M. (1979) *Assertive Discipline Phase 1 In-Service Workshop Leaders Manual*. Santa Monica, CA, Lee Canter Associates.

Centre for Studies on Integration in Education (1992) *Segregation Statistics 1988–1991*. London, CSIE.

Chapman, J. (1988) 'Special education in the least restrictive environment; mainstreaming or maindumping?' *Australia and New Zealand Journal of Developmental Disabilities*, 14, 2.

Clark, A. and Warlberg, H. (1968) 'The influence of massive rewards on reading achievement in potential school dropouts'. *American Educational Research Journal*, 5, 3.

Clay, M. (1979) *Reading: The Patterning of Complex Behaviour*. London, Heinemann.

Clay, M. (1981) *The Early Detection of Reading Difficulties: A Diagnostic Survey with Recovery Procedures*. London, Heinemann.

Clement, M. (1980) 'Analysing children's errors on written mathematical tasks'. *Educational Studies in Mathematics*, 11, 1.

Cockcroft, W. (1982) *Mathematics Counts: Report of the Committee of Enquiry into the Teaching of Mathematics*. London, HMSO.

Coleman, M. and Gilliam, J. (1983) 'Disturbing behaviours in the classroom: a survey of teachers' attitudes'. *Journal of Special Education*, 17, 2.

Coverdale Organization (1986) *Coverdale: A Systematic Approach*. Materials from courses run by the Coverdale Organization, Dorland House, 14–16 Regent Street, London SW1Y 4PH.

Craig, F. (1990) *The Natural Way to Learn: The Apprenticeship Approach to Literacy*. Worcestershire, The Self Publishing Association.

Croll, P. and Moses, D. (1985) *One in Five*. London, Routledge.

Cronbach, L. and Snow, R. (1977) *Abilities and Instructional Methods*. New York, Irvington.

Davidson, J., Coles, D., Noyes, P. and Terrell, C. (1991) 'Books that talk', in Singleton, C. (ed.) *Computers and Literacy Skills*. Hull, British Dyslexia Association Computer Resource Centre.

Davidson, P. (1988) 'Word processing and children with specific learning difficulties'. *Support for Learning*, 3, 4.

Davies, M. (1989) 'Microchip gives new life to rote learning method'. *Times Educational Supplement*, 19 May.

DES (1981) *Education Act*. London: HMSO.

DES (1989a) Circular 15/89: Education Reform Act 1988: Temporary Exceptions from the National Curriculum. London: DES.

DES (1989b) *Discipline in Schools*. London, HMSO.

DES (1989c) *English in the National Curriculum*. London, HMSO.

DFE (1993) *Education Act*. London: HMSO.

DFE (1994) *Code of Practice on the Identification and Assessment of Special Educational Needs*. London, DFE.

DFE (1995) *Key Stages 1 and 2 of the National Curriculum*. London, HMSO.

DoH (1989) *The Children Act*. London: HMSO.

Dring, J. (1989) 'The impact of a tape-cassette library on reading progress'. *Special Children*, November issue.

Dudley-Marling, C., Snider, V. and Tarver, S. (1982) 'Locus of control and learning disabilities: a review of research'. *Perceptual and Motor Skills*, 54.

Engelmann, S. (1969) *Preventing Failure in the Primary Grades*. Chicago, Science Research Associates.

Evans, G. (1992) *Child Protection: A Whole Curriculum Approach*. Bristol, Avec Designs.

Evans, L. (1990) 'What to Wear?' *Special Children*, 41, 8–10.

Fry, E. (1972) *Reading Instruction in Classroom and Clinic*. New York, McGraw-Hill.

Fullan, M. (1991) *The New Meaning of Educational Change*. London, Cassell.

Gains, C. (1994) 'Editorial: new roles for SENCOs'. *Support for Learning*, 9(3).

Galton, M., Simon, B. and Croll, P. (1980) *Inside the Primary Classroom*. London, Routledge.

Galvin, P., Mercer, S. and Costa, P. (1990) *Building a Better Behaved School*. London, Longman.

Good, T. and Brophy, J. (1977) *Educational Psychology: A Realistic Approach*. London, Holt, Rinehart and Winston.

Gordon, T. (1974) *Teacher Effectiveness Training*. New York, David McKay.

Gottlieb, J. (1981) 'Mainstreaming: fulfilling the promise?' *American Journal of Mental Deficiency*, 86, 2.

Gross, J. (1991) *Special Needs in the Primary School: A School Development Programme*. Bristol, Redland Centre for Primary Education, Bristol Polytechnic.

Gubbay, S. (1975) *The Clumsy Child – A Study of Developmental Apraxic and Agnosic Ataxia*. London, W. B. Saunders.

Gurney, P. (1988) *Self Esteem in Children with Special Educational Needs*. London, Routledge.

Hall, P. and Tomblin, J. (1978) 'A follow up of children with articulation and language disorders'. *Journal of Speech and Hearing Disorders*, 43.

Hanilton, D. (1987) 'Working with parents – the key to learning'. *Support for Learning*, 2, 3.

Hanson, D. (1991) 'Assessment: the window on learning', in *Differentiating the Secondary Curriculum*. Trowbridge, Wiltshire County Council.

Hargreaves, D., Hopkins, D., Leask, M. et al. (1989) *Planning for School Development: Advice to Governors, Headteachers and Schools*. London, DES.

Haring, N., Lovitt, T., Eaton, M. and Hansen, C. (1978) *The Fourth R: Research in the Classroom*. Columbus, OH, Merrill.

Harrison, P. (1989) 'Numbers Game'. *Times Educational Supplement*, 17 February.

Haylock, D. (1991) *Teaching Mathematics to Low Attainers 8–12*. London, Paul Chapman Publishing.

Henderson, A. (1989) 'Multisensory Maths'. *Special Children*, 34.

Henderson, S. and Hall, D. (1982) 'Concomitants of clumsiness in young school children'. *Developmental Medicine and Child Neurology*, 24.

Hersov, L. and Berger, M. (1980) *Language and Language Disorders in Childhood*. Oxford, Pergamon Press.

Hickey, K. (1992) *The Hickey Multisensory Language Course*, 2nd edn, London, Whurr Publishers.

HMI (1989a) *A Survey of Pupils with Special Educational Needs in Ordinary Schools*. London, HMSO.

HMI (1989b) *Reading Policy and Practice at Ages 5–14*. London, HMSO.

HMI (1989c) *Educating Physically Disabled Pupils*. London, HMSO.

HMI (1990a) *Education Observed: Special Needs Issues*. London, HMSO.

HMI (1990b) *Information Technology and Special Needs in Schools*. London, HMSO.

HMI (1990c) *The Teaching and Learning of Reading in Primary Schools*. London, HMSO.

Holdaway, D. (1982) 'Shared book experience'. *Theory into Practice*, 21.

Horner, E. (1990) 'Working with peers'. *Special Children*, November issue.

Hornsby, B. and Shear, F. (1975) *Alpha to Omega: The A–Z of Teaching Reading, Writing and Spelling*. London, Heinemann.

Hornsby, B. and Farrer, M. (1990) 'Some effects of a dyslexia-centred teaching programme', in Pumfrey, P. and Elliott, C. (eds) *Children's Difficulties in Reading, Spelling and Writing*. Basingstoke, Falmer Press.

Hughes, M. (1986) *Children and Number: Difficulties in Learning Mathematics*. Oxford, Basil Blackwell.

Hunt, M. (1992) 'Meeting primary needs'. *British Journal of Special Education*, 19, 1.

Ireson, J., Evans, P., Redmond, P. and Wedell, K. (1989) *Pathways to Progress*. London, University of London Institute of Education.

James, J., Charlton, T., Leo, E. and Indoe, D. (1991) 'A peer to listen'. *Support for Learning*, 6, 4.

Jewell, T. (1986) 'Involving parents and teachers in individual education programmes'. *Educational Psychology in Practice*, July issue.

Joffe, L. (1981) quoted in *Mathematical Difficulties and Dyslexia*. Reading, British Dyslexia Association.

Johnson, D. and Johnson, R. (1987) *Learning Together and Alone: Cooperation, Competition and Individualisation*, 2nd edn. New Jersey, Prentice Hall.

Johnstone, M., Munn, P. and Edwards, L. (1991) *Action Against Bullying*. Edinburgh, Scottish Council for Research in Education.

Joyce, B., Murphy, C., Showers, B. and Murphy, J. (1991) 'School renewal as cultural change', in Ainscow, M. (ed.) *Effective Schools For All*. London, David Fulton.

Kavale, K. and Forness, S. (1985) *The Science of Learning Disabilities*. Windsor, NFER-Nelson.

Keogh, B. (1982) 'Children's temperament and teachers' decisions', in CIBA Foundation Symposium 89, *Temperamental Differences in Infants and Young Children*. London, Pitman.

Krutetskii, V. (1976) *The Psychology of Mathematical Ability in School Children*. University of Chicago.

Lane, C. (1990) 'ARROW: alleviating children's reading and spelling difficulties', in Pumfrey, P. and Elliott, C. (eds) *Children's Difficulties in Reading, Spelling and Writing*. Basingstoke, Falmer Press.

Lawrence, D. (1973) *Improved Reading through Counselling*. London, Ward Lock.

Lawrence, D. (1988) *Enhancing Self Esteem in the Classroom*. London, Paul Chapman.

Leeves, I. (1990) 'Now hear this'. *Special Children*, April issue.

Lewis, A. (1995) *Primary Special Needs and the National Curriculum*. London, Routledge.

Lewis, M. and Wray, D. (1994) *Writing Frames: scaffolding children's non-fiction writing in a range of genres*. Exeter, EXEL, Exeter University School of Education.

Lewis, M., Wray, D. and Rospigliosi, P. (1994) 'Making reading for information more accessible for children with learning difficulties', *Support for Learning*, 9(4).

Limbrick, E., McNaughton, S. and Glynn, T. (1985) 'Reading gains for underachieving tutors and tutees in a cross-age tutoring programme'. *Journal of Child Psychology and Psychiatry*, 26, 6.

Lindsay, G. (1989) 'Evaluating integration'. *Educational Psychology in Practice*, 5, 1.

Lindsay, G., Evans, A. and Jones, B. (1985) 'Paired reading versus relaxed reading: a comparison'. *British Journal of Educational Psychology*, 55.

Long, M. (1988) 'Goodbye behaviour units, hello support services: home–school support for pupils with behaviour difficulties in mainstream schools'. *Educational Psychology in Practice*, 4, 1.

Losse, A., Henderson, S., Elliman, D. et al. (1991) 'Clumsiness in children – do they grow out of it?' *Developmental Medicine and Child Neurology*, 33.

Lunzer, E. and Gardner, K. (eds) (1979) *The Effective Use of Reading*. London, Heinemann.

Luton, K., Booth, G., Leadbetter, J. et al. (1992) *Positive Strategies for Behaviour Management: A Whole-School Approach to Discipline*. Windsor, NFER-Nelson.

Madden, N. and Slavin, R. (1983) 'Mainstreaming students with mild handicaps'. *Review of Educational Research*, 53, 4.

Maher, C. (1984) 'Handicapped adolescents as cross-age tutors'. *Exceptional Children*, 51, 1.

Maines, B. and Robinson, G. (1989a) *Bag of Tricks*. Bristol, Lame Duck Publishing.

Maines, B. and Robinson, G. (1989b) *B/G Steem: A Self Esteem Scale*. Bristol, Lame Duck Publishing.

Maines, B. and Robinson, G. (1992) *Michael's Story: The No Blame Approach*. Bristol, Lame Duck Publishing.

McConnon, S. (1989) *Your Choice*. London, Nelson.

Mcnally, J. and Murray, W. (1984) *Keywords to Literacy*. London, Schoolmaster Publishing.

Merrett, J. and Merrett, F. (1992) 'Classroom management for project work: an application of correspondence training'. *Educational Studies*, 18, 1.

Merrett, F. and Wheldall, K. (1987) 'Natural rates of teacher approval and disapproval in British primary and middle school classrooms'. *British Journal of Educational Psychology*, 57.

Miles, E. (1989) *The Bangor Dyslexia Teaching System*. London, Whurr Publishers.

Miller, A., Jewell, T., Booth, S. and Robson, D. (1985) 'Delivering educational programmes to slow learners'. *Educational Psychology in Practice*, 1, 3.

Montgomery, D. (1990) *Children with Learning Difficulties*. London, Cassell.

Mortimore, P., Sammons, P., Stoll, L. et al. (1988) *School Matters: The Junior Years*. Somerset, Open Books.

Mosely, D. (1989) 'How lack of confidence in spelling affects children's written expression'. *Educational Psychology in Practice*, 5, 1.

Moses, D. (1982) 'Special educational needs: the relationship between teacher assessment, test scores and classroom behaviour'. *British Educational Research Journal*, 8, 2.

Moses, D., Hegarty, S. and Jowett, S. (1988) *Supporting Ordinary Schools*. Windsor, NFER-Nelson.

Mosley, J. (1993) *Turn Your School Around*. Wisbech, LDA.

Mosley, J. (1992) 'Value added pacts'. *Special Children*, March issue.

Moss, G. (1992) 'The right to teach'. *Special Children*, 58.

National Curriculum Council (1989) *A Curriculum For All*. York, NCC.

National Oracy Project in Avon (1991) *Children's Voices*. Bristol, Avon County Council.

Nelson-Jones, R. (1988) *Practical Counselling and Helping Skills*, 2nd edn. London, Cassell.

Newell, P. (1985) 'The children's legal centre', in Lindsay, G. (ed.) *Integration, Possibilities, Practice and Pitfalls*. Leicester, British Psychological Society.

Norman, K. (1990) *Teaching, Talking and Learning*. York, NCC.

Nottingham County Council Advisory and Inspection Service (1990) *Pupil Exclusions from Nottingham Secondary Schools*. Nottingham Education Department.

Oxley, L. and Topping, K. (1988) 'Cued spelling', in Topping, K., Scoble, J. and Oxley, L. (eds) *The Cued Spelling Training Pack*. Huddersfield, Kirklees Paired Reading Project.

Pasternicki, J. (1986) 'Teaching handwriting: the resolution of an issue'. *Support for Learning*, 1, 37–41.

Pearsall, E. and Wollen, E. (1991) *Differentiating the Secondary Curriculum – DARTS: Directed Activities Related to Text*. Trowbridge, Wiltshire County Council.

Pearson, L. and Lindsay, G. (1986) *Special Needs in the Primary School: Identification and Intervention*. Windsor, NFER-Nelson.

Phillips, D. (1989) 'Teachers' attitudes to pupils with learning difficulties', in Ramasut, A. (ed.) *Whole School Approaches to Special Needs*. Lewes, Falmer Press.

Reason, R. and Boote, R. (1995) *Helping Children with Reading and Writing*. London, Routledge.

Rieser, R. and Mason, M. (eds) (1990) *Disability Equality in the Classroom*. London, ILEA, now published by Disability Equality in Education.

Rutter, M., Tizard, J. and Whitmore, K. (eds) (1970) *Education, Health and Behaviour*. London, Longman.

Rutter, M., Maugham, B., Mortimore, P. and Ouston, J. (1979) *Fifteen Thousand Hours*. London, Open Books.

Safran, S. and Safran, J. (1985) 'Classroom context and teachers' perceptions of problem behaviours'. *Journal of Educational Psychology*, 77, 1.

Sawyer, C. and Knight, E. (1991) 'A fast method for calculating text readability levels'. *Support for Learning*, 6, 2.

SEAC (1991 and 1992) *Teacher Handbook for the SAT*. London, SEAC.

Share, D., Jorm, A. and Maclean, R. (1984) 'Sources of individual differences in reading acquisition'. *Journal of Educational Psychology*, 76.

Sharpley, A. and Sharpley, C. (1981) 'Peer tutoring: a review of the literature'. *Collected Original Resources in Education*, 5, 3.

Shaw, L. (1990) *Each Belongs: Integrated Education in Canada*. London, Centre for Studies on Integration in Education.

Sheridan, M. and Peckham, C. (1975) 'Follow up at 11 years of children who had marked speech defects at 7 years'. *Child Care and Health Development*, 113.

Singleton, C. (1991) 'Computer applications in diagnosis and assessment of cognitive deficits in dyslexia', in Singleton, C. (ed.) *Computers and Literacy Skills*. Hull, British Dyslexia Association Computer Resource Centre.

Solity, J.E. (1991) 'Special needs: a discriminatory concept?' *Educational Psychology in Practice*, 7, 1, 12–19.

Somerville, D. and Leach, D. (1988) 'Direct or indirect instruction? An evaluation of three types of intervention programmes for assisting students with specific reading difficulties'. *Educational Research*, 30, 1.

Southgate-Booth, V., Arnold, H. and Johnson, S. (1981) *The Effective Use of Reading Project*. London, Heinemann.

Sparks, D. and Hiley, A. (1989) 'Setting up a resource base in a primary school', in Widlake, P. (ed.) *Special Children Handbook*. London, Hutchinson Education and Special Children.

Spivack, G. and Shure, M. (1974) *Social Adjustment of Young Children: A Cognitive Approach to Solving Real-life Problems*. San Francisco, CA, Jossey-Bass Publishers.

Sprick, R. (1981) *The Solution Book*. Chicago, IL, Science Research Associates.

Stott, D., Green, L. and Francis, J. (1988) *The Guide to the Child's Learning Skills*. Stafford, NARE Publications.

Thacker, J. (1983) *Steps to Success*. Windsor, NFER-Nelson.

Thompson, P. (1992) 'Raising reading standards: the reader-leader scheme'. *Support for Learning*, 7, 2.

Thomson, M. (1989) 'Evaluating teaching programmes for children with specific learning difficulties', in Pumfrey, P. and Elliott, C. (eds) *Children's Difficulties in Reading, Spelling and Writing*. Basingstoke, Falmer Press.

Thomson, M. (1991) 'The teaching of spelling using techniques of simultaneous oral spelling and visual inspection', in Snowling, M. and Thomson, M. (eds) *Dyslexia: Integrating Theory and Practice*. London, Whurr Publishers.

Tizard, J., Schofield, W. and Hewison, J. (1982) 'Collaboration between teachers and parents in assisting children's reading'. *British Journal of Educational Psychology*, 52.

Topping, K. and Wolfendale, S. (eds) (1985) *Parental Involvement in Children's Reading*. London, Croom Helm.

Topping, K. (1987) 'Children as teachers'. *Special Children*, October issue.

Topping, K. (1988) *The Peer Tutoring Handbook*. London, Croom Helm.

Topping, K. (1990) 'Outcome Evaluation of the Kirklees Paired Reading Project'. PhD thesis, Division of Education, University of Sheffield.

Veit, D., Scruggs, T. and Mastropieri, M. (1986). 'Extended mnemonic instruction with learning disabled students'. *Journal of Educational Psychology*, 78, 4

Warnock, M. (1982) 'Children with special needs in ordinary schools: integration revisited'. *Education Today*, 32, 3, 56–61.

Waterhouse, P. (1990) *Classroom Management*. Network Educational Press.

Webster, A. and McConnell, C. (1987) *Children with Speech and Language Difficulties*. London, Cassell.

Wells, G. (1981) *Learning through Interaction*. Cambridge, Cambridge University Press.

Westmacott, E. and Cameron, R. (1981) *Behaviour Can Change*. London, Globe Education.

Westwood, P. (1982) 'Strategies for improving social interaction of handicapped children in regular classes'. *Australian Journal of Remedial Education*, 16, 1.

Wheldall, K. (1988) 'The forgotten A in behaviour analysis: the importance of ecological variables in classroom management, with particular reference to seating arrangements', in Thomas, G. and Feiler A. (eds) *Planning for Special Needs*. Oxford, Blackwell.

Wheldall, K. and Merrett, F. (1984) *Positive Teaching: The Behavioural Approach*. London, Unwin Education.

Wolfendale, S. (1987) *Primary Schools and Special Needs: Policy, Planning and Provision*. London, Cassell.

Womack, D. (1988) *Special Needs in Ordinary Schools: Developing Mathematical and Scientific Thinking in Young Children*. London, Cassell.

Wood, D. (1986) *Teaching and Talking with Deaf Children*. London, John Wiley and Sons.

Wooster, A. and Leech, N. (1982) 'Improving reading and self concept through communication and social skills training'. *British Journal of Guidance and Counselling*, 10, 1.

Wragg, E., Bennett, S. and Carre, C. (1989) 'Primary teachers and the National Curriculum'. *Research Papers in Education*, 4, 17–46.

Youdan, J. (1991) 'Support for learning: an aid to differentiation', in *Differentiating the Secondary Curriculum*. Trowbridge, Wiltshire County Council.

Young, P. and Tyre, C. (1983) *Dyslexia or Illiteracy? Realising the Right to Read*. Milton Keynes, Open University Press.

Zigler, E. and Hodapp, R. (1986) *Understanding Mental Retardation*. Cambridge, Cambridge University Press.

AUTHOR INDEX

SUBJECT INDEX

EDUCATING THE WHOLE CHILD
CROSS-CURRICULAR SKILLS, THEMES AND DIMENSIONS

John and Iram Siraj-Blatchford (eds)

This book approaches the 'delivery' of the cross curricular skills, themes and dimensions from a perspective emphasizing the culture of primary schools and the social worlds of children. The authors argue that the teaching of skills, attitudes, concepts and knowledge to young children should not be seen as separate or alternative objectives, but rather as complementary and essential elements of the educational process. It is the teacher's role to help children develop and build upon the understandings, skills, knowledge and attitudes which they bring with them into school. Learning for young children is a social activity where new skills and understandings are gained through interaction with both adults and with their peers. Each of the approaches outlined in the book is thus grounded in an essential respect and empathy for children and childhood as a distinct stage in life and not merely a preparation for the world of adulthood. For instance, the authors argue that responsibilities and decision-making are everyday experiences for children and that they need to be able to develop attitudes and skills which enable them to participate fully in their own social world.

Contents
Cross-curricular skills, themes and dimensions: an introduction – Little citizens: helping children to help each other – Effective schooling for all: the 'special educational needs' dimension – Racial equality education: identity, curriculum and pedagogy – 'Girls don't do bricks': gender and sexuality in the primary classroom – Children in an economic world: young children learning in a consumerist and post-industrial society – Catching them young: careers education in the primary years – Understanding environmental education for the primary classroom – Health education in the primary school: back to basics? – The place of PSE in the primary school – Index.

Contributors
John Bennett, Debra Costley, Debbie Epstein, Peter Lang, Val Millman, Lina Patel, Alistair Ross, Ann Sinclair Taylor, Iram Siraj-Blatchford, John Siraj-Blatchford, Balbir Kaur Sohal, Janice Wale.

192pp   0 335 19444 3 (Paperback)   0 335 19445 1 (Hardback)

BEGINNING TEACHING: BEGINNING LEARNING IN PRIMARY EDUCATION

Janet Moyles

- How can beginning primary teachers not only survive but enjoy their chosen career?
- What can newly qualified and student teachers do to recognize and address the many complexities of primary teaching?
- What are the issues which continually challenge both new and experienced teachers?

This book sets out to explore with beginning primary teachers, and the people who support them in schools and institutions, some of the wider issues which need to be considered when working with primary age children and how these are woven into the broad framework of teaching and teachers' own learning. Cameos and examples of classroom practice help to illustrate the many different aspects of teaching: what it is to be an effective and competent teacher; classroom processes such as planning, observation and assessment; the variety of ways in which children learn and develop thinking and skills; social interactions and support networks; equal opportunities; and 'in loco parentis' responsibilities.

Written in an accessible style, the aim throughout is to offer guidance and encouragement in the challenging and complex task of primary school teaching.

Contents

Introduction – Part 1: Teaching to learn – Do you really want to cope with thirty lively children and become an effective primary teacher? – The classroom as a teaching and learning context – Observation in the primary classroom – Competence-based teacher education – Part 2: Learning to teach —– Primary children and their learning potential – Planning for learning – children's and teachers – Developing investigative thinking and skills in children – Developing thinking and skills in the arts – Developing oracy and imaginative skills in children through storytelling – Developing children's social skills in the classroom – Developing writing skills in the primary classroom – Part 3: Responsibilities, roles and relationships – Assessing, monitoring and recording children's progress and achievement – Equal opportunities in practice – Working with experienced others in the school – Primary teachers and the law – Concluding remarks – Index.

Contributors

Tim Brighouse, Martin Cortazzi, Maurice Galton, Barbara Garner, Linda Hargreaves, Jane Hislam, Morag Hunter-Carsch, Tina Jarvis, Neil Kitson, Mark Lofthouse, Sylvia McNamara, Roger Merry, Janet Moyles, Wendy Suschitzky, David Turner, Martin Wenham.

288pp   0 335 19435 4 (Paperback)   0 335 19436 2 (Hardback)

CREATIVE TEACHERS IN PRIMARY SCHOOLS

Peter Woods

Is creative teaching still possible in English schools? Can teachers maintain and promote their own interests and beliefs as well as deliver a prescribed National Curriculum?

This book explores creative teachers' attempts to pursue *their* brand of teaching despite the changes. Peter Woods has discovered a range of strategies and adaptations to this end among such teachers, including resisting change which runs counter to their own values; appropriating the National Curriculum within their own ethos; enhancing their role through the use of others; and enriching their work through the National Curriculum to provide quality learning experiences. If all else fails, such teachers remove themselves from the system and take their creativity elsewhere. A strong theme of self-determination runs through these experiences.

While acknowledging hard realities, the book is ultimately optimistic, and a tribute to the dedication and inspiration of primary teachers.

This book makes an important contribution to educational theory, showing a range of responses to intensification as well as providing many detailed examples of collaborative research methods.

Contents
Introduction: Adapting to intensification – Resisting through collaboration: A whole-school perspective of the National Curriculum – The creative use and defence of space: Appropriation through the environment – The charisma of the critical other: Enhancing the role of the teacher – Teaching, and researching the teaching of, a history topic: An experiment in collaboration – Managing marginality: Aspects of the career of a primary school head – Self-determination among primary school teachers – References – Index.

208pp   0 335 19313 7 (paperback)   0 335 19314 5 (Hardback)